# The End of the Innocence

Lawrence R. Samuel

# The End of the Innocence

The 1964–1965 New York World's Fair

 SYRACUSE UNIVERSITY PRESS

First Paperback Edition 2010
10  11  12  13  14  15        6  5  4  3  2  1

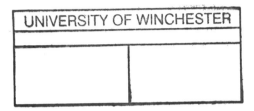

All photographs are courtesy of Bill Cotter.

The paper used in this publication meets the minimum requirements of
American National Standard for Information Sciences—Permanence of
Paper for Printed Library Materials, ANSI Z39.48–1984 ∞™

For a listing of books published and distributed by Syracuse University Press,
visit our Web site at SyracuseUniversityPress.syr.edu.

ISBN (paper): 978-0-8156-0956-8
ISBN (cloth): 978-0-8156-0890-5

**Library of Congress Cataloging-in-Publication Data**

The Library of Congress has catalogued the hardcover edition as follows:
Samuel, Lawrence R.
   The end of the innocence : the 1964–1965 New York World's Fair / Lawrence R. Samuel.
      p. cm.
   Includes bibliographical references and index.
   ISBN 978-0-8156-0890-5 (hbk. : alk. paper)
   1. New York World's Fair (1964–1965)—History. 2. Moses, Robert, 1888–1981. 3. Fairs—New York (State)—New
York—History. 4. National characteristics, American—History—20th century. 5. Nineteen sixty-four, A.D. I. Title.
II. Title: 1964-1965 New York World's Fair. III. Title: 1964 New York World's Fair.
T7861964.B1 S36 2007
907.4'747243—dc22                                                                                    2007012973

*Manufactured in the United States of America*

✦

*To my parents, who brought me to the Fair*

**Lawrence R. Samuel** is the author of *Pledging Allegiance: American Identity and the Bond Drive of World War II* and *Brought to You By: Postwar Television Advertising and the American Dream*. He lives in Miami Beach.

# Contents

# Illustrations

# Acknowledgments

THANKS TO GLENN WRIGHT and all the other fine folks at Syracuse University Press. Much gratitude to all the information specialists at the New York Public Library and the New-York Historical Society who helped steer me the right way. Special thanks to Bill Cotter for the photos used in this book (information on his collection can be found at http://www.worldsfairphotos.com) as well as to Doug Lapham, Janet Rosen, Brendan O'Malley, and Lary May. Finally, a word of recognition to Robert Kopple who, a half century ago, suggested to a few friends that there be another world's fair in New York City.

# Introduction

NEXT TIME YOU'RE IN THE CITY so nice they named it twice, take a walk in the park. Not Central Park, but one that's half again as big and is even more of a central park, located in the geographic and population bull's-eye of New York City. It's Flushing Meadows–Corona Park in Queens where, before the soccer players, picnickers, and best tennis players on the planet took it over, the last great world's fair took place. Between April and October 1964 and again in 1965, some fifty-two million people from the four corners of the earth gathered there to be part of what Fair officials predicted would be the greatest single event in history. The park is an enduring legacy of the Fair, transformed from the dismal "valley of ashes" that F. Scott Fitzgerald described in *The Great Gatsby* into a big, beautiful thing that is the pride of the borough.

Few people today, of course, would say that the 1964–65 New York World's Fair achieved, or even came close to achieving, this more than lofty, perhaps ridiculous claim of becoming the greatest event in history. Besides the sheer attendance, however, which made it not just one of the most popular world's fairs but perhaps one of the most popular events of any kind ever to be held, consider what a typical fairgoer could experience in a single day in Flushing Meadows. In between seeing color television for the first time at the RCA Pavilion and taking a ride in a brand-new car from Ford called the Mustang, one might have stopped by Bell Telephone's pavilion to try something named the Picturephone that let you see (and, a little concerning, be seen by) the person you were speaking to. One's next stop might be the IBM Pavilion to see what the huge fuss was over this new business machine, the computer, followed by a visit to GE's pavilion to watch a real demonstration of thermonuclear fusion in which a million amperes of "free energy" were released. Then, after strolling through the Space Park to check out a few rocket ships that had actually been in orbit—quite a thrill in these heady days of the race to the moon—one might go back in time to see a few of the Dead Sea Scrolls followed by Michelangelo's *Pietà*, especially since this event was the first time that masterpiece had left the Vatican since it was sculpted 465 years earlier. Then just for fun, one might swing over to Pepsi's pavilion to take in a new ride

built by Walt Disney called "It's a Small World" and then over to the Illinois Pavilion to see another Disney creation, an eerily lifelike (or just plain eerie) robotic
Abraham Lincoln that reportedly looked, spoke, gestured, and even smiled like
the dead president. Finally, for sustenance, you might head over to the Chun King
Inn for its seven-course dinner (for just ninety-nine cents, thankfully, now that
one was nearly flat broke) and, on the way out, one of those Bel-Gem waffles that
everybody said was the best damn thing at the Fair.[1]

Some, perhaps many of you, had such a day or something like it in your own
visit to Flushing Meadows in 1964 or 1965. I was lucky enough to, giving me firsthand knowledge of the amazing experience that was the Fair, especially for an
eight year old. "Anyone who has attended [a world's fair] has a story to relate about
the[ir] experience," says Ilene Sheppard in her essay in *Remembering the Future:
The New York World's Fair from 1939 to 1964,* and this Fair was no exception. Sheppard rightly believes that world's fairs are "cultural common denominators that
cut across social and class distinctions" and "shared experiences among diverse
groups of people," powerful ideas that certainly describe the biggest one of all held
in the most polyglot of cities. Still, despite the incredible array of sights, sounds,
smells, and tastes that more than fifty million people took in some forty years ago,
the 1964–65 New York World's Fair has been either discounted or simply ignored by
both scholars and general writers alike. Not as beautiful as the Columbia Exposition's White City in Chicago in 1893, not as progressive as the St. Louis World's Fair
in 1904, and not as optimistic as the 1939–40 New York World's Fair, the 1964–65
Fair is considered, in short, the ugly duckling (or perhaps Ugly American) of global
expositions. Overshadowed by its financial losses, European no-shows, heavy commercial orientation, and, above all, the looming and rather sinister presence of its
president, Robert Moses, the Fair has been summarily dismissed by critics as the
world's fair that permanently put an end to major world's fairs.[2]

In what is the most thorough survey of world's fairs in the United States, *Fair
America,* for example, Robert W. Rydell, John E. Findling, and Kimberly D. Pelle
sum up the 1964–65 New York World's Fair as "a large, rambling, unfocused exposition." Rydell (who legitimately calls himself "the venerable patriarch of the
world's fair field") and his coauthors make no mention that the Fair was the nation's
most attended or, amazingly, bother to describe how any of the fifty-two million
visitors actually felt about the time they spent there. Similarly, in his 2003 memoir
*City Room,* Arthur Gelb, a former editor of the *New York Times,* writes that "while
it did provide entertainment for some fifty million visitors, [the Fair] ended as an
embarrassing failure." More evidence of the Fair's B-team official status within the
history of global expositions is *Times* writer Sam Robert's dismissive thinking in
2005 that "the 1964 fair paled in comparison [to the 1939–40 fair] but did expose
Michelangelo's *Pietà* to millions and popularized the Belgian waffle."[3] These kinds
of analyses of the Fair, typical of the precious little that has actually been written
about it, are not so much wrong as they are incomplete, a partial telling of the tale.

Filling in the gaps with the most important part of the story—what people could see, hear, eat, and, most important, learn there—tells us that the Fair was not a failure at all, but rather a major success, offering millions of people a wonderful, unforgettable experience unlike any other. Besides doing a disservice to the Fair's public, popular memory, such top-down, producer-oriented, operation-focused tellings of history are very much out of sync with one that puts people ahead of institutions, recognizing that the latter exist only to serve the former. As the growing body of scholarship dedicated to the relationship between history and memory illustrates, it is not uncommon for official and popular memories to construct different versions of the past, something I believe is very much the case for the 1964–65 New York World's Fair. A big part of my mission here thus is, rather simply, to repair and restore the reputation of the Fair, something that is long overdue, by bringing its official and popular memory closer together.

Past and present critics' myopia is also responsible for misinterpreting the Fair's undeniable conservatism, which was largely a product of Robert Moses's traditional, septuagenarian tastes. (Moses's brother-in-arms, Walt Disney, was sixty-three when the Fair opened and would die a year after the exposition closed.) Whereas the intellectual and creative elite, then and now, labeled the Fair's Eisenhower-style aura passé and stifling ("Curved, finned, corporate Tomorrowland, as presented at the 1964 World's Fair, was over before it began," wrote former Merry Prankster Robert Stone forty years after his visit), regular folks found the 1950s overtones comforting and reassuring, a sanctuary from the cultural storm that was rapidly approaching in the mid-1960s.[4]

Outside the fairgrounds, cracks in the nation's foundation were becoming too large to simply ignore, cracks that were threatening the golden age in which the country had achieved unprecedented power abroad and prosperity at home. Along with these cracks, which were dividing Americans along political, social, and economic lines, a growing sense of cynicism and disillusionment was palpable in the air. "There is a mood of uneasiness," Barry Goldwater observed in a September 1964 campaign speech. "We feel adrift in an uncharted and stormy sea."[5] Despite America's triumph over both the Depression and its enemies in the war, the utopian world of tomorrow that was promised by the nation's leaders in business and government throughout the 1940s and 1950s had not been realized. The brief, shining moment of Camelot had come and passed, replaced by a time in which economic woes and social unrest seemed to be everywhere one looked. For the first time since the Great Depression, it appeared that it might be the end of the American Dream, if it wasn't over already.

Its opening day held just five months after the assassination of President Kennedy, the 1964–65 New York World's Fair thus took place at a key turning point in American history and during a period of remarkable cultural upheaval (much like the previous New York fair). In the eighteen months from the beginning of season one in April 1964 and end of season two in October 1965, a bevy of key events related to the two major sources of conflict in the mid-1960s—civil rights and the Vietnam War—took place. While fairgoers munched on their Bel-Gem waffles and rode Avis's Antique Car Ride at a top speed of six miles per hour, thousands were marching (and a few dying) in Mississippi to register black voters during the Freedom Summer of 1964. Other seminal milestones of the civil rights movement—the assassination of Malcolm X in February 1965, the Selma to Montgomery marches the following month, and the Watts riots in August—were also happening as "peace through understanding" reigned in Flushing Meadows. Similarly, the amazing string of civil rights laws that were signed by LBJ during the run of the Fair—the Civil Rights Act in July 1964, the Voting Rights Act in August 1965, and affirmative action the next month—stood in stark contrast to Moses's city-state in Queens where America's "Negro problem" did not exist and time appeared to stand still.

The Vietnam problem too was rapidly becoming a nightmare as global harmony, or at least Moses's version of it, ruled at the Fair. From the Tonkin Gulf Resolution in August 1964 to Operation Rolling Thunder in March 1965 and the start of "search and destroy" missions in June of that year, Vietnam was top of mind for most Americans exactly at the time when millions were gathering in Flushing Meadows in celebration of international brotherhood. As more troops were sent to Southeast Asia throughout 1964 and 1965, students and organizations such as the Students for a Democratic Society marched and "sat-in" in protest of the escalation of the war. Against the backdrop of all this conflict and social unrest, Robert Moses created a space that was essentially free from the turmoil of the mid-1960s.

American popular culture also revealed the massive upheaval the country was experiencing that could not be detected at the Fair. Whereas 1964 was still largely steeped in classic postwar-era pop culture (Broadway shows that hit the stage that year included *Funny Girl, Hello Dolly,* and *Fiddler on the Roof,* for example), it was equally clear by 1965 that the wheels of what was left of the Eisenhower legacy were flying off. During that pivotal year, the countercultural triumvirate of sex, drugs, and rock and roll came onto the national scene in full force as what we commonly refer to as "the sixties" actually begun. In the first arena, two events—the Supreme Court's overturning of the law prohibiting birth control and the invention of the miniskirt in the U.K. (and its immediate appearance in the States)—clearly suggested that a seismic shift was taking place in sexual politics, especially among women. On the drug front in 1965, Timothy Leary's *Psychedelic Reader* was published and the term *flower power* coined by Allen Ginsberg, each a sign of the emerging trippy times. And in rock and roll, a variety of milestones, including the British invasion, Dylan going electric at the Newport Folk Festival, and the forming of the Grateful Dead in San Francisco, signaled a radical transformation of America's musical landscape and the culture that went along with it. Another major blow to the foundation of the postwar consensus in 1965 was the publishing of Ralph Nader's book *Unsafe at Any Speed,* which challenged the accepted tenet that what was good for General Motors was good for America. The advent of a much more permissive climate for sex, drugs, and rock and roll was one thing, but a serious (and, in retrospect, entirely valid) threat to the nation's automobile industry was perhaps too much to keep the nation on its smooth postwar track.

While change, uncertainty, and angst reigned outside the fairgrounds, the world inside Robert Moses's tightly controlled universe (patrolled by thousands of Pinkerton guards) remained known and safe. (A few groups tried to use the Fair as a stage to voice their concerns, most successfully on opening day, but Moses and his World's Fair Corporation [WFC] adeptly used the law and, when that failed, good old muscle to keep protesters at bay.)[6] For the overwhelming majority of visitors, the Fair's conservative tone was thus not a liability, as critics have argued, but I believe a key asset, contributing heavily to its tremendous popularity. Rattled by immense cultural upheaval—racial unrest; an escalating, unpopular war; increasingly fuzzy gender roles; and a growing, unprecedented divide along generational lines—American visitors in particular found the Fair's postwar swagger and bravado to be a welcome anchor providing stability and ballast. The Fair's imaginary universe looked backward as much as forward, offering visitors a bridge over the troubled waters of the times. (Guy Lombardo, a personal favorite of Robert Moses, headed the unofficial house band at the Fair.) The postwar world may have had its anxieties, but, after twenty years, they were known, familiar, and contained, the Fair told visitors, whereas the post-postwar world represented completely uncharted territory that the nation appeared unprepared to navigate. And by bypassing the uninviting near future for a more palatable far-distant one, the Fair offered its millions of visitors hope and confidence that utopia or something like it was not an entirely lost cause. In short, the American Dream was still very much alive in these 646 acres of land in Queens, an oasis of faith and optimism.

Heavily inspired by Walt Disney, whose theme park in Anaheim had been open for a decade by 1964 (and who wanted to open his second park on the Fair's site after its run), Moses thus sought and succeeded in creating a safe bubble that was virtually free from worldly concerns in order to make the event a popular success. As the quintessential fantasy world that offered visitors refuge from the often less-than-magical realities of everyday life, the Magic Kingdom provided an ideal blueprint for Moses to follow in building his own interpretation of the happiest place on earth. Chaos may have reigned in the WFC's boardrooms and in the offices of elected officials, but precious little of it could be detected on the fairgrounds. "Any hint of inequality, conflict, or injustice was excluded from the social purview of the Fair," observes Morris Dickstein in his own essay in *Remembering the Future,* an accurate assessment of the protective cocoon that was Flushing Meadows.[7] Within its grounds, foreign nations sang in harmony, corporations existed to produce things that made life better, and, most important, the future looked brighter than ever. The same formula of success that had proved so reliable the past couple of decades—science and technology—would lead America to an even more abundant promised land, this one made up of limitless energy, computerized efficiency, and push-button convenience. The make-believe universe of the 1964–65 New York World's Fair was, in short, the final gasp of American innocence, the last time and place in which the harsh realities of the mid-1960s could be ignored on such a large scale.

With all due respect to Don Henley, titling any work *The End of the Innocence* is admittedly a risky proposition. One could easily make the solid case that America never lost its innocence because it was never truly innocent to begin with. Jon Margolis, author of *The Last Innocent Year*, says this very thing, that "no notion is more naïve (which is not the same as innocent) than the one supposing America ever had an innocence to lose, a peculiar conceit in a country that began as a slave society in the process of exterminating the folks who got here first."[8] Even if one buys into the belief that there was once an innocence to be lost (which Margolis himself ultimately does), one could very well argue it occurred during the Civil War or, as Henry Farnham May suggests in his book *The End of the American Innocence,* in the few years before and during World War I when the nation shook off the last vestiges of Victorianism. If asked, most would probably locate America's loss of innocence in the 1920s, when the "lost generation," shattered by the trauma of World War I and disillusioned by its aftermath, rejected a bourgeois lifestyle and embraced the pleasures to be found in the new, thoroughly modern age. I don't take issue with any of these views but do believe there was a kind of renaissance of innocence after World War II, as many Americans settled into a period of self-imposed naïveté following a decade and a half of depression and war. It was this brand of innocence that I think disappeared from American culture in the mid-1960s, never to be seen again, with the 1964–65 New York World's Fair its final hurrah.

Telling the full story of this world's fair is also an opportunity to locate it as a major intersection for many if not most of the world's most influential people and institutions in politics, business, and the arts. Directly in the center of the intersection as both heroic and villainous protagonist stood, of course, the maddening figure of Robert Moses, whose reputation and power were already seriously fading as the cultural winds shifted away from his style of scorch-the-earth urban planning. Much of the overreporting of bad news and underreporting of good news about the Fair was, in fact, Moses's own fault, his self-destructive streak and hypersensitivity to criticism heavily imprinting how the first draft of the event's history was written.[9] All the key players of New York City and New York State politics of the 1960s were naturally somehow involved with the Fair as well. Governor Nelson Rockefeller, Mayor Robert Wagner (and, later, John Lindsay), city controller Abe Beame, Senator Jacob Javits, and a host of local congressmen and city council members played instrumental roles in the highly charged political dynamics of the Fair. The story of the Fair represents an opportunity to fill in some of the gaps of the history of New York City, whose geographic and cultural landscape was irrevocably altered by the event and its aftermath. In fact, the Fair (along with the opening of the Verrazano Bridge and Lincoln Center, naturally also both Moses projects) was originally conceived as a three hundredth birthday celebration for the city, although this idea was overshadowed like much else when the man took over, his primary motive being to turn Fitzgerald's "valley of ashes" into a world-class park that bore his name. Big, loud, and contentious, this Fair was a mirror image of its host city, just as the 1939–40 fair held on the same site was in its day, making it hard to conceive that it could have taken place anywhere else. And if nothing else, the 1964–65 Fair was able to capture the attention of New Yorkers for a couple of years. What other event besides the previous fair and, much later, 9/11 can claim that?

At the national political level, the U.S. Congress (rather reluctantly) supported the Fair when Moses and his World's Fair Corporation colleagues came knocking in the early 1960s in search of funds to build the United States Pavilion. The Fair also crossed the paths of no fewer than three presidents. President Eisenhower chose New York City as the Fair's site, President Kennedy was an early and enthusiastic champion of the event, and President Johnson was the (loudly heckled) keynote speaker at the opening ceremonies. As Johnson discovered firsthand, the Fair emerged as a brief but important site of the mid-1960s civil rights movement, with both the Congress of Racial Equality (CORE) and the National Association for the Advancement of Colored People (NAACP) using the event to try to advance their cause. Few people likely know that Martin Luther King, not long after he won the Nobel Prize, too became entwined in one of the many controversies that bubbled up out of the Fair's volatile political mix.

Most exciting, however, was when the world's fair became a major feature on the international stage. With the cold war still very chilly, especially in the early sixties during the planning of the exposition, the Fair was used as a political pawn by both the United States and the USSR. The State Department worked right alongside the WFC in its (unsuccessful) attempt to get the Soviets to come to Flushing Meadows as they had in 1939, an interesting but generally forgotten game of cat and mouse played between the superpowers during JFK's one thousand days in office. International politics also came into play in a skirmish between Arabs and Jews, a foreshadowing of the Palestinian-Israeli conflict that would explode in a couple of years after the Fair and, of course, continues today. On a more positive note, a steady stream of foreign dignitaries and heads of state visited the Fair for groundbreaking ceremonies and throughout its two seasons, making Flushing Meadows in the mid-1960s an important site of international diplomacy (and, occasionally, faux pas). Not just one pope but two—Pope John XXIII and Pope Paul VI—are characters in the Fair's story, the latter actually coming to Queens to bless the Vatican Pavilion (and probably check up on his *Pietà*). The international character of the Fair proved to be one of its most appealing and enduring features as, more so than any fair before it and arguably any other single event, visitors were exposed to a phenomenal range of global culture. Some of it was as kitschy as kitsch can get—Hong Kong Burgers served by waitresses in motorized rickshaws and *The Last Supper* done in wax, to name just a couple of things one was not very likely to run across anywhere else in the world—but much else was as authentic as possible.

Although the local, national, and international political fireworks surrounding the Fair were, of course, unplanned, the exposition was designed from the get-go as a commercial enterprise for both itself and its exhibitors. Virtually all world's fairs before 1964 had a strong trade orientation, but this one, as critics were quick to point out, took the proverbial cake. Moses himself expressed this thought best, saying that he would not consider the Fair to be a success unless the three most powerful organizations in the world—the U.S. government, the Vatican, and General Motors—took part. In addition to the Big 3 automakers who reprised their significant roles from the 1939–40 New York World's Fair, a bevy of corporate-America heavyweights, including General Electric, IBM, Bell Telephone, Du Pont, Kodak, and Coca-Cola, invested heavily in their pavilions and exhibits. This new Fair, executives believed, represented an unprecedented opportunity to build goodwill among tens of millions of consumers from all around the world, a promotional vehicle that promised to pay dividends for decades. International exhibitors too, many of their pavilions sponsored not by governments but by private interests, also marketed themselves heavily, eager to claim their stake in the fast-growing global economy. Perhaps more than anything else, the Fair served as a pronounced endorsement of American-style consumer capitalism, offering visitors everything from a hair-color analysis from Clairol to an underground home complete with painted scenes of nature at the Better Living Center.

It was precisely this pervasive commercialism that made the 1964–65 New York World's Fair different from all others and forever changed the landscape of global expositions. With corporate America more powerful than ever in the mid-1960s and consumer culture at an all-time high, the 1964–65 New York World's Fair would make all previous expositions pale in comparison in terms of their commercial nature. Corporate sponsors had of course been represented at world's fairs since the turn of the century, when American consumer culture became much more standardized and dominated by nationally advertised and distributed brands.[10] Visitors to the Louisiana Purchase Exposition in St. Louis in 1904 sipped on Dr. Pepper, for example, and Henry Ford set up an actual assembly line at the Panama Pacific International Exposition in San Francisco in 1915 (which produced forty-four hundred cars over the run of the fair). Dozens of corporations proudly showed off their wares at each of the two biggest American fairs during the Great Depression, the 1933 Century of Progress in Chicago and the 1939–40 World of Tomorrow in New York, this at a time when business was viewed by many as the principal cause of the economic mess.[11] The consumer paradises that lay ahead would no doubt make our lives easier and more enjoyable, these fairs and previous ones promised, with the miracles of science making it all possible.

Following the scientific wonderland that was the World of Tomorrow, world's fairs were suspended during the war, putting utopia understandably on hold.[12] The idea of an idyllic tomorrow would be revived at another world's fair, however, once again grounded in the seemingly limitless possibilities of science. The 1958 Brussels Universal Exposition, or Expo '58 as it was popularly called, put world's fairs back on the international stage but, in the atomic age of the postwar years, was the first to suggest the dystopia that science could also bring about. Although Expo '58 drew a hefty forty-two million visitors over its six-month run—a clear sign that, almost twenty years after the last major one, world's fairs were far from passé in the public's imagination—the pure, unadulterated optimism of global expositions would forever be tempered. The fair's official, unusually clunky theme—Evaluation of the World for a More Human World—was grounded in standard exposition-speak of peace and progress, but the now undeniable possibility of atomic war between the two superpowers pervaded the proceedings.[13]

Much of this atomic muscle-flexing had to do with the unequivocal star of Expo '58, the Atomium, a 355-foot steel and aluminum sculpture of the crystal molecule that held the key to producing copious amounts of cheap energy for whatever purposes man had in store. Still a popular tourist attraction (having recently undergone an extreme makeover), the Atomium was the Eiffel Tower or Perisphere and Trylon of its particular fair but, unlike these other decidedly forward-looking architectural centerpieces, also symbolized a darker side of its time and place, specifically the underlying tensions of the nuclear age. Beyond the colossal atomic iconography of Expo '58, the fair served as an ideal opportunity for the superpowers to play their cards at the height of the cold war. Having launched Sputnik just nine months before the start of the fair, the Soviets parlayed this coup with a pavilion that showed off their scientific know-how and military strength. In its pavilion, however, the United States chose a softer approach, focusing on its consumer-based lifestyle as a propagandist tool. In his *Pavilions of Plenty*, Robert Haddow discusses how the United States used world's fairs in the 1950s, especially Expo '58, to exhibit and, the country hoped, export the American way of life to a global audience. With backing from both the federal government and the business community, American consumer culture served as a "silent ambassador for democratic ideals," according to Haddow, and a counterpoint to Soviet-style communism.[14]

In the why-Johnny-can't-read era of the late 1950s and early 1960s, however, mere ideology was simply not going to fly. Embarrassed by its showing at Brussels and concerned that the country was falling further behind in the science race, the federal government was determined to use another fair as a platform to show the world it had the right stuff. Following a small fair in Turin in 1961, it would be the Century 21 Exposition in Seattle in 1962 that would bring larger nations and American corporations together again with the purpose of celebrating, at least officially, international understanding and free trade. With the space race now in full swing, however, global harmony and laissez-faire commerce took a backseat to rocket power. Century 21 was positively space happy, topped off, of course, by the 606-foot Space Needle complete with revolving restaurant. The exposition was in many ways a cold war–era version of the 1933 Century of Progress and 1939–40 New York fairs, a revisiting of the science-as-secular-religion trope in the space age. In the United States's Science Pavilion, fairgoers moved from a Charles Eames film about science to the educational "Spacearium" to a National Aeronautics and Space Administraton (NASA) exhibit featuring the very craft that Alan Shepard had ridden into suborbit a year earlier. More revealing (quite literally) of Century 21's space mania were the topless showgirls at Planet Eve, a lounge on the grounds, who did their thing alongside performers dressed as astronauts.[15]

Both atomic energy and space would also be heavily represented at the 1964–65 New York Fair, but, with the Soviets' decision to opt out, American-style capitalism clearly stole the show. Robert Moses made a conscious decision to fill the obvious void of countries absent because the Fair was not sanctioned by the Bureau of International Expositions (BIE) (the governing body of world's fairs) with corporations who were positively ecstatic at the opportunity to show off their products and services at what promised to be the biggest trade fair ever held. Besides serving as a jumbo-sized promotional tool for marketers, the world's fair also, thankfully, offered visitors entry into a creative (and often surreal) wonderland. As the biggest game in town in 1964 and 1965, some of the world's best and brightest were eager to showcase their talents to a global audience of tens of millions. Even though they were temporary events, their contents fully intended to be either scattered or, more likely, unceremoniously destroyed, world's fairs had always attracted the creative elite within a healthy competitive spirit, and this one too brought together an all-star cast of players. Where else might one see in a single place the architecture, design, and music of Eero Saarinen, Philip Johnson, Walt Disney, Charles Eames and Ray Eames, Saul Bass, and Elmer Bernstein? The art at the Fair, something roundly criticized as lacking, included the work not only of Michelangelo but of Goya, Velázquez, and Picasso as well, not to mention leading pop artists such as Roy Lichtenstein, James Rosenquist, Robert Indiana, and Robert Rauschenberg. (A controversial mural by Andy Warhol hung briefly on the New York State Pavilion before being taken down before opening day.) And despite the brouhaha over the Fair's architecture, which, unlike most past expositions, lacked a consistent theme, the overall effect was, just as intended, carnivalesque, a multicolor, space-age spectacle that left many visitors dazzled if not dazed.

THE END OF THE INNOCENCE tells the story of the 1964–65 New York World's Fair in two ways. Part I, "Peace Through Understanding," traces the history of the Fair chronologically, from its conception in early 1958 through its demolition in 1966. In its three chapters, this part examines the who, what, and why of the Fair, providing a broad overview of the dynamics leading up to the event, in season one, and in season two. Part II, "Tomorrow Begins Today," traces the history of the Fair thematically, its three chapters focusing on the event's commercialism, national and international identity, and emphasis on science, technology, and the future. This dualistic approach is designed to create a kind of synergy that either approach alone could not by combining a linear narrative with a more subjective take on what I feel were the most interesting and significant things and ideas at the Fair.

All of the photographs in the book were taken by Bill Cotter who, like me, believes that our time spent at the Fair left a lasting impression that shaped our careers and lives. Rather than use formally commissioned, often staged photos now kept in archives, libraries, and museums, I intentionally wanted to use ones taken by an "average" visitor to capture some of the real Fair experience. Almost all of the book's sources are "period," that is, from the era of the Fair rather than subsequent reflection, as, although I'm as big a fan of oral history as anyone, I felt it was important to capture events as they occurred for accuracy's sake. I love hearing personal anecdotes from anyone and everyone who visited the Fair but, for historical purposes at least, tend to take forty-year-old memories (including my own) with a large grain of salt. In addition to relying on the words of the many journalists who were on the scene as it happened, I reviewed primary materials produced by the WFC and exhibitors that can be found at various libraries, archives, and museums and, less formally, via the thriving world's fair subculture operating both off- and online. My ultimate hope is that this book will help preserve the memory of the Fair so that future generations will have some idea of what once took place in what is now a big park in Queens, New York City.

# PART ONE

# ✦ Peace Through Understanding

# 1  The Greatest Event in History

*Pick up your left foot, pick up your right.*
*Walk away from every care.*
*This is your fun time, you are entitled to it,*
*Fair is Fair.*
 —The official world's fair song,
  "Fair Is Fair," by Richard Rodgers

IN 1958, FOUR MEN IN NEW YORK CITY found themselves chatting about the problems of modern education. After considerable banter, the men came to the conclusion that American schools were not very good at teaching children about other people, especially people from other countries. One of the men, Robert Kopple, a forty-eight-year-old lawyer with a wife and two daughters, knew this was especially true among his own children. Over a recent dinner at home with his family, he told his friends, he had been surprised at his daughters' ignorance of life outside the United States. "We were discussing the world," Kopple later recalled, "and I found that my daughters, who were then 9 and 12, had very little contact with what was going on in it. Everything was black and white; everything was hate. And it occurred to me that I would like to bring home to them that people around the world were basically the same. And I thought it would be nice to bring the nations of the world together again."[1] Kopple, who had been a concessionaire at the 1939–40 New York World's Fair, suggested to his friends that another world's fair would be the perfect way to fill in the holes of a child's education. All of the other men too had attended or worked at the last New York fair, and they were soon recalling fond memories of the spectacular event.

The story could and by all rights should have ended there, but Kopple decided to take action. In May of that year, after eating lunch at the Mutual Admiration Society, a New York club the four men belonged to, Kopple offered the idea of another world's fair in the city up for discussion. The members of the club, many of them businessmen who remembered the economic boom that had coincided

3

with the 1939–40 World of Tomorrow, liked what they heard. Realizing he was on to something, Kopple now became nearly obsessed with the prospect of New York hosting another world's fair. Over the next few months, he read through the complete minutes of the 1939–40 fair; tracked down and interviewed its president, Grover Whalen; and went to Washington, D.C., to propose the concept to Senators Kenneth Keating and Jacob Javits (both Republicans from New York), the State Department, and the Department of Commerce. He then visited with Billy Rose, the famed theatrical producer who had put on the popular "Aquacade" water show at the last fair, to get his perspective and support. With the help of one of his friends, Charles Preusse, who as fate would have it happened to be city administrator, Kopple got a meeting with Mayor Robert F. Wagner and pitched the idea to him. The rest, as they say, is history. City hall was, it turns out, looking for a way to celebrate the three hundredth anniversary of the British takeover from the Dutch in 1664, that is, when the city became known as New York, and another world's fair seemed like an ideal way to commemorate the occasion.[2] The fact that 1964 would also be the twenty-fifth anniversary of the 1939 fair was another fortuitous aligning of the planets. Wagner appointed Kopple the city's official representative in planning a tercentennial celebration for 1964, planting the seeds for another New York world's fair to become a reality.

Despite his enthusiasm, the mayor was not ready to go public with the idea until he was sure the city's business community would support it. Lenders to the last New York fair had lost sixty-eight cents on every dollar they had put in, and Wagner knew it would be difficult to raise money for another one. He asked Kopple and Preusse to do some more groundwork before he officially threw New York's hat in the ring to try to host another major exposition. Kopple filed an application with the Bureau of International Expositions in Paris—the governing body of world's fairs—and formed a private committee, headed by Thomas J. Deegan, the public relations counselor to the 1958 Brussels fair and the Moscow fair about to be held. After Kopple, Preusse, and Deegan met with a group of thirty-five enthusiastic businessmen in August 1959 at 21, the famed New York restaurant, to formally gain their support, Mayor Wagner became confident the city had a legitimate shot at the fair. Wagner named these same thirty-five businessmen the "Mayor's Committee" for a 1964–65 fair, each of whom (along with another fifty soon added to the committee) was promptly asked for one thousand dollars as working capital.[3] In the year and a half since Kopple's impromptu chat with his buddies, another New York world's fair was on the way to becoming more than a dream.

Right on cue, the legendary Robert Moses, New York City's commissioner of parks since 1934, announced that the site of the 1939–40 fair, which was now the largely undeveloped Flushing Meadows Park, would be available for another exposition for the rock-bottom price of one dollar a year.[4] Before the 1939–40 fair, Flushing Meadows was known as Corona Dump, the very same dump described by F. Scott Fitzgerald as a "valley of ashes" in his 1925 novel *The Great Gatsby*.[5] With support from local politicians and businessmen, a little money in the bank, and the ideal location, Kopple, Deegan, and Wagner were off and running. The World's Fair of 1964–65 Corporation was formed in 1960, setting up camp rent free on the seventy-sixth floor of the Empire State Building and receiving tax-exempt status as a nonprofit entity. Based on Kopple's wish for his daughters, a member of his team, Jerome Weinstein, came up with the Fair's theme, Peace Through Understanding, while Deegan proposed that the time capsule buried at the 1939–40 fair be opened in 1964, linking the fondly remembered event to the proposed one. Meanwhile, Mayor Wagner extended an invitation to Premier Nikita Khrushchev for the USSR to take part in the Fair, an olive branch in the red-hot cold war. Khrushchev tentatively accepted, but there was a hitch, the first of many to come.

## A Fair Is Born

As it turned out, New York was not the only American city thinking about hosting another world's fair in 1959 (Vienna dropped out in October). Officials in Washington, D.C., and a Los Angeles real estate developer were also pursuing a global exposition for their respective cities, knowing it would pump millions of dollars into the local economies. Approval from President Dwight Eisenhower and Congress was needed, however, before anyone was hosting anything, as private citizens were not allowed to invite foreign governments to build pavilions. The president, rather sensibly, refused to take sides in the geographic battle (even though his brother-in-law was lobbying heavily for a Washington, D.C., fair). After a couple of months of stalling, Eisenhower agreed to set up a three-person committee to determine first if the nation should even host a world's fair so soon after Seattle's Century 21 Exposition planned for 1961. Representatives from Seattle were making a hard case that 1964 was simply too soon for the United States to hold another major exposition, fully aware that another major New York fair could very well make its upcoming event suddenly seem rather puny and off the beaten track.

President Eisenhower, however, had a particular interest in trying to make another major world's fair in New York happen. The Brussels Universal Exposition of 1958 had turned into something of a confrontation between the United States and the Soviet Union, with many believing that the Russians had fared better. The Soviets put on an impressive display of military hardware and technology (including Sputnik), making the Americans' exhibit centered around popular culture appear rather lightweight and the nation less than superpowerful. Eisenhower was personally embarrassed by America's showing in Brussels and relished another chance to fire a peaceful missile on a global stage. While the upcoming Seattle exposition could plant the seed, a world's fair in what had become, after the war, the most important and influential city on the planet presented an unprecedented opportunity to flex the nation's scientific and military muscle. Such machinations were hard evidence that despite proposed world's fair themes like

Peace Through Understanding, there was no denying that the tensions of the cold war lurked underneath the rhetoric of international harmony. There had been no world's fairs in the United States since the end of World War II precisely because of these tensions, but the time seemed right for the nation to host a major global exposition that showed off its technological superiority and, as well, celebrated international-style corporate capitalism.[6]

As Eisenhower's committee weighed the various issues, the New York and Washington, D.C., contingents lobbied heavily. (Los Angeles was a long shot at best—even the city's Chamber of Commerce did not want it—and a late bid by Mayor Richard Daley for Chicago to host a fair was never taken seriously.) The Washington group made a compelling case by proposing that its fairgrounds be part of a new, permanent community in Prince George County, Maryland. The New York group took an equally aggressive approach, ticking off its key advantages—dense population, hometown of the United Nations, and plenty of hotel rooms (108,000, in fact). The New Yorkers also flaunted their cheaper-than-cheap lease and argued that holding the event on the same site as the 1939–40 fair would save $50 million by using existing sewer and utility connections.[7] Turning up the heat even more, one of Kopple's friends asked Bill Bernbach, president of Doyle Dane Bernbach, the hottest ad agency in town, to create a brochure for the committee that praised the benefits of another New York world's fair.

After a week of intense deliberating in October 1959, Eisenhower's committee recommended that New York City host the world's fair on the basis of it being "a symbol of freedom to millions."[8] The president gave his official blessing (confirmed by President Kennedy after his inauguration a few months later), as did Congress, which reminded the New York group that part of the deal was that no federal funds would go toward the event. To pay for the Fair, the WFC planned to ask the state legislature to sell $150 million in bonds (lowered from $500 million and then $200 million), pledging to pay back the state out of the $200 million it expected to bring in from leases, concessions, and admissions. No city, state, or federal funds would be requested or needed, the WFC made clear, making it, theoretically, a virtually no-lose proposition.[9]

The next line of business was for the WFC to find a permanent president. Deegan was more than willing to give up the top job to, as the vernacular of the day went, "the right man." The job qualifications were quite specific, especially in these pre–Equal Employment Opportunity Act days. "He" had to, one, come from a top position in business or the military; two, be between fifty and sixty years old and be in excellent health; three, be successful enough not to want to use the position for "bigger things"; and four, be financially and politically savvy (but not a politician). The financial package being offered was a hefty $100,000 a year (interestingly, the same amount that Grover Whalen had made in 1939). Although a flood of applications arrived at the WFC's office (including one from an active army captain and another from a twenty-two year old whose credentials included having "lived in Paris"), it was virtually inevitable that the job would be offered to one man: Robert Moses.[10]

Moses, then seventy years old (seventy-five when the Fair opened), was not only commissioner of parks for both the city and the state but also head of the New York State Power Authority, the Triborough Bridge and Tunnel Authority (TBTA), the Slum Clearance Committee, and all arterial-road construction.[11] By 1960, Moses had, over the past forty years, already earned a famous and, to others, infamous reputation as "New York's master builder." In his definitive study of the man and his works, *The Power Broker*, Robert Caro claims that Moses had a more complete vision of the city than any other individual ever had. Having remade the city for the automobile age since the days of Al Smith, Moses was arguably the most influential builder in the history of the world. It is not an exaggeration to say that the only thing that changed the physical landscape of New York more than Robert Moses was the ice age. Depending on whom you listened to, the man was either a hero, leading New York into a better, more intelligently designed future, or a villain, destroying healthy, vibrant communities if they stood in the way of "progress." For example, *Newsweek* at the time referred to him as the city's "most articulate, pugnacious, and spectacular builder of roads, parks, beaches and bridges," and *Esquire* considered him "one of the few men in New York public life who combines energy, efficiency, and incorruptibility." Others, however, were less kind, referring to him as a "dictator" or even "generalissimo" in his efforts to complete such mammoth undertakings as the St. Lawrence power project and Jones Beach. Recognizing Moses's propensity to be a "lightning rod for criticism," *Business Week* aptly captured this ambiguity, considering him to be the Fair's greatest asset and its greatest liability. "Critics liken his technique to a steamroller aimed downhill," the magazine observed in 1963, with "the fair no exception." *Time* concurred, saying that Moses "is the sort of man who likes to knock things over rather than walk around them."[12]

With the Fair an incredibly complex project involving a disparate group of constituencies, however, someone with a clear vision and proven track record of rolling or knocking things over if necessary seemed like just the right stuff for the job. Perhaps even more important, Moses was one of the few men on the planet who could convince both public and private interests to lend the WFC the kind of money it needed. For Moses, the Fair job not only was a way to achieve his lifelong dream in Flushing Meadows but also represented what Caro calls "a graceful exit" from a scandal related to a city housing program he was in charge of that had tarnished his reputation.[13] The high-salary position was also, not incidentally, a way for Moses to pay doctor bills for his daughter Jane, who had cancer. After the WFC reportedly could not find another qualified candidate for the position (two generals declined it), Moses was offered the job in February 1960 and accepted it two months later after a bill was signed exempting him (and another Parks Department employee, Stuart Constable) from the New York City Ethics Code, which would have created conflicts of interest when the two resigned their city posts. In a decision that would have long-term consequences for the Fair, Moses's only demand in accepting the job was that Robert Kopple—the man who had conceived and launched the project without any compensation—be let go from the WFC. Besides arguing against Moses's appointment as president of the WFC, saying he was too old and too much of a bully, Kopple had had a previous run-in with the power broker, bravely opposing him on his proposed, ill-conceived elevated Manhattan Expressway, some years earlier. Kopple resigned before getting the ax, receiving a $35,000 cash settlement for his efforts and a free pass for the Fair, good every day.[14] The financial windfall for Moses was undoubtedly a lot more sizable than the peanuts Kopple was given to disappear. Upon his appointment, Moses received a seven-year (1960–67) contract for $75,000 in salary and $25,000 in expenses per year plus a $27,500 annuity for seven more years, resulting in a total package of almost $900,000.[15] In addition to what amounted to financial security for the rest of his life, Moses also received good-wish messages from President Eisenhower and former presidents Harry Truman and Herbert Hoover, firm proof of the significance of the future Fair and the importance of the job. (Moses later repaid them by appointing all three as honorary chairmen.) Moses hired about 160 staff members, many if not most of them loyal associates who went back with him as much as thirty years ("Moses men" who unfailingly called him "R. M.").[16] This initial number of employees was just a fraction of the 3,700 people hired to organize and manage the previous New York fair, a step Moses reportedly took so that his Fair would make money.[17]

The key players on Moses's team not surprisingly reflected R. M.'s own skill set grounded in political connectivity and a proven ability to accomplish huge undertakings. As a high-profile public relations executive (a classic postwar man in the gray flannel suit), Deegan had an ideal professional background to lead the immense effort of persuading millions of folks to come to the Fair. Deegan, who personally extended the top Fair job to Moses and would chair the WFC's executive committee from its formation in 1959 to the corporation's dissolution in 1971, traveled in VIP circles of not just the political and corporate worlds but also sports and the Catholic Church as well. He not only advised LBJ during the candidate's run for the Democratic nomination for the presidency in 1960 but consulted on matters of importance with the Vatican for more than twenty years as well (earning him a Knight Grand Cross of the Holy Sepulchre by Pope Pius XII, appointment as a Knight of Malta by Pope John XXIII, and recognition as Catholic Layman of the Year in 1965).[18]

Charles Poletti, in charge of international or foreign exhibits, had an equally impressive background to help lead the Fair. Lieutenant governor of New York in 1942, Poletti became governor of the state for a whopping twenty-nine days when his boss, Herbert H. Lehman, resigned to direct war-relief efforts in Europe. Poletti, the first American of Italian ancestry to serve as a governor, himself soon joined the cause when the Office of War Information asked him to appeal to Italians, via a short-wave radio broadcast, to "throw out both Hitler and Mussolini." Poletti was later appointed by Governor W. Averell Harriman to the New York State Power Authority, working under none other than Robert Moses during the years in which both the St. Lawrence and Niagara Projects were largely completed. (The Charles Poletti Power Project in Astoria, Queens, was renamed in 1982 to honor him.) Extroverted and gregarious, "Governor," as he was nicknamed, would use every bit of his wartime salesmanship experience and peacetime organizational skills to recruit dozens of international exhibitors and then help keep them from declaring World War III at the Fair.[19]

Another key member of Moses's team was Major General William E. Potter, who supervised the Fair's construction. Potter's thirty-two years in the U.S. Army included helping plan the invasion of Normandy and orchestrating the massive moving of men and supplies in Western Europe (the "Red Ball Express" operation). After the war, Potter worked for the Corps of Engineers, supervising such projects as the controlling of the Missouri River, and then served as military governor of the Panama Canal Zone.[20] As with Deegan and Poletti, Potter's experience managing vast, complex projects would prove to come in very handy during the next five years.

## The Olympics of Progress

One of Moses's first responsibilities was to try to figure out how many people would come to the Fair, as this number would determine the admission price for visitors and the cost structure for exhibitors. In April 1960, consultants hired by Moses forecast that 40 million people would visit the Fair during the 1964 season (April 22 to October 18) and another 33 million in 1965 (April 21 to October 17), 28 million more than the 1939–40 fair. After lowering the 1965 estimate by 3 million to be on the safe side, Moses used the 70-million figure for the full run as the official forecast right up until opening day.[21] Coming up with such figures was, however, as much art as science, employing a methodology that could only be described as "weird math." To arrive at the 70-million estimate, Fair officials started by taking the first year's attendance figures for the previous exposition in the area, which was 26 million in 1939. The next step was to bump up that figure by the average of population growth since 1939 in the nation (38 percent) and the city (42 percent), or 40 percent. That figure in turn was lowered by 11 percent to account for the greater (four times) planned admission cost in 1964 versus 1939, bringing them to 32.4 million. To that figure, officials added another 7.5 million to account for repeat visits resulting from the absence of a competing fair (as there was in 1939), easier traveling (especially from Europe), and a healthier economy. The result was 39.9 million, or a rounded-up 40 million. For the second year, officials first multiplied the 40-million figure by the relative attendance of the second year of the 1939–40 fair (72 percent), arriving at 28.8 million. Tack on an extra 5 percent to 10 percent because 1940 was a war year in Europe and—presto!—a nice round 30 million for 1965, or 70 million for the two seasons.[22]

With Seattle officials forecasting just 7.5 million visitors over its single-season fair, it was clear that the New York event would be a major world's fair, whereas the former would be a minor one. In terms of sheer physical size as well, there was no real comparison. New York officials were planning a fair spreading over 646 acres (about a square mile), whereas Seattle's Century 21 Exposition would cover just 74 acres. And compared with New York's planned $1 billion expenditure, the Seattle group was spending a putative $80 million. Even the New York Fair's alternative theme, Man's Achievement in an Expanding Universe, seemed bigger than Seattle's theme of Man in the Space Age.[23]

But the Seattle exposition could claim one key advantage over the New York Fair: official recognition from the Bureau of International Expositions. The BIE was formed in Paris in 1928 when delegates from thirty-one countries agreed to a set of provisions regulating international expositions. Such an organization was some twenty years in the making, as it became clear there should be some common guidelines regarding expositions in what was arguably the heyday of world's fairs. The BIE was especially interested in the frequency of fairs and the rights and obligations of exhibitors—issues that the organization remains focused on to this day. The BIE's guidelines were last modified in 1965—no doubt at least in part a reaction to the huge amount of attention the previously obscure organization received when it ran smack into Robert Moses.[24]

The complete breakdown in communications between Moses and the BIE resulted from the power broker's inability to persuade the French organization to relax its guidelines so that the Fair could be officially sanctioned. According to the BIE's rules, a single country could not host more than one major exposition in a ten-year period, a fair could run six months at most, and fair organizers could not charge governments for exhibition space. The New York group had decided to ignore all these regulations, meaning that the organization's then thirty member nations (which did not include the United States) could have government-sponsored exhibits at the Seattle fair but not the New York one. To take part in the latter, exhibitors from member nations would have to either have an unofficial presence, that is, sponsorship from private (corporate) interests rather than the government, or simply decide to violate the BIE's rule. This situation was remarkably similar to the one in 1939, when New York launched its world's fair without official sanction from the BIE and still ended up having some sort of representation from member nations through some heavy persuasion by Whalen. "We don't take this B.I.E. business very seriously," Moses said in 1962. "You won't find anybody around here worrying about it." In classic Moses style on the rare occasions he did not get what he wanted, he described the BIE as "three people living obscurely in a dumpy apartment in Paris" or, alternatively, "that bunch of clowns in Paris."[25]

When it became clear in late November 1962 that the Century 21 Exposition was a hit, exceeding its 7.5 million estimate by a full third, New York Fair officials came to believe their estimate may have been on the low side, viewing Seattle's success as a very good omen. Rather than think the Seattle fair had stolen the thunder from its upcoming Fair, an initial fear, the belief now was that it proved there was still a market for global expositions, something that was by no means ensured. The president of the Century 21 Exposition, Joseph E. Gandy, recognized this fact as well, stating, "The New York boys are banking heavily on our success." He added, "If the Seattle World's Fair is a flop, they might as well quit. Fairs will have had it."[26] With the Century 21 Exposition proving that world's fairs were not an anachronism, at least not yet, corporate America, which had been somewhat reluctant to commit to the New York Fair, now eagerly signed up. Smaller companies remembered that when Borden introduced "Elsie the Cow" at the 1939–40 fair, the company instantly became a major player in dairy foods. Dozens of companies, both large and small, began making significant financial commitments to the event, knowing that most Fair visitors would be, as the *Nation* described them, "the world's single most important consumer market—the solid, well-heeled American middle class."[27]

Indeed, although the Fair was officially about "peace through understanding," it was really mostly about dollars and cents. In fact, from the very first world's fair in 1851, London's Crystal Palace Exhibition of the Works of Industry of All Nations, global expositions celebrated, above all, commerce. World's fairs themselves were business ventures as well, although they had a rather dismal financial history. Chicago's Century of Progress in 1933 made a little money (about $700,000 on a $47 million investment), but it was a rare exception. New York's 1939–40 fair lost $22 million, a much more representative financial performance for major expositions. Despite this track record, Moses and his staff were confident that their Fair would be a profitable one. Based on his estimate of 70 million in attendance, Moses was by late 1963 forecasting $120 million in profits, $80 million less than the WFC's original estimate but still a hefty piece of change, especially when most fairs had finished in the red.[28] Moses even knew where profits from the Fair should go, proposing that $23 million of it be prioritized for building a seven-mile chain of parks in Queens as a "gift to the city." Moses consistently and freely admitted that the "main attraction" would actually come after the Fair, when Flushing Meadows Park would be considered the most important park in the city, or, as he described it, "a new sort of super Central Park."[29] Moses had tried to achieve this very thing after the previous New York fair but had failed when all revenues from the event went back to the city to pay off as much of its loans as possible. As he told *Reader's Digest,* in September 1964, "Parks are the big thing in my life, and I decided to turn this dump into a great park. When they started planning the 1939 World's Fair, I saw my opportunity. Well, I made the fairgrounds all right, but the fine park never materialized, because we didn't have the money." Just as in 1939,

Moses was looking at this fair as, as Marc H. Miller later wrote, "a high-budget, high-priority enterprise that he could latch onto for advancing his main business: park and roadway construction." Given a second chance, Moses was determined to not let "the fine park" slip out of his hands, planning for the WFC to build it before the site was turned back over to the city. "With all due respect to City Hall," Moses said, "if we hand over our profits to the city government and ask them to make the park, the park will never be built."[30] By viewing the Fair as one more opportunity to remake New York City and leave another lasting personal legacy, however, Moses was blatantly ignoring the WFC's lease with the city for Flushing Meadows Park that clearly stated that any profits from the exposition would first go to education. Moses even kept a colored map of the future park in his office, detailing the exact location of its lawns, picnic areas, athletic fields, day camp, zoo, botanical gardens, and archery courts, along with a step-by-step timetable for its completion in 1967.[31]

Knowing that huge profits to build his park relied on realizing the equally huge forecasted attendance, Moses and his WFC colleagues quickly became experts at the art of hyperbole. Almost as soon as he was appointed president, Moses announced that the Fair would be the first "billion-dollar" exposition in history, a figure that became permanently attached to the event. It was a catchy factoid but actually a bit of a stretch, including $95 million in construction costs for roadways to the Fair, $120 million to improve the Throgs Neck Bridge, and millions more to build the adjacent baseball stadium.[32] Moses also repeatedly referred to the event as "the Olympics of progress" or "the Olympics of global industry," but was outdone by his colleague Deegan, who claimed that the Fair would be "the greatest single event in history."[33] A big part of Fair officials' wild optimism was the response to their advance ticket sale. Discounted tickets for $1.35 (65 cents off the regular $2 fare for adults) were sold from April 22, 1963 (exactly one year before opening day), until February 29, 1964, with Fair officials reporting that 1 million such tickets had been sold by September 1963 and 2 million by November.[34] Advance tickets became a very popular Christmas stocking stuffer that year, so much so that another million discounted tickets were reportedly sold over the holidays. Fair officials proudly announced that almost 4 million tickets had been sold by January 1964—75 percent more than they had expected—and an incredible 28 million advance sale tickets (three times what the WFC had expected) had been sold by the end of the discounting program.[35] Major exhibitors such as IBM and United Airlines each had bought 100,000 advance tickets for its employees and AT&T a whopping 250,000, helping the advance ticket program considerably.[36] With advance ticket sales almost three times the actual attendance of Seattle's fair, critics who had consistently predicted the New York exposition would lay an egg were hushed. Some in the media began talking about possibly 100 million people coming to the Fair, with an average daily "population" equal to the size of Wichita (230,000) and, on a really good day, that of Washington, D.C. (764,000).[37] Maybe the Fair would be the biggest single event in history after all.

If Moses's ultimate purpose for the Fair was to build a world-class park, his penultimate objective was to create a lasting infrastructure for a lot of people to get there. Although the jet set would get whisked to the fairgrounds by helicopter from the Pan Am building in Manhattan, many more would be tossing the kids in the back of family sedans and station wagons. The early 1960s was a golden age for the American automobile, of course, as our postwar love of the freedom of the road was fueled by new and better highways. Moses, already famous (or infamous) for making New York City more vehicular-centric (and, correspondingly, less pedestrian friendly), seized the opportunity presented by the Fair, using the forecasted high attendance figures to sell the need for additional and improved highways and bridges (and parking lots). As soon as Flushing Meadows was announced as the likely site for the Fair in 1959, in fact, Moses immediately announced that $85 million was needed to upgrade the city's highways and transit system.[38] A huge highway construction program was in the works by the end of 1961 (Caro calls it "the biggest, most lucrative schedule in the history of New York or any other metropolis"), with funds allotted for no fewer than five different highway projects in Queens.[39] One early project involved a six-lane traffic link in Forest Hills, a decidedly bucolic urban neighborhood, drawing the wrath of many local residents and the Long Island Safety Council. Millions of dollars were soon allocated to extending what was officially called the Clearview Expressway but known to critics as "the road to nowhere" (a nod to another of Moses's Herculean projects, the Triborough Bridge, which, during the years it took to be built, was often referred to as "the bridge to nowhere"). Millions more were approved to improve the Grand Central Parkway and the Van Wyck Expressway, the other major arteries near the park.

As commuters faced horrendous traffic snarls for the next three years of construction, Moses's highway expansion plan and the man responsible for it were widely rebuked. New Yorkers were remaining rather ambivalent about the upcoming Fair in large part because the principal roadways of Queens had been turned into "the world's biggest parking lot" (a moniker that stuck for the Long Island Expressway) as a result of it. "For the present at least," *Time* noted in October 1962, "New Yorkers are most aware of their fair in terms of the bumper-to-bumper embolisms the highway expansion program is causing in the borough of Queens."[40] Road construction was continually behind schedule and in danger of not being finished by the Fair's opening day. The New York Mets could not occupy the new stadium being built next to the fairgrounds in the spring of 1963 as planned because it too remained unfinished and behind schedule. Even worse, parts of the Long Island Expressway were buckling and cracking from the huge vibrations caused by construction associated with the Fair, and air pollution in the area had risen considerably because of the building going on. Local mechanics were busier than ever, repairing the wheels, springs, and other parts of cars damaged by the rough roads, and motorists detoured to areas of Queens they never knew existed and, often, could not find their way out of. Moses's plans for the city of the future were, as usual, wreaking havoc with the city of the present.

As millions of dollars were poured into New York's private transportation grid, leaders of the city's public transportation network insisted that it too needed upgrading. Moses had successfully argued against a subway extension to Flushing Meadows (even though the city had built one for the previous fair), a clear sign of his passion for roads (and distaste for people who could not afford a car).[41] Fearing that the current system would be inadequate to get the millions of visitors to and from the Fair, however, New York City Transit Authority (NYCTA, later the Metropolitan Transit Authority) executives lobbied city officials for eighty extra subway cars and various station improvements at a cost of $10 million. Like the WFC, the NYCTA was expecting a windfall from the Fair, forecasting $9 million in additional revenue from increased ridership, and it wanted to make sure its financial ship would come in.[42] Subway fares were 15 cents in the early 1960s, a cheap and efficient way to get to and from the Fair, but there would simply not be enough cars to handle the event if the daily attendance forecasts were at all accurate. City officials agreed to the NYCTA's request for more cars, although not as many as it wanted. In May 1962, ten brand-new Redbirds made a successful test run from Times Square and were scheduled for the IRT line between Manhattan and Flushing for the two seasons of the Fair. The Redbirds, at a cost of $110,000 a piece, not only were technically state of the art but also, according to the Transit Authority, had "interior color schemes recommended by psychologists for relaxed riding."[43] Two cars were added to the line in September 1963, complete with twenty "picture windows" so that visitors could enjoy the scenery on the elevated portion of the fifteen-minute trip (complementing the many sit-back-and-enjoy-the-ride activities possible at the Fair).[44] It remained difficult for Brooklynites to get to and from the Fair by public transportation, however, as the subway lines between most of the borough and Flushing Meadows were less than direct. After politicians from Brooklyn complained that the NYCTA was not making it easier for residents from the borough to get to the upcoming Fair via mass transit (more than half of its residents and families did not own automobiles at the time), the authority agreed to run two special bus lines from Brooklyn to Flushing Meadows. Brooklyn may have lost the Dodgers, but residents of the country's fourth-largest city would have their day at the Fair.

## Sumae over Flushing Meadows

Although transportation was obviously critical, perhaps the most important decision Moses and his staff had to make was what the Fair should look like. As the builder of builders, Moses had definite opinions on the matter. His initial idea was to model the Fair on Tivoli Gardens in Copenhagen, but he soon gave up on the concept when the WFC could not find anyone who would or could build such a thing.[45] Replicating the nineteenth-century gardens and amusement park did not prove "practical under conditions which prevail here," Moses said disappointingly, exactly what the puzzled Danes said would happen when they heard he wanted to knock off their cherished Tivoli.[46] Moses then decided to appoint an all-star committee to come up with an original plan, which is exactly what it did. The committee, which included the renowned designers Wallace Harrison, Edward D. Stone, Henry Dreyfus, and Emil Praeger, envisioned a single circular pavilion to house the exhibits in order to project a common, unified theme. Moses, however, was disgusted with what he termed the "doughnut building," calling the proposal (which borrowed from the design of the Paris fair of 1867) "constipating and stultifying."[47] Moses and his staff decided instead that participants should have separate exhibition buildings laid out on the 1939–40 grid, ostensibly for variety's sake. Upon learning of the WFC's decision in December 1960, four members of the Fair's design committee resigned, feeling their talents were being wasted. "Why should architects hang around four years beating an old cat?" reasonably asked Gordon Bunshaft, one of the committee members who quit.[48]

Most architectural critics, not surprisingly, sided with their colleagues, viewing Moses's vision as both bland and scattered. One critic claimed, "Moses doesn't believe in anything progressive except Progress," while another said that as a result of Moses's rejection of a single building or unified design theme, the Fair was going to consist of "the most horrendous hodgepodge of jukebox architecture that has yet been assembled." In response to such criticism, Moses pointed out the "devastating effects" of the all-encompassing classic revival architectural style of the World's Columbian Exposition of 1893 in Chicago, which was blamed for setting back modern architecture by decades or even generations. It was true that the beaux arts marble temples making up the fair's "white city" reinforced the principles of the City Beautiful movement but slowed down the progressive ideas being pioneered by Louis Sullivan, Frank Lloyd Wright, and other visionaries. "The fair administration belongs to no architectural clique," Moses sniped at modernists in 1961, and "worships at no artistic shrine." He added, "This will produce endless variety, if not uniformity."[49]

Allowing (or forcing) exhibitors to build their own pavilions also provided a climate of healthy competition, pitting leading architects such as Skidmore, Owings, and Merrill against Eero Saarinen. But Moses had another equally rational purpose for his controversial architectural policy, reasonably asking in 1962, "You mean you're going to tell General Motors what kind of building to put up?"[50] Moses was keenly aware that the Fair would attract more and bigger exhibitors if he simply allowed them control over the design of their own pavilions. Besides the aesthetic and control factors, one large common building also would not be possible within the business model that Moses had decided upon for the new Fair.

Moses was well aware of the mistakes made during the 1939–40 fair, when officials decided to construct buildings with the $27 million in bonds the fair had floated. Rather than pay for buildings out of this fair's own pocket, Moses decided to instead rent out the two million square feet they sat on, a much smarter business decision for a temporary event like a fair.[51] Allowing exhibitors free rein to put up whatever they wanted on the still-existing 1939–40 fair template or grid was also a way to get them to pay the high rental fees Moses was asking, serving as yet another revenue source to go toward his dream park after the Fair. Foreign countries and corporations would pay rent ($6 and $200 a square foot, respectively), while states and religious exhibitors would get in rent free as a public service and way to make sure the Fair did not completely resemble a giant trade show.[52]

Sticking to their guns despite criticism from the design and architectural community, Moses and the WFC would put up only three buildings at their own expense—a small administration building, the 2,000-seat domed World's Fair Pavilion, and the 20,000-seat Singer Bowl. With its laissez-faire policy, the WFC allowed exhibitors generally to do whatever they wanted in terms of architecture and design, subject to the corporation's approval and height and size restrictions. Moses's plan for the Fair to be as self-supporting as possible, relying less on government subsidies and loans and more on paying guests and exhibitors, was undeniably brilliant. The great builder, realizing that in this case the real estate business was more financially attractive than the construction business, laid out his village of corporations and governments along the same grid of streets created for the 1939–40 fair, dividing the grounds into five major areas: Industrial, International, Federal and State, Transportation, and Lake Amusement. By not taking on significant construction projects, Moses not only avoided putting the WFC into considerable debt but also limited the number of people on the corporation's payroll, ensuring that thousands of people would not have to laid be off when the Fair ended (something that had happened in 1940). Moses's decision proved to be especially smart in retrospect, as almost all the exhibitors went over their construction budgets. Rather than the $150 million the WFC initially thought it needed from the state, the corporation ended up borrowing just $24 million from the city and floating only $35 million of 6 percent bonds, just $3 million in bonds more than for the 1939–40 fair.[53]

Despite granting exhibitors virtually complete architectural freedom, the WFC was spending more time than it had hoped to renting out the full 646 acres of the grounds. Less than 60 percent of the Fair's space had been reserved by January 1963, a little concerning, as it typically took at least a full year to build a major pavilion.[54] Indeed, one of Moses's primary tasks was to urge participants to start early and work fast, knowing that exhibitors—particularly foreigners—often underestimated how long it took to construct a building. Fair officials remained relatively calm, however, planning to sell as much space as possible and simply landscape the rest (a clever way for Moses to get a head start on his future park). In fact, despite the Fair's commercial orientation, the WFC ensured that the grounds would be heavily landscaped with grass and trees by not allowing any pavilion to occupy more than 60 percent of its site.[55] Moses and his colleagues breathed a sigh of relief a year before the Fair's kickoff, when 80 percent of the available space was committed and forty pavilions were under construction. "Girders for the pavilions of nations, states, industrial firms, and religious groups [are] sprouting like sumae over Flushing Meadow [*sic*]," a reporter for the *New Yorker* observed in June 1963. Equally encouraging, most observers were truly impressed by what was taking shape, architecturally speaking. In February 1963, for example, with about thirty pavilions in various states of completion, *Time* predicted that the grounds would consist of "a maze of pleasure domes, some dazzling and some merely elaborate." Not surprisingly, Moses concurred, considering the pavilions going up "an extraordinary array of originality, talent, ingenuity, and stimulating competition."[56]

As might be expected, building the Fair was not your typical construction project; it was a mammoth undertaking by any measure. By opening day, a million cubic yards of dirt would be picked up and moved and fifty miles of pipe and five hundred miles of cable laid underground for water, gas, and electricity.[57] Beyond the sheer scale, however, the creation of the fairgrounds was an event unto itself, as a host of personalities came to Flushing Meadows to inspect the site and to give their personal blessings. Over the course of about four years, there were almost daily dedications, "shovel-wielding" ceremonies, and ribbon-cutting celebrations among dignitaries and corporate executives for the groundbreaking and topping off of pavilions. A parade of political figures and honorary guests visited the grounds as they took shape, most of the dignitaries awarded the Fair's silver medallion embossed with the Unisphere by Charles Poletti. Just a couple months after the Cuban missile crisis, for example, President Kennedy attended a groundbreaking ceremony, promising to be there on opening day. (President Johnson made the same promise exactly two months after the assassination of Kennedy.) Mrs. Indira Gandhi, wearing a green sari and plastic hard hat, broke ground for the Indian Pavilion in April 1963, a Shinto priest purified the site of the Japanese Pavilion before ground was broken there that same month, and Queen Frederika of Spain took a look at the site from a helicopter in early 1964.

As Moses in typical fashion became "a lightning rod of criticism" for his design sense (or lack thereof), critics took sharp aim at the principal architectural symbol of the Fair. Because the icons of the 1939–40 fair, the Trylon and Perisphere, so compellingly symbolized that exposition's theme of World of Tomorrow, the WFC was faced with a considerable challenge if it wanted to achieve its goal of creating the greatest single event in history. The new symbol would stand on the same spot as the Trylon and Perisphere, making the comparisons to the modern pyramid and sphere that much more apparent. The popularity of the architectural icon of the Seattle's fair, the 606-foot Space Needle (not to mention the Eiffel Tower built for the 1867 exposition in Paris, which, at 984 feet, was the tallest structure in the world at the time), also made it important that the WFC come up with some-thing extraordinary. What would or could equally represent in tangible terms the new fair's vague and nebulous theme, Peace Through Understanding?

Consistent with its strategy to partner with corporate America whenever pos-sible to avoid out-of-pocket costs, the WFC joined forces with the still-reigning heavyweight champion of the world in construction: U.S. Steel. The company de-livered on the WFC's demand for something that would make an impression, and then some. In 1961, Moses revealed plans of the Unisphere, at 140 feet in height and 120 feet in diameter the largest globular structure or representation of earth ever to be built. Designed by Gilmore Clarke (with a little help from Moses himself), the Unisphere was (and is) a twelve-story, 940,000-pound, stainless-steel globe girded by three orbiting satellites, with illuminated points marking world capitals. The Unisphere would not just be built by U.S. Steel but also be officially sponsored by the company, a public monument to its status as an icon of American muscle and know-how and an immensely powerful promotional tool. Based on the (dubious) claim that Native Americans have little or no fear of heights and thus make ideal bridge workers, the company brought a team of fifty Mohawk Indians from the Caughnawaga reservation on the St. Lawrence River near Montreal to Pittsburgh to build the sphere. Surrounded by a 350-foot-diameter pool smack in the heart of the fairgrounds, the Unisphere was always intended to be permanent, unlike the Trylon and Perisphere, which were demolished and melted down to make weap-ons during World War II.[58]

Again the critics jumped on Moses's aesthetics steeped in traditional and representational form, pointing to the Unisphere as precisely what was wrong with the Fair's emerging architecture. Modern art was, of course, all the rage in the early 1960s, its proponents waging a passionate war against Old World, old-fashioned narrative that looked backward rather than forward. The mother of all globes was criticized by those individuals wanting or expecting something more leading edge and, on a larger level, was considered as a missed opportunity to advance the field of design. One group of art critics and designers called the plans "trite" and "uninspired" in February 1961, while *Esquire* considered the thing that was taking shape "incredibly corny." *Newsweek* was even crueler, describing it as "the world's biggest birdcage."[59] Unfazed, Moses continually defended the choice of design by relating it back to the Fair's alternative, or subordinate, theme, Man's Achievement in an Expanding Universe. In 1961, for example, Moses told an audi-ence at Brandeis University that the Unisphere was "certainly distasteful to lovers of abstract art, but we believe easily recognizable by the average visitor as symbol-izing the interdependence of all people on a small shrinking planet in an expand-ing universe."[60]

Because of its size, central location, and easy-on-the-eyes familiarity, the Uni-sphere (almost called Earth and Orbits) immediately became the primary visual symbol of the Fair. Even before the Fair opened, the Unisphere's ubiquity was

*1. The largest representation of the earth ever made, the Unisphere was and remains the principal symbol of the 1964–65 New York World's Fair. Photo © Bill Cotter.*

ensured by means of the WFC's decision to license the image to a plethora of marketers wanting to align themselves with the upcoming event. (The Trylon and Perisphere were also licensed by marketers, their images appearing on everything from soap to underwear.) *Advertising Age* considered the spherical symbol of peace through understanding "the greatest tie-in coup at the fair," a hot property that was popping up on clothing, toys, and sugar wrappers.[61] The WFC itself was naturally sticking the Unisphere on a tremendous array of souvenirs to be sold at the Fair, including wastebaskets, motorized fans, egg timers, salt and pepper shakers, jackknives, bow ties, lighters, and, of course, snow domes. New York City too appropriated the Unisphere as a universal code to let visitors know how to get to the Fair. "Orange-and-blue Unisphere directional signs have broken out like German measles all over town," *Newsweek* observed two days before opening day.[62] Retailers too jumped on Unisphere-mania. When Macy's announced it would feature a model of the Unisphere in its annual Thanksgiving Day Parade in 1963, archrival Gimbel's announced it would put a model of it in front of its building. After hearing of this scheme, Macy's then decided to put a 400-square-foot replica of the entire fair in its store so visitors could preplan their trip, with the promotion becoming an unexpected hit, as millions flocked to get a preview of the real thing. Gimbel's (now calling itself "the world's fair-est store"), however, then outdid Macy's, plopping a "colorful World's Fair spectacular" on top of its building. The exhibit was nothing less than the largest display ever placed on a building in New York City, encompassing the entire width of the store and reaching six stories in height.[63] It was clear that the coming world's fair had finally caught the attention of busy New Yorkers.

## Holy Moses

Although Moses had a very clear opinion on the Fair's design and architecture, he and his staff were at somewhat of a loss when it came to what kind of entertainment should be offered in the Lake Amusement Area (which would remain open until two in the morning every day, four hours after the rest of the Fair closed). H. L. Hunt, the famous Texas right-wing billionaire, was eventually hired to build an amusement park for the twenty-eight-acre area but was fired by Moses in October 1963, even this fair not big enough for the two larger-than-life men and despite the fact that the park was to be inspired by Moses's beloved Tivoli Gardens. Hunt claimed that he was "pressured and taken in" by Moses and denied that his park was going to be "gaudy," as Moses suggested.[64] Moses was, in fact, highly sensitive to "gaudiness" and anything else that smacked of vulgarity in any sense of the word. This aversion directly affected what amusements would appear at the Fair or, more accurately, what amusements would not appear. From the very beginning, Moses was adamant that the Fair not include a "midway" with shills, con men, or sideshow freaks—standard features of a fair's ne'er-do-well cousin, the carnival. There was little doubt that bright and shiny Disneyland would be the model for attractions and rides at the Fair, offering wholesome, sanitized entertainment instead of the bawdy, seedy atmosphere of the carnival. Here too Moses was breaking with world's fair tradition. All or virtually all of the major expositions of the past had offered entertainment charged with sexuality appropriate to the time. At Chicago's World's Columbian Exposition of 1893, for example, Little Egypt did her *danse du ventre* in the Streets of Cairo Area of that fair, the first time belly dancing was so widely seen in the United States. Dancing girls appeared at the racy Streets of Seville exhibit of the 1904 St. Louis Fair, Sally Rand did her famous fan dance at Chicago's 1933 Century of Progress, and, six years later, Gypsy Rose Lee performed her "Streets of Paris" burlesque at the 1939–40 New York fair.

Such naughty doings, however, would have no place at all at Moses's Fair. Despite the youth-driven revolutions in both entertainment and sexuality that lay just around the cultural corner, and the fact that strip clubs were a very popular form of entertainment for men at the time, Moses insisted that amusements at the Fair be "free of honky-tonk," reflecting his clear bias toward middle-class, family-oriented values and his distaste for any form of grit.[65] Like his highways and this former ash dump, it appeared, Moses wanted his Fair clean and pure, to minimize the effects of actual human occupancy and physicality. A bemused writer for *Atlantic Monthly* poked fun at Moses's insistence that there be "no strip-teasers, no razzle-dazzle and whoop-dee-do" and that "a husband will not have to leave his wife and children for ten minutes to see any of the features." (The rumor was that Moses even made the puppets in the "Les Poupees de Paris" show wear bras.) Poletti reinforced the WFC's official position, telling the media that the Fair would have "plenty of amusement . . . but no belly dancers," referring to Little Egypt's scandalous (and very popular) performance. Not wanting to be seen as a prude or party pooper, Moses argued that he simply wanted to raise the bar of entertainment at the Fair. "We are not against gaiety," he said in March 1962. "We shall inaugurate many new inventions infinitely more diverting than whiskered women, tattooed giants and nudes on ice—such as worldwide color television."[66] Spotting an opportunity, some Manhattan nightclub operators began talking about adding stripteasers to close what *Newsweek,* mocking the "gap"-drenched rhetoric of the cold war, referred to as the Fair's "nudity gap."[67]

In the place of such a gap, what gradually emerged was a genre of entertainment that was highly theatrical and sensational yet decidedly free from eroticism or even sensuality. With Flushing Meadows on the shore, much of the entertainment was planned to be watery, just like at the 1939–40 fair. In addition to commissioning a "Dancing Waters" show, the WFC hired the folks from Radio City Music Hall to produce "Wonderworld," a musical extravaganza in the amphitheater on Flushing Meadows Lake. Other amusements included "Ice-Travaganza" (an ice show created and performed by Olympic skating star Dick Button in the New York City Pavilion), a Ringling Brothers circus, and a wax museum, which included not only the figures of Cleopatra, Dr. Kildare, Lady Godiva, the Beatles, Superman, and Jesus but also another cultural icon—Robert Moses.[68]

Moses had another idea of how to make the Fair squeaky clean and wholesome as apple pie, free from the sinful trappings of the carnival: old-time religion. Moses ensured that considerable space—eight pavilions on seven acres—was devoted to religion, covering his bases by inviting all major Christian faiths to participate.[69] (The 1939 fair had just one faith-based pavilion, the Temple of Religion.) The decision to make religion a significant presence at the Fair was in some ways a curious one, as the Supreme Court had just banned official prayer in public schools, deeming it a violation of the First Amendment's guarantee to separate church and state. With the Fair a public event (but run by a private corporation), a strong religious and specifically Christian orientation could have been construed as somewhat inappropriate. Regardless of the way the cultural winds were blowing, religion would be heavily represented at the Fair, contributing to its overall conservative tone. "Into the gap left by the departing Communists," Moses said in 1962 after the Soviets announced they would not make a return to Flushing Meadows, "the saints have come marching in." The Church of Jesus Christ of Latter-day Saints, or the Mormon Church, was given a land grant for its exhibit and promised to bring its world-famous Tabernacle Choir from Salt Lake City. There would also be a Protestant and Orthodox Center, a Christian Science Pavilion, a Greek Orthodox

*2. Among the 160 figures in the Fair's wax museum (the largest collection in the United States) were the Beatles who were, of course, all the rage during the run of the exposition. Photo © Bill Cotter.*

Church exhibit, a Christian Life Convention pavilion, and, of course, the Vatican's pavilion.[70] None were so swaying, however, as the Billy Graham Evangelical Association Pavilion, at which the most famous preacher in America vociferously held court. To give his voice a break, however, the Reverend Graham decided to show a movie between sermons, making a pilgrimage to Jerusalem to produce his three hundred thousand–dollar film, *Man in the Fifth Dimension,* shot in high-tech Todd-AO cinematography. A Jewish Pavilion too was planned, but the American Synagogue Council would not support it, making it appear that Judaism would be the only major religion in the United States to be a no-show. A group of American Jews ultimately decided, however, to cosponsor the American-Israel Pavilion, ensuring that the Jewish people would have some representation at the Fair. Meanwhile, the Protestants were having a difficult time deciding how they should be represented at their pavilion. The Roman Catholics were planning to bring Michelangelo's *Pietà* from the Vatican (the first time the statue would leave St. Peter's Church since it was placed there in 1479), and both Israel and Jordan were planning to exhibit their respective portions of the Dead Sea Scrolls, two very tough acts to follow. Besides being inherently fragmented, the Protestant Church was facing somewhat of a crisis in the early 1960s, losing followers and lacking a clear sense of what it should be. This ecumenical fuzziness made it very difficult for church leaders to choose an architectural symbol for their pavilion, considering everything from an open Bible to a representation of Albrecht Dürer's famous drawing *Praying Hands.* (A more cynical follower suggested a better symbol of contemporary Protestantism might be "a dying tree, leaning toward the left.") The *Christian Century,* the foremost journal of Protestantism, was especially concerned about this issue, observing that "the divided state into which Protestantism has fallen since its sixteenth-century beginning seems to necessitate a whole caseful of symbols rather than a single representation."[71] The Protestants settled on the Charred Cross of Coventry, a wooden cross constructed from the beams of the roof of Coventry Cathedral in England, which was destroyed by German bombing in 1940. Like Graham, the Protestants too planned on showing a film to visitors to its pavilion. When some leaders of the church saw it, however, they were outraged, calling it "sacrilegious" and "improper." Upon seeing the twenty-two-minute film, titled *Parable,* Moses agreed and asked its sponsors, the Protestant Council of New York City, to not show it at the Fair, questioning its "propriety, good taste, and validity." Much of the controversy related to the fact that Jesus was depicted in *Parable* as a mime or, from the perspective of *Christianity Today,* a "donkey-riding circus clown," seemingly enough reason to keep it in the can.[72] As a compromise, the council agreed to withdraw it if audiences found it similarly distasteful.

As New Yorkers finally began to get excited about the Fair in the fall of 1963, the world's fair became a major battleground between Moses and city leaders. Consistent with Robert Kopple's original concept of the Fair, local educational leaders, including Calvin Gross, superintendent of schools, thought the event would offer "a major educational experience" for New York City's 1.4 million schoolchildren and requested that the WFC offer students in groups a reduced admission fare (25 cents, versus the regular $1 fare for children) to make it easier for them to attend.[73] Moses, however, rejected the request on economic terms, claiming that the Fair would lose as much as $9 million if it did so (and adding that even a movie cost a buck in New York City).[74] Moses unapologetically admitted he viewed the Fair as a business enterprise, surprising many people who, upon hearing the theme, thought the event was about education and finding common ground with our international neighbors. Wanting to maximize the Fair's profits in order to build his dream park after the event (and probably dreading the scenario of thousands of poor African American and Puerto Rican children invading Flushing Meadows), Moses was determined to make kids in groups pay the full price. The Democratic candidate for city council, Paul O'Dwyer, pounced on Moses's Scrooge-like decision, scoring points with voters by insisting that the WFC grant the Education Board's request. Not to be outdone, the Republican candidate for the same position, Richard S. Aldrich (a cousin of Governor Nelson Rockefeller), announced he would organize a drive, the "Children's World's Fair Committee," to raise the estimated $762,500 needed to subsidize schoolchildren visits. Even the Liberal and Socialist Party candidates for the job chimed in, saying they too thought kids should pay less than adults ("Moses thinks he's God," quipped Amos Basil, the

*3. Although it could have fitted right into Disney's Magical Kingdom, the Fair's Mormon Church was actually a three-quarter-size replica of the east end of the Mormon Temple in Salt Lake City. Photo © Bill Cotter.*

Liberal, "but fortunately he's only Moses").[75] Seeing which way the wind was blowing, Mayor Wagner was soon in support of reduced fares for kids, the first public disagreement regarding the Fair between the mayor and Moses. Other local politicians joined the fray by preparing a formal resolution demanding that pupils of both public and parochial schools get to attend the Fair at a discount. Reduced fares for schoolchildren were apparently the only thing that members of every political party could agree on.

With the WFC refusing to budge, local politicians turned up the heat by suggesting that the Fair's internal operations be examined, suspecting that there might be some funny financial business going on. Although Moses called those individuals insisting on a reduced fare for groups of students "assorted Santa

Clauses" whose demand would "bring about the financial collapse of the fair," a WFC representative, probably fearing an audit, announced that it would review the proposal. A few days later, looking for a way out of the mess, Moses announced that the WFC would consider offering reduced rates for groups of schoolchildren on Mondays during July and August, hardly the most generous gesture.[76] Mayor Wagner recognized the offer was a clever tactic by Moses, as the latter was certain to know that it would be difficult for schoolchildren to come as a group during their summer vacation. The city council stuck to its guns, insisting that students attending in groups get into the Fair for 25 cents anytime. The WFC remained equally firm, approving instead its very limited discount plan.[77] It was high noon in Flushing Meadows as Moses took on the entire city of New York, which was turning out to be a pretty fair fight. Knowing that it was probably the last thing Moses wanted to happen, the city council made the next move by threatening to probe the WFC's finances and audit its books. Also wanting to score points with the little man, state politicians in Albany, including Governor Rockefeller, began to consider legislation to force the WFC to extend the discount policy or else cancel the corporation's tax exemption and other special privileges. His back against the wall, Moses offered a compromise: schoolchildren in groups would get the blanket 25-cent fare in the *second* year of the Fair *if* the event was profitable. He also told the city council it had no authority to go ahead with its threat to examine the WFC's books and, quoting the corporation's legal counsel, that neither the city nor the state could legally revoke its tax exemption. As lawyers on both sides studied the case, one councilman half-jokingly proposed another idea: cut WFC executives' salaries 10 percent and use the money to subsidize the 25-cent fare.[78]

Throwing himself into the breach, city controller (and later mayor) Abe Beame came up with an alternative plan, suggesting that the city buy tickets at the bulk rate of 67.5 cents and then resell them to schoolchildren for 25 cents. Not surprisingly, however, his boss, Mayor Wagner, rejected this idea, not wanting the city to pick up the tab. The mayor instead proposed a compromise, that the Fair offer the discounted 25-cent admission for groups of pupils three days a week during the regular school year. Equally not surprising, Moses hailed Beame's plan, wanting the discount to come out of the city's pocket versus his own. A couple of weeks later, however, after some details of the WFC's financial operations (alleged noncompetitive bidding and extravagant legal fees and public relations expenditures) started to become public, Moses raised the white flag by agreeing to admit groups of children from a fifty-mile radius to the Fair during the school year for 25 cents.[79] It was a rare loss for Moses, and a considerable victory for schoolchildren from the area who would indeed come to Flushing Meadows for a kind of extracurricular education, just as Robert Kopple had imagined.

The controversy was not completely over, however. Fair officials from other states soon began to complain that the policy was unfair by favoring only children from New York City schools. Also, as some noted, the discount did not apply to special exhibits that carried an additional entry fee, making the Fair still a pricey proposition for disadvantaged kids. Additionally, various organizations for the elderly began to complain that they too deserved a price break and petitioned for a Senior Citizens Week with a 25-cent admission fare. Moses was less than enthralled with this development, claiming that the only group who legitimately should get preferential treatment was the Mohawk Indians. The WFC made it clear that because of a 1684 land deed between New York City and the Mohawks stating that the latter had unfettered access to the area "to cut bulrushes," the tribe could get into the Fair anytime free of charge. "Ye Indians hath reserved Liberty to cut bulrushes for them and their heyers for ever in any place within ye Tract," the deed said, the tract being "all Meadows, feeding marshes, woodes, underwoodes, waters and ponds . . . scittuate upon ye North Shore of Long Island knowne by ye name of fflushing within Queenes County." Even this deal, written a couple of centuries before the area became a valley of ashes, caused dissent, however. One Princess Sun Tamo of the Matinnecocks promptly came forth to argue that it was her tribe, not the Mohawks, who had the legal right for free admission to the Fair. Experts in Indian history supported her claim, and it was agreed that the Mohawks, like everyone else except the Matinnecocks (and Robert Kopple), would have to fork over two bucks if they wanted to experience the greatest event in history.[80] Would any aspect of the Fair reflect its theme of "peace through understanding"?

## Countdown

When it came to the intersection of race and the 1964–65 New York World's Fair, the answer to that question was a definitive no. The early 1960s was, of course, a high point of the civil rights movement, defined by such seminal events as the 1960 lunch counter sit-in in Greensboro, the 1961 "Freedom Riders" bus trips, and the 1963 demonstration in Birmingham and the March on Washington. It was not surprising, then, that African Americans' struggle for equal rights crossed paths with the Fair, especially when it came to jobs. The fireworks began in June 1961, when Dr. Edward Lewis, director of the Urban League of Greater New York (ULGNY), charged that he was getting the "runaround" in his efforts to get the WFC to make a pledge of fair employment opportunities for blacks.[81] Over the next few years, the ULGNY became a pesky adversary to Moses (who disparagingly called its members "professional integrationists"), as the organization publicly claimed that blacks were being discriminated against when it came to the Fair's hiring practices. Lewis astutely recognized the contradiction between the Fair's utopian theme and social realities, noting that the phrase "peace through understanding" would "ring hollow" if qualified blacks were not treated equally.[82] As with many if not most of Moses's projects, it was undoubtedly true that no blacks (or Puerto Ricans, for that matter) had been hired for professional or technical jobs despite the ULGNY's best efforts to make it happen, something that attracted the attention of city and state politicians. In March 1962, Representative Adam Clayton Powell Jr. ordered a federal investigation into the absence of blacks in executive positions, prompting a Fair spokesman to admit that there were indeed no blacks in such positions but that there were many in lesser jobs and two on the WFC's board of directors.[83] As a response to the charges, the WFC set up the new area of "Inter-Group Relations" and appointed Dr. George H. Bennett, an educator and member of the National Urban League, to the executive staff of the corporation's international division. The ULGNY hailed these steps as a "good beginning" and a "professional breakthrough" but was unrelenting in its demand that more blacks be given profession and technical jobs.[84]

With the situation a ticking public relations time bomb as the rest of the nation and world watched the Fair take shape, Governor Rockefeller asked Lieutenant Governor Malcolm Wilson to try to resolve the conflict. Little progress was made, however, and the ULGNY continued its campaign to end the WFC's discriminatory practices. In June 1963, the organization sent telegrams to the governor, President Kennedy, and a number of unions, urging that construction crews of government-sponsored projects at the Fair be immediately integrated. The ULGNY reported "some movement" in their effort to get blacks hired on the construction crew for the Federal Pavilion, but threatened to picket the site if more progress was not made.[85] The next month, Louis E. Lomax, an author, echoed that demonstrations would be held to force the Fair's craft unions to integrate their crews. This threat was made even more real when a study prepared by a local political organization, the East River Reform Democrats, found that both blacks and Puerto Ricans were indeed being discriminated against in building projects at the Fair. Out of a total of sixty-eight workers at the New York State Pavilion, the group found, only two were black, more than sufficient cause for protests of some kind. Passage of the Civil Rights Act of 1964, which prohibited racial discrimination in employment and union membership, was still about a year away, making such threats especially necessary to force change.[86]

True to its word, the Joint Committee on Equal Employment Opportunity (JCEEO) picketed the United Nations in August, appealing to African and Latin American countries to join the organization in its fight for equal hiring practices at the Fair. Picketers carried signs saying "End Apartheid at the Fair" and "African Pavilions Built with Lily White Labor," astutely drawing the parallels between American and African racism. The very next day, a UN group from Guinea toured the fairgrounds to see if any blacks were helping construct its pavilion and, just as the JCEEO claimed, found none. The (white) builders there denied any intentional attempt to keep blacks off the job, but this of course did little to satisfy the JCEEO or its new African allies.[87] Just a few days before opening day, the situation became even more highly charged when the New York State chapter of the NAACP and the Brooklyn chapter of the Congress of Racial Equality learned that Louisiana would be featuring a minstrel-style show called "America, Be Seated" in its pavilion. CORE, a more radical group, had had enough, announcing that it planned a "stall-in" (inspired by the ever growing number of "sit-ins" that were taking place) by having two thousand cars "run out of gas" on Moses's new highways leading to the Fair. Isaiah Brunson, chair of Brooklyn's CORE chapter, came up with the stall-in idea, announcing that "we're going to block every street that can get you anywhere near the World's Fair and give New York the biggest traffic jam it's ever had."[88] Brunson, soon backed up by James Farmer, CORE's national chair, even took out ads in the *New York Times* to promote the protest. New Yorkers, civic leaders, Mayor Wagner, President Johnson, and famously unflappable New York cabbies became alarmed, knowing that opening day at Shea Stadium a few days earlier had snarled traffic on the same roads. Besides traffic ruining the big day, would this Fair become forever known as the "Un-Fair"?

Despite the myriad of problems that Moses and his staff were facing on a daily basis, excitement about the Fair was growing. This frenzy was of course no accident, a result of an intense publicity campaign supervised by Thomas Deegan, whose day job remained a leading public relations consultant. (Deegan's own firm, in fact, was being paid $100,000 a year by the WFC, just one of many apparent conflicts of interests embedded within the Fair's Byzantine financial operations.)[89] One of Deegan's programs was three annual "Preview Days" where hundreds of invited guests, most of them VIPs and members of the media, visited the fairgrounds to see the site, listen to speeches from WFC officials, and eat lunch.[90] At the last Preview Day on April 22, 1963, exactly one year before opening day, Moses and Wagner arranged for President Kennedy to participate in the festivities. Dialing the numbers 1-9-6-4 on a "special telephone," the president gave the go-ahead for a clock to begin the year's countdown to the Fair's opening and promised to be there when the last of the 31.5 million seconds ticked off. "We have a deadline to meet and by dialing 1-9-6-4, I launch the final phase of this great effort," Kennedy declared. (A constant reminder of how much there still was to do in so little time, the clock soon became known as the "Ulcer Machine" by WFC staffers.) In typical Fair fashion, however, the publicity stunt did not go smoothly when a bus ran over a cable and the five hundred special guests at the fairgrounds to hear the president's message had to wait for it to be retransmitted, this time on tape. Deegan made light of the snafu with some cold war humor, remarking, "It's reassuring . . . that this is not the hot line to Moscow."[91] (A hot line between Washington, D.C., and Moscow had recently been set up to facilitate communication between political leaders in order to avoid an accidental nuclear war.) The "Ulcer Machine" itself turned out to be less than precise when two days before the Fair opened, people realized that the clock had miscalculated the countdown.

Deegan pressed on with the publicity blitz in the fall of 1963, having models of some of the Fair's exhibits displayed in the lobby of the Time and Life Building. A public-address system was set up in front of the building (conveniently located across the street from Radio City Music Hall), loudly inviting passersby to "Come on in!"[92] The first public display of Pepsi's "It's a Small World" ride also took place that fall when Moses, Walt Disney, Herbert Barnet (the president of Pepsi-Cola), and Helenka Pantaleoni (the president of the United States Committee for UNICEF) hosted a lunch to show off pictures and a scale model of the boat ride to the media. Even more impressive (and a lot bigger) were the eight Fiberglas dinosaurs that floated down the Hudson River on a barge in October, heading to their ultimate destination in the Sinclair Oil exhibit. The West Side Express Highway, as it was known then, was jammed as motorists stopped to gawk and take pictures, while some parents let their kids skip school to see the prehistoric migration. In January 1964, two thousand colored lights on the dome of General Electric's pavilion were switched on by Ann McKeon, the World's Fair and Summer Festival Queen (remaining on every night until the Fair's closing in October 1965), giving passersby in Queens a small inkling of what lay in store for them in a few months. With its movies, speakers, advertising, and other tactics, the WFC's promotion effort was nothing less than, according to Robert Caro, "perhaps one of the most extensive ever undertaken on behalf of any enterprise except a presidential election."[93]

As New Yorkers started to catch fair fever (distracted a bit by the Beatles' visit in February to *The Ed Sullivan Show* and Carnegie Hall), city officials began to lick their chops at the thought of millions of tourists sure to spend money and boost the local economy. Mayor Wagner predicted that the Fair would generate six billion dollars for the city's economy, and city controller Beame too was rejoicing over the prospect of the city's coffers overflowing because of the event.[94] Local businesses were equally excited. Gimbel's, again trying to trump Macy's, announced it would offer Fair visitors back and foot massages in a special room on the store's sixth floor. Broadway producers anticipated packed houses, Manhattan nightclubs like the Latin Quarter and the Copacabana were hoping that the flood of visitors would fill bars like the old days (new IRS rules limiting expense-account deductions and the assassination of JFK had seriously hurt the club scene), and hotels and parking lots were raising rates to get in on the action.[95] Hilton was racing to finish its new flagship 2,153-room hotel in midtown Manhattan and shake the bugs out before the hordes arrived, knowing many would spring for the special occasion. Although the Fair was months away, IBM had in fact already booked the hotel's five hundred–dollar-a-day penthouse for executives who would be in town for the big event.[96] Some companies were instead renting out apartments for executives planning to catch the Fair (Seven-Up leased a pied-à-terre for its men in gray flannel suits), while other companies were buying cooperative apartments, giving a modest boost to the local real estate market.

Other businesses took full advantage of the promotional opportunities the coming world's fair offered. Banks offered "World's Fair savings accounts," department stores were holding "World's Fair fashion shows," and one clever shoe-maker introduced a special "Fair-hopper" model specially designed to traverse the grounds' 646 acres.[97] New York cabbies were both anticipating and dreading the Fair, knowing it would bring in a lot of new tourists to town but worried about getting stuck in the inevitable traffic jams. Although they could lose their license for doing it, some cabbies were saying they would refuse passengers wanting to go the Fair because of the expected traffic nightmare. The WFC, concerned that some Manhattan-based drivers might get lost in Queens, invited hundreds of cabbies to the fairgrounds to get a tutorial on how to get to and from Flushing Meadows.[98] Staffers (and police) were also worried about price gouging and an increase in an old standby, going via the "scenic route," thinking cabbies might charge more than the usual four dollars for a ride to or from Manhattan and concerned that travelers arriving at the just-renamed Kennedy Airport too might get pinched. However, at least one New York taxi driver was willing to go the extra mile, quite literally, to make sure the Fair was a success. Picking up on the theme of the previous New York fair, the cabbie offered to turn his taxi into a "Cab of Tomorrow" and drive it around the world as a promotional gimmick for the new one. The driver said he would even keep the meter running just to find how much it would cost to take a taxi around the world, in case anyone was interested.[99]

Not only New Yorkers had the Fair on their minds as opening day approached. Phyllis Pennell, the prom chair of Rocky Ford High School in Colorado, planned to use the world's fair as a theme for the party, while in Sault Sainte Marie, Michigan, Tony Calery was getting ready to row the seventeen hundred miles to Flushing Meadows Lake via the St. Lawrence Seaway.[100] Meanwhile, back in Queens, hundreds and even thousands of people were starting to gather around the fairground's perimeter daily, trying to get in even though opening day was still a few weeks away.[101] All were turned away, of course (even kids "wanting to see their father who worked there" and adults "going to Europe tomorrow"), but two eleven year olds (perhaps the ghosts of Tom Sawyer and Huck Finn?) bragged that they had been enjoying the Fair for the past three weeks, having slipped through various holes in the fence. "It's great," said one of them, Frank Mendez of Corona, especially excited to have ridden down the neck of one of Sinclair's dinosaurs.[102] Fifteen thousand people were still working around the clock in the final days before the Fair's opening, racing against the "Ulcer Machine." Eighty-five percent of the total project would be finished by opening day, not bad considering the magnitude of the event and the host of problems encountered along the way.[103] Sixty-six nations, twenty-four states, and some three hundred U.S. companies had accepted invitations to what had started out five years earlier as a three hundredth birthday party for New York City, a gathering as big as any other world's fair ever held.[104]

On April 21, the night before opening day, Americans across the country got a sense of the wholesome, familiar, and, above all, happy experience that was waiting for them in New York City when the popular NBC TV show *The Bell Telephone Hour* aired its prime-time "Salute to the New York World's Fair of 1964." A national audience saw host Donald O'Connor, a star whose career had peaked about a decade earlier, perform Richard Rodgers's new song, "Fair Is Fair," as well as sing and dance his way through a few numbers that recalled previous world's fairs. O'Connor sang "Daisy, Daisy" and danced the cakewalk as a tribute to the 1893 World's Columbian Exposition in Chicago, performed the Charleston to commemorate the (rather feeble) 1926 Sesqui-Centennial International Exposition in Philadelphia, did the jitterbug to remember the 1939–40 New York World's Fair, and, finally, tried the twist to celebrate the Fair kicking off the next day.[105] Also on the eve of opening day, a twelve-billion candlepower beam of light was turned on over the fairgrounds, visible from New Haven, Connecticut, to Atlantic City, New Jersey, and outshining Times Square. Soon the world's largest fountain would be turned on, and a 610-bell carillon would ring out "There's No Business Like Show Business."[106] Already a highly contentious political battleground and social phenomenon, "the single greatest event in history" was finally about to begin.

# 2  Heigh Ho, Ho Hum

*Today we may well be marking the end of one era and the beginning of another.*
    —Mayor Wagner on opening day of the Fair

AT EXACTLY 9:00 A.M. ON APRIL 22, 1964, Bill Turchyn, an eighteen-year-old student from New Jersey, entered Gate 1 at the fairgrounds in Flushing Meadows, becoming the first official visitor to the 1964–65 New York World's Fair. Right behind Mr. Turchyn was Michael Catan, who claimed he was the first to enter the last New York world's fair in 1939, and Al Carter, who said he was first in line at the recent Seattle fair.[1] The three men were the first of 92,646 people (63,791 paid) who would enter the grounds on opening day, a chilly, rainy Wednesday morning.[2] Four thousand people marched in the morning parade, which featured not only Montana cowboys, kimono-clad Japanese geishas, Hawaiian hula dancers, and a group of Shriners but also such beauties as Miss America, Miss Universe, and Donna Reed. Music included Scottish bagpipes, a Caribbean steel-drum band, an Israeli accordionist, strolling Spaniards with guitars, and the University of Pennsylvania marching band.[3]

The multicultural parade, almost like a real-life version of Disney's animatronic "It's a Small World" ride that was kicking into gear over in Pepsi's pavilion, was an apt tribute to the Fair's theme of Peace Through Understanding. America and the world as a whole were indeed more peaceful and understanding places in 1964 than in 1939, when rampant racism and unemployment in the States and the outbreak of World War II in Europe were the social, economic, and political backdrop for the last fair held in the very same spot. Over the course of a generation, the United States had become a more equitable and prosperous nation and an international superpower, but, according to the dignitaries who spoke at the Fair's opening-day dedication ceremonies, it was just the beginning of a truly great society that lay ahead. "Today we may well be marking the end of one era and the beginning of another," correctly predicted Mayor Wagner, although the future he imagined had nothing to do with America's cultural revolution and economic decline that were just around the corner. It was President Johnson, how-ever, swooping in by marine helicopter while Indira Ghandhi was speaking, who offered the rosiest picture of what lay ahead for the nation and the world. In his address to some 10,000 invitation-only guests in the Singer Bowl, LBJ (reprising FDR's presidential opening-day appearance in 1939 and, for that matter, Grover Cleveland's showing at the 1893 World's Columbian Exposition in Chicago and Teddy Roosevelt's at the 1904 St. Louis fair) referred to both World War II and the cold war but made no mention of the country's increasing involvement in Vietnam. "I prophecy peace is not only possible in our generation," Johnson de-clared, "I predict that it is coming much earlier." (He would in fact escalate the war in Vietnam in early 1965.) The president then predicted that by the time of the next world's fair, the United States would be a place in which "no man need be poor" and "no man is handicapped by the color of his skin," each a key theme in what would come to be known as his Great Society domestic agenda.[4] What better place and time to spread the seeds of a Great Society than on opening day of a world's fair whose theme was Peace Through Understanding?

## Black Eye

Unfortunately, President Johnson's utopian vision contrasted sharply with real-ity, a fact brought home even as he spoke. Many visitors outside the Singer Bowl, trying to listen to his speech that was being broadcast over loudspeakers, could not hear it because of the louder shouting of "Jim Crow Must Go!" by hundreds of civil rights activists. This day—opening day—would be the only one in which the contained universe of the Fair would be disrupted by the outside world in any significant way. The activists were led by James Farmer, national director of CORE, and Bayard Rustin, the organizer of the March on Washington, which had been held less than a year before opening day of the Fair. Many of the activists (who were mostly college age and white) had arrived carrying suitcases, prepared to be arrested and spend a night or two in jail.[5] Security for LBJ was understand-ably extremely tight, not just because of the recent assassination of JFK but also because those individuals knowing their history remembered that another presi-dent, William McKinley, was mortally wounded at a previous world's fair, the 1901 Pan-American Exposition in Buffalo. After his address at the Singer Bowl, the president was escorted to the Federal (or United States) Pavilion, giving another speech as he dedicated the nation's official building. There, hundreds of protestors in different groups, holding placards and shouting "Freedom now!" disrupted the president's speech, often making it unintelligible.[6] Apparently prepared for such a scenario, Johnson deftly referenced the picketing, saying, "We do not try to mask our national problems. We do not try to disguise our imperfections or cover up our failures. No other nation in history has done so much to correct its flaws." When the president envisioned "a world in which all men are equal," however, the protestors laughed derisively, even more cause for police, waiting patiently for the speech to end, to drag the protestors into nearby paddy wagons.[7]

Hundreds more "integrationists" or "sit-ins," as reporters alternatively referred to them, however, were scattered around the Fair. Groups of demonstrators—chanting slogans, singing songs, and sitting in front of pavilion entrances—had gathered at dozens of different locations on the grounds. "Bearded and untidy, the seats of their pants muddied from sitting on the soggy ground, the pickets repelled and fascinated the fairgoers," a *New York Times* reporter wrote. (Arthur Gelb, the managing director of the newspaper, would later remember that "visitors to the fair [were] by turns supportive of and angered by the picketers.") Both Rustin and Farmer were arrested at the New York State Pavilion, the latter having led a march of about 300 people in front of the building and barricading it. Farmer's goal at the Fair was to publicize what he referred to as "the melancholy contrast between the idealized, fantasy world of the Fair and the real world of brutality, prejudice, and violence in which the American Negro is forced to live," as accurate an appraisal of the situation as one can imagine as the Civil Rights Bill simmered in the Senate. Farmer's first stop was the Louisiana Pavilion, to which he carried a three-foot electric cattle prod and a sign saying that such a device was used on Negroes in that state. Discovering that the building had not yet been completed and therefore no visitors would or could try to enter it, however, he and his group had to settle on New York. Meanwhile, at the Florida Pavilion, about 50 shouting protestors were fighting with police outside the building while the governor of that state tried to hold a news conference inside. By midafternoon, though, the protests were over, a relief to officials and visitors who were, exactly as intended, distracted and disturbed by the vivid reminder of America's "Negro problem." "The fair was a gayer place after the demonstrators had departed," the *Times* reporter observed, himself apparently relieved that the real world had not overly intruded on the fantasy world in Flushing Meadows.[8]

Although CORE's demonstrations at the fairgrounds did just what they were designed to do, the group's other two disruptive strategies proved to be unequivocal duds. Unless the CORE's Brooklyn chapter's demands—integrated crews on all city construction sites, better inner-city housing conditions, total desegregation of public schools, and a citizen-based review board of complaints of police brutality—were met, the group planned its massive stall-in on the highways and bridges leading to the Fair. The two thousand automobiles that Isaiah Brunson, chairman of the chapter, had said would appear, however, failed to materialize, no doubt pleasing national director Farmer, who was against the stall-in. The major flaw of the protest, which certainly looked great on paper, was that it was left up to each volunteer to choose the time and place where he or she would stall and then how to deal with the inevitable arrival of the police and tow truck. The lack of a coordinated plan of attack discouraged most would-be stallers, as did a court injunction declaring the protest illegal, the disagreeable weather, and the simple fact that many had reservations about possibly never seeing their cars again. Fearing the worst, however, the city mobilized an army of wreckers, which waited patiently on the Triborough Bridge and Grand Central Parkway and scooped up the dozen or so cars that did "run out of gas." A helicopter capable of lifting a car hovered above, a clear sign that city officials believed the stall-in might indeed ruin the day.[9] CORE's other planned protest—pulling the emergency-stop cords on subways to prevent visitors from going to the Fair by mass transit—was also thwarted by some of New York's finest in a rather ugly club-swinging melee that left 4 of the group's members and 3 officers injured.[10]

Although less than a great victory, CORE's protest received national attention via a CBS News special live broadcast covering the Fair's opening ceremonies. Anchor Harry Reasoner covered the demonstrations on the grounds and the failed stall-in, while reporter Mike Wallace talked with Farmer and Rustin in a taped interview. Roger Mudd reported that many lawmakers in Washington, D.C., feared that the protest would negatively impact passage of the Civil Rights Bill in Congress rather than help it.[11]

Political leaders, clearly embarrassed by the situation, were quick to speak out. At a news conference back in Washington, President Johnson called the demonstrations "rude" and said that they "serve[d] no good purpose . . . of promoting the cause they profess to support." Senator Jacob Javits personally apologized to the president for the shouting, not because he did not support the protesters' cause but because he considered it to be an act of disrespect. Governor Nelson Rockefeller claimed he "didn't see any demonstration," something extremely hard to believe, while Mayor Wagner, admittedly ashamed about the chanting over the president's speech, was happy about the "sensible conduct of almost all of our Negro fellow citizens [who] refused to be stampeded into ill-chosen action." Police Commissioner Michael J. Murphy was proud as a peacock to have successfully "closed the lid on the kettle of chaos" but unwittingly confirmed exactly what the protestors were trying to convey. April 22 was "a day in which the President came to the world of fantasy and encountered the world of fact," the commissioner said in an address to the Bronx Board of Trade, perfectly summarizing the disparity between America's rhetorical democracy and blacks' actual experience.[12]

Despite their mixed results on opening day, civil rights activists continued to make their presence known at the Fair through legal tactics. Just a few days after opening day, in fact, 4 women picketed the Florida Pavilion, challenging the WFC's rule to disallow any form of protesting on the fairgrounds. Both CORE and the American Civil Liberties Union (ACLU) were behind the protest, disagreeing with Moses's claim that the grounds were private property and, if they were, testing the right to picket on private property. The women were careful not to cause any form of civil disobedience by shouting or by blocking the entrance to the pavilion, simply carrying signs reading "We Don't Want a World's Fair. We Want a Fair World." Although no fairgoers at all complained to officials about the demonstration, the women were soon arrested for "obstructing the sidewalk" and "causing a crowd to gather" and carried away in Moses's trusty paddy wagon.[13] CORE and the ACLU believed that because the Fair was funded through federal, state, and city bonds, the grounds were, in effect, public property and filed a motion to enjoin the WFC from banning picketing on the grounds. The groups were astutely using the case to push the limits of the First and Fourteenth Amendments to the Constitution, which protected free speech and, therefore, the right to demonstrate peacefully. In June, however, a Queens Criminal Court judge ruled that the grounds were, as the WFC argued, private property and convicted the 4 women of trespassing and disorderly conduct.[14]

The case, and Moses's desire to keep the Fair politics free, did not end there, however. The NAACP promptly joined CORE in its use of the courts to test the breadth of the First Amendment and, ultimately, to use the Fair as a stage to make more people aware of America's institutional racism. The next month, a federal judge ruled that although the WFC could maintain its ban on picketing, it would be legal for handbills to be passed out on the grounds, as they were on opening day in front of the Florida and Louisiana Pavilions. This ruling was just the first in a series of disappointments for the WFC, which feared that any and all forms of protesting would, in one of its lawyer's words, "convert the fairgrounds into an ideological battlefield."[15] A couple of weeks after the latest court ruling, 150 Spanish civil war veterans and their families congregated outside the Spanish Pavilion, circumventing the WFC's no-protesting rules by wearing giant buttons reading "Amnesty for All Political Prisoners in Spain." The WFC's frustrated police force, realizing that they could not arrest the demonstrators because many people at the Fair wore all sorts of buttons, were forced to keep the paddy wagon in its garage.[16] Much more to the WFC's dismay, another Queens judge soon acquitted 12 leaders of the American Jewish Congress who had been arrested for disorderly conduct resulting from picketing the Jordan Pavilion for an allegedly offensive mural back in May. The judge decided that the Fair was a "quasi-public operation" whose grounds had the "character of public streets," and thus "all guarantees of the United States Constitution appl[ied]," including the right to picket. As a coup de grâce, an appellate court in Brooklyn in October reversed the convictions of the 4 women arrested for trespassing and disorderly conduct at the Florida Pavilion, finding insufficient evidence of the demonstrators' guilt.[17]

Despite the brave and savvy efforts by civil rights activists to use the Fair to promote their cause, the WFC and many exhibitors believed the event was a perfect example of America's creed of *e pluribus unum*. Even the *New York Times* considered the Fair "a showcase for civil rights, where Negroes and whites work together in virtually every phase of the operation," reflecting the state of equal opportunity employment in the United States in 1964. Such a claim was simply untrue, with people of color allowed to hold only subordinate positions. Knowing that issues of race and racism would no doubt continue as the civil rights movement intensified through the early 1960s, both Fair officials and managers of pavilions and businesses implemented what they believed to be a progressive form of affirmative action in their hiring practices, an attempt to present an enlightened image to visitors. "We knew we'd have visitors here from all walks of life," said T. H. Roberts, manager of GM's Futurama, where 19 of 38 hosts and hostesses were black, "[so] we wanted our personnel to reflect this." Ford was pleased as punch to claim that 26 of its 200 greeters were black, and Du Pont was equally happy that visitors would notice that 8 of its 45 hosts and hostesses were African American. GE considered its hiring of 10 black hostesses out of a total of 110 at its Progressland exhibit such a progressive step that the company proudly made it known in its in-house magazine for employees and shareholders. Working with the National Urban League as a job clearinghouse, the WFC asked the Brass Rail, the largest food service operator at the Fair, to actively recruit workers from black colleges such as Howard University, Morgan State, Fisk University, and Florida A&M as part of its drive to fill its staff with energetic (and affordable) college students. Members of the local New York chapter of the National Urban League seemed pleased to see a lot of black workers on the grounds but were not ready to laud the Fair as a civil rights victory quite yet.[18]

## Fair Sailing

Almost as soon as the cowboys, geishas, hula dancers, and Shriners got off the opening-day parade route, controversy started to swirl around Moses's plan to use the fairgrounds as the centerpiece of a world-class park system. Moses was intent on using virtually all of the expected $27.5 million Fair surplus for his chain of six parks in Queens, even though the WFC's lease with the city suggested, at the very least, that the future funds were supposed to go to the city's schools. "All net revenue [from the Fair] shall be paid to the city and shall be used for the restoration and improvement of Flushing Meadows Park, and the balance of such revenue remaining thereafter shall be used by the City of New York for educational purposes," the lease stated, sufficiently unclear to allow for the significant difference in opinion. Moses's "restoration and improvement" encompassed no less than 2,816 acres worth of park stretching for more than 7 miles, a mammoth project obviously beyond the parameters of the lease. As well, if all of the Fair's forthcoming profits were to be "paid to the city," why did the WFC—a private corporation—presume that it was going to manage the project? Mayor Wagner and the city council were behind Moses, however, as was Governor Rockefeller who signed a New York State bill on April 25 that extended the life of the WFC for two years after the Fair closed to allow it to develop park facilities on the site. In his dedication speech for the New York State Pavilion, in fact, Rockefeller backed Moses's proposal to make the building a permanent part of the future park at Flushing Meadows, using his power to gain popular support for the idea.[19]

One man, however, was doing everything he could to block Moses from adding another key piece to his creation of a reconfigured New York City. City controller Abe Beame considered Moses's attempts to use the Fair to pay for his collection of parks an "elaborate scheme" and wanted the money to go to where he believed it was originally intended and was needed most—school repairs, new textbooks, lab equipment, and other educational needs.[20] Organizations such as the Citizens Union, the United Federation of Teachers, and the United Parents Association not surprisingly sided with Beame, but so did a number of parks groups, the latter naturally concerned that a private corporation believed it had the right to build public parks with public money. Also curious, to say the least, was that included in Moses's plan was the appointment of a special parks commissioner for Queens to supervise the project. The proposed salary for the new position was $100,000—precisely the total compensation Moses was making as president of the WFC. Newbold Morris, the city's current commissioner of parks, was making just $25,000 a year, but Morris was backing Moses all the way, no doubt knowing where his career bread was buttered.[21]

As the clouds of opening day—the gloomy weather, fears of major civil rights protests, and bickering over what to do with money that did not yet exist—cleared, many critics and, especially, visitors seemed to be impressed with what they saw, heard, smelled, and tasted at the bright and shiny Fair. "The sophisticated visitor approaches the fair ready to dismiss it as 'Disneyland East,' Newsweek wrote five days after opening day, "but he—or she—will find it hard to resist being swept up by the exuberant shapes and sights and sounds of the world's biggest playground." Life chirpily called it "the biggest exposition of all time" and "a smash-eroo of a world's fair," while Ebony was equally ecstatic, considering it both "the biggest show ever conceived and staged by man" and "the most expensive and extravagant spectacle of all times." By the end of the first week, a million people had already passed through the ground's eight gates and eighty-nine turnstiles, buoying Fair officials' dream of hosting the greatest event in history.[22]

An even tougher audience than the media, however, seemed to be impressed with what Moses had delivered to the people. By the end of opening week, the Fair had already become a popular hangout for teenagers, especially at night when most of the exhibits had closed but the bars remained opened. Officials' reaction to what the New York Times referred to as "bands" of teens who "invaded" the Fair "mainly for mischief" was very much consistent with authoritative figures' fear of and obsession with "juvenile delinquency" in the postwar years. Francis X. Clines of the Times seemed to have just seen West Side Story before filing his report about various teenagers "travel[ing] aimlessly" at the Fair, one whose major offense seemed to be his wearing of "tight black trousers" and another for being named "Chick." Although no teenagers had yet committed a crime, both the Fair's Pinkerton security force and the city police were closely watching them "just in case," as one guard put it. During the day, teens seemed to be causing no such ruckus,

merely making full use of the Fair's technological innovations for their own particular purposes. "Teen-agers," observed *Newsweek*, "dig the no-hands telephones,
which free them for doing the frug." Another young person especially enamored
with the Fair was 12-year-old Dominic Tucci, who had been reported missing for
nine days from his Port Washington home on Long Island. The boy was discovered on the grounds, having spent the entire time there quite happily, living off of
change he plucked out of the Fair's numerous fountains. "I slept in the Gas Pavilion for three nights, four nights in the Continental Insurance Pavilion, one night
at Coca-Cola and one night in the Johnson's Wax Theater," Tucci told police. Also
very impressed with the sights and sounds of the Fair was 101-year-old Edward
Everett Cauthorne, who compared this one to the New Orleans Exposition of 1884,
which he had attended 80 years earlier. Cauthorne, who was Harvard University's
oldest living alumnus, recalled trying to guess how many beans were in a jar at
the Louisiana fair, with the grand prize a horse and carriage.[23]

Another sign that the Fair seemed to be a success early on was its popularity
among another bellwether group: panhandlers. A few of Times Square's most visible panhandlers had moved their operations to Flushing Meadows, working the
gates near the main entrance and the boardwalk that visitors had to cross after
pouring out of or into the IRT subway. A blind man who had been raising money
for an "eye transplant" for more than a decade in midtown Manhattan was doing
gangbusters business at the Fair, finding happy visitors heading back to the city
relatively easy pickings. Not too surprisingly, pickpockets and confidence men
too were active at the Fair, moving to where the action was. Arrests by the New
York City Police Department's Pickpocket and Confidence Squad were way up,
as both uniformed and plainclothes officers caught petty thieves trying to take
advantage of the large crowds of tourists. Two classic cons in circulation at the
Fair—the Spanish handkerchief switch and the pocketbook drop—required that
victims put up cash in the belief they would profit from the deal, but unsuspecting
fairgoers were falling for the schemes nonetheless.[24]

An even more important group—the rich and famous—was also showing up
at the Fair, with a trip to Flushing Meadows quickly becoming a requisite stop for
many in the public eye, especially politicians. Upon arrival, congressmen, mayors,
governors, senators, and presidents of nations were escorted around the grounds
by a Fair official and often given a "special" medal as a parting gift. Moses himself
hated to serve as tour guide even for heads of state from foreign countries and
thus would very rarely do it, although he did personally show the 94-year-old el-
der statesman and financier Bernard Baruch around the grounds.[25] The Duke and
Duchess of Windsor showed up on May 6, escorted by Thomas Deegan, while a
horde of congressmen from thirty-eight states along with their families—a group
of five hundred people—arrived a week later for three full days of fairgoing. Jac-
queline Kennedy, along with her daughter, Caroline, and Mrs. Stephen Smith, the
late president's sister, and her children, visited the Fair on April 30 (John-John had

a cold and couldn't make it). The Kennedy party declined to take part in any official functions, a condition of Jackie's year in mourning, choosing to spend their six hours at the Fair much like any other family. The group took in the flume ride in the Lake Amusement Area, and, despite the obligatory soaking, even did an encore plunge at Caroline's insistence. The group's lunch at the Terrace Club also suggested they were just another typical American family, with the kids ordering hamburgers and hot dogs at the exclusive restaurant. Disappointed to be told that the gourmet establishment did not serve such fare, they settled for roast beef and got their epicurean wish later at one of the many Brass Rail snack bars. Robert Kennedy, his wife, and seven of their eight children came out to the Fair on October 17, just making it before the first season closed the next day. Running for the United States Senate as New York's Democratic candidate, Kennedy used the Fair as a scenic backdrop to promote his campaign issues centered around education, public housing, and medical care for the aged. The former attorney general also knew a good photo op when he saw one, kissing each of his kids as they boarded a Glide-a-Ride car in front of the IBM Pavilion.[26]

Despite his mixed reception on opening day, President Johnson returned to the Fair on May 9, using the highly publicized event to continue making his case for a great American society. In a speech before the Amalgamated Clothing Workers Association convention, Johnson lent his support for the Civil Rights Bill then before Congress and emphasized his commitment to fight poverty by announcing a federal grant of one million dollars for improvements in schools, job training, employment services, and crime prevention in Harlem. "The nation must open wide the door of equality and invite all the nation to walk through that door," the president said, "not from charity, not from coercion but from a deep commitment to justice." Johnson reminded the audience that it was the one hundredth anniversary of Abraham Lincoln's Emancipation Proclamation, but America was not yet free of bigotry. "Until education is unaware of race, until employment is blind to color, emancipation may be a proclamation but it is not a fact," the president declared, words very much like those of civil rights activists who had been booing him just a couple of weeks earlier in the same spot.[27] The Civil Rights Bill, which made segregation illegal, passed in July, perhaps in part because of the protests at the Fair on opening day that brought international attention to African Americans' inequalities.

Senator Jacob Javits too was an early visitor to the Fair, arriving by subway on opening day to promote the use of the city's mass transit systems, especially the IRT's new express run. Over the first week, 42 percent of visitors had arrived by bus or subway, an impressive figure and good news to elected officials like Javits who pushed for additional trains going to and from the Fair. To prove that mass transportation was a good way to get to the Fair, the transit authority decked out one of its trains in red carpeting, crystal fixtures, pink and blue drapes, and snazzy furniture on May 13, and then filled it with celebrities such as Shirley MacLaine,

Gene Kelly, and Dick Van Dyke (a publicity stunt not just for the NYCTA but also for Twentieth Century-Fox, whose film *What a Way to Go* starring these same actors premiered at the Fair). Still, despite these efforts to get more visitors on subways and buses, many of the grounds' parking lots (which Moses had prioritized over a temporary subway extension from the inner city) were often full. In May, some fifteen thousand people waiting for buses to the parking lot nearly rioted, with police brought in to control the crowd and metal barriers and more guards added to prevent another ugly scene. The NYCTA was taking aggressive steps to get folks to use mass transit, such as distributing leaflets in Brooklyn to promote the express buses to the Fair and screening the movie *What a Way to Go,* which hailed the benefits of getting to the grounds by the transit authority's brand-new blue cars. The NYCTA even devised a speedier method to sell subway tokens at the Times Square IRT station, where bottlenecks were throwing a monkey wrench into the mass transit works. In June, another form of mass transit, the Circle Line, canceled its boat trip to the Fair from West Forty-third Street in Manhattan because of a lack of demand, visitors apparently not too interested in traveling to the event by sea. Nationwide, the Fair was being credited for a big increase in train travel, with many Americans still avoiding airplanes because of both safety concerns and the high cost. One Houstonite, Paul Kepner, however, was not interested in getting to the Fair by plane, train, or automobile, choosing instead to cover the two thousand or so miles by bicycle. The sixty-eight-year-old former professor was an avid cyclist, explaining his ability to pull off such a feat as simply to "act half your age."[28]

## Motleyland, USA

Although millions of people were devoting considerable time, effort, and expense to get to the Fair and were very glad to have done so, architectural critics continued to be a tougher crowd. Upon taking in what had sprung up on the grounds, some critics panned the disparate collection of buildings, believing that what had arisen fared the worse compared to other recent global expositions. At Brussels in 1958, there was a palpable, cold war–fueled feeling of tension and excitement in the air, turning the architecture into part of an ideological contest. Not only did Russia—conspicuously absent from the new world's fair—have a pavilion in Brussels, but Eastern European countries such as Czechoslovakia and Hungary did as well, creating a highly charged, "us versus them" architectural atmosphere. Even the most recent fair in Seattle, with its rather daring Space Needle, was viewed by many as more architecturally interesting than New York's.[29] Ada Louise Huxtable of the *New York Times* found most of the Fair's architecture inferior, a result of Moses's laissez-faire, anything-goes policy. Huxtable believed pavilions in the International Area especially suffered from the lack of a clear identity, a result of their often privately funded but government-sanctioned status. "The public-private approach has produced an uneasy design blend in which the official portion peters out rapidly into trade show clichés," she noted in May. Although Huxtable, like almost everyone, was mightily impressed with the Japanese Pavilion's stone exterior, for example, she thought the interior "degenerates into a salesman's sample room." China's was "like an elaborately bad Oriental furniture store," she added, whereas "Greece is better not mentioned at all."[30]

Other critics took swipes at Moses's controversial decision to forego a grand plan and allow exhibitors to put up buildings of their own design. "Left on their own, many exhibitors predictably put up the sort of eyecatchers that suggest refreshment stands on U.S. 1," *Time* snickered. One writer for the *Saturday Review* commented that "no architectural style was taboo, and as a result we have a rather dazzling Motleyland, USA," while another for the magazine saw the Fair as "a triumph of the engineer and not the artist." Writing for the *New Republic,* Wolf Von Eckardt wrote, "This American surreality [*sic*] ca. 1964, like our new suburban never-never lands, dazzles the eye with a chaotic accumulation of architectural stunts and colossal banalities." A. G. Odell Jr., the president of the American Institute of Architects, was of similar mind, simply calling it "Coney Island." Some European critics, seeing no real theme (and likely angry that the Yanks had the audacity to ignore the Paris-based BIE rules), were even referring to the event not as a world's fair but as an especially large "street fair." Another design critic saw the architectural grab bag of the Fair as a metaphor for something much bigger and more important, believing that "its inability to send men home exploding with ideas [is] a real indication of the decline of the nation." Vincent Scully Jr., writing for *Life,* pretty much said it all just in the title of his article, "If This Is Architecture, God Help Us."[31]

Mixed in with the slams, however, were some views that all of it wasn't bad. John Canaday of the *New York Times* found most of what he saw at the Fair tawdry, confused, and vulgar but somehow also tolerable, a form of "folk art." Though critical, *Time* also had some good things to say about the Fair's architecture in its initial reviews. "Much of it, to be sure, has a tacky, plastic, here-today-blown-tomorrow look, as if it were a city made of credit cards," the magazine reported. "But much of it has grace and substance," it was quick to add, "and somehow, in its jostling, heedless, undisciplined energy, it makes a person happy to be alive in the 20th century."[32] And like many fairgoers, the magazine was especially enthralled with the grounds when the sun had set. "At night, when the ticky-tacky disappears and the jewelling lights go on, the happy, hoppy daydream becomes a garden of visual delight," a reporter swooned. Horace Sutton of the *Saturday Review* was similarly charmed with the Fair after dusk, writing that the grounds "look like a city in a book of fairy tales at night."[33]

## Technical Difficulties

Besides the random nature of the Fair's architecture, critics and average visitors alike were disappointed to find not all the exhibits open for business early in the first season. Lebanon's pavilion was not complete on opening day, for example, nor was Morocco's or France's (the latter, a privately funded affair, was also in arrears).[34] Construction on various unfinished buildings was continuing around the clock through the spring, with the nearly four-acre Belgian Village the most egregious slowpoke. The village was actually designed in 1930 and shown in Antwerp, then constructed for the 1933–34 Chicago world's fair and then again in Brussels in 1958 for its fair. Work on the village, described in the Fair's *Official Guide* as "a meticulous copy of a walled Flemish village as it might have appeared in 1800," came to a screeching halt for a week in May after funds to finish the job ran out. "Picturesque Belgium," as it was also called, consisted of no less than a hundred houses, a replica of the fifteenth-century Gothic church of Saint Nicholas in Antwerp, a town hall with an underground rathskeller, forty shops, a canal, and an arched stone bridge, formally opening in early August despite it still not being totally installed.[35] Investors in the project, which was finally completed in October—just in time for the closing of the first season—took a whopping two million–dollar Belgian bath. The owner of the village, Robert Straile, had an idea, however, of how to recoup his losses the second season. Straile had been talking with Hugh Hefner about putting in a Playboy Club in the town hall, the two of them planning to dress up the "bunnies," according to the former, "in medieval

*4. At the Belgian Village, a visitor might have mistaken twentieth-century Flushing Meadows for eighteenth-century Antwerp. With 124 buildings on its four-acre plot, however, the Flemish town proved to be an overly ambitious enterprise, at least for its investors. Photo © Bill Cotter.*

Flemish costumes à la Breughel." Upon hearing how Picturesque Belgium might be even more picturesque in 1965, Charles Poletti threw up his hands and said, in effect, over his dead body.[36]

Although exhibitors brought in their own architects and interior designers, the construction work itself was done by members of dozens of local unions under contract with the WFC. Some exhibitors believed that workers had intentionally delayed the completion of their buildings so that overtime pay would kick in, a claim the unions of course denied.[37] Union leaders had agreed early on to the WFC's demand that there be no strikes, walkouts, or other forms of work stoppages, but labor problems proved to be a running theme throughout the run of the Fair. However, a number of events—the "Dancing Waters" show, Dick Button's "Ice-Travaganza" show, and the Continental Circus—did not open on time because of a dispute between the corporation's management and IATSE Local 829. KLM's Cinerama presentation, "To the Moon and Beyond," too was delayed because of union issues when management and Local 638 metalworkers had it out.[38]

These were minor spats, however, compared to the brouhaha between managers of the Spanish Pavilion and the Teamsters. Upon learning that the Spaniards had hired some nonunion workers, Teamsters Local 1034 prevented garbage collectors from picking up the pavilion's trash, causing quite a political (and literal) stink. The Spaniards threatened to dump the trash into the Unisphere's fountain if it was not collected, with the Teamsters saying they would then retrieve the garbage from the fountain and throw it back into the pavilion. Luckily, the skirmish, which became known at the Fair as the "Great Garbage Controversy," was resolved before it escalated into another Spanish-American War.[39]

With New York City local unions charging anywhere from $11.50 an hour for a carpenter to $17 for a plumber, very high rates back in 1964 and a reflection of the immense power of labor in the mid-1960s, many exhibitors suffered from a severe case of sticker shock upon receiving bills for routine maintenance on their buildings.[40] Interestingly, the maintenance contract was awarded to a company, Allied Maintenance, with no competitive bid process, the first of what would soon be a stream of questions about the WFC's financial and bookkeeping practices. Complaints about the high costs flooded into the WFC's offices in May and June, especially from foreign governments not used to paying American, much less New York City, union rates.[41] Former Olympic champion Dick Button, operator of the "Ice-Travaganza," canceled his contract with his union-run maintenance company after being charged $200 a week for a sweeper. "At those prices," Button said, "I'll give up skating and sweep." Two days later, forty industrial exhibitors called a meeting with WFC executive Colonel J. T. O'Neill, hoping to discuss the high maintenance costs with the man they believed headed up the area. It turned out, however, that the colonel was in charge of security, not maintenance, but since they had the man's attention, they talked with him about security concerns, another problem area.[42]

Even before opening day, things were disappearing from some of the build-ings, with the Japanese, Indonesian, Philippine, Maryland, and a few other pavil-ions reporting cases of pilferage. Sudan had lost a large, decorated ostrich egg, for example, while Hong Kong was continually losing and then recovering twelve foot-long spears taken from its exhibit's sampans.[43] Many exhibitors added more security guards to prevent future thefts, but a wide variety of items continued to go missing, with laborers (who had been allowed to park their cars near construc-tion sites) considered the primary suspects.[44] Over the first three weeks of the Fair, for example, 109 baby strollers worth more than $10,000 had evaporated from the Hertz concession, turned into souvenirs. In May, two Pinkerton employees were charged with stealing 3,000 admission tickets that they no doubt planned to sell somehow to unsuspecting visitors, while in June the Carriage House, a restaurant in the Transportation and Travel Pavilion, was robbed of $10,000 in a rather dar-ing holdup. Most puzzling was the disappearance of a stuffed, seven-foot, fifty-four-pound white marlin from the Long Island Rail Road exhibit that jumped ship in September.[45]

Another source of angst among exhibitors was the expected but still disturb-ing series of snafus that come with an operation the magnitude of a world's fair. A fire at Maryland's pavilion on opening day caused it to close, and a few days later seven people were injured when a Glide-a-Ride bus hit the General Foods arch near the ground's entrance were not happy to discover that the hospital on the fairgrounds remained unfinished and closed for business. (The prefab "Atom-edic" hospital finally opened in late June.)[46] By the end of just the first week of the Fair, many of Greyhound's three-wheeled, four-passenger "Escorters" were already breaking down, perhaps causing some visitors to wonder if the utopian world of transportation being presented would ever be realized if man couldn't make a golf cart work. In early July, twelve persons were trapped for four hours in the Aerial Tower Ride after an electrical failure, an experience made even the more miserable because of an intense heat wave that settled over New York around the July 4 holiday.[47]

Ford, however, was the unlucky poster child for technology running amok at the Fair, sometimes quite literally. At the end of the opening week, 2,000 visi-tors had to be evacuated from the company's pavilion because of a fire in a trans-former, and, in June, a Pinkerton guard was run over by one of its 144 automatic convertibles. The next month, the building again had to be evacuated because of another small fire, causing one woman to angrily ask a guard, "You mean we have to leave? We stood in line an hour." The series of mishaps was, perhaps, a bad omen for Ford, which was again being clearly shown up by its perennial rival, General Motors. GM's Futurama was turning out to be the undisputed hit of the Fair, just as its earlier incarnation was in 1939 and 1940. In September, GM passed its 1939–40 Futurama attendance of 13,180,000 and celebrated by holding a photo op with the visitor who set the new record. The lucky winner turned out to be

5. *A well-dressed foursome travels in style aboard a Greyhound Escorter. The vehicles proved to be less than reliable, although they did later find service on the Atlantic City boardwalk. Photo © Bill Cotter.*

a five-year-old boy who, after being given a Fair medallion by Moses, asked his mother for a salami sandwich. The mom was given a 24-karat gold bracelet and a GM-made washer-dryer, but the seemingly perfect public relations ploy went awry when she told officials that she already had two such machines, adding, "I always hang the clothes outdoors anyway."[48]

## Trouble in Paradise

Although the plethora of technical difficulties—unfinished buildings, union problems, fires, and stuffed fish gone missing—were glitches the Fair certainly could have done without, the single largest problem the first season was without a doubt the Lake Amusement Area. The area was a trouble spot since the Fair's early planning stages, with no clear theme, no originality, and no compelling reason for being. Just as many critics thought, Moses's idea of good entertainment—wholesome, risk free, and, in a word, boring—was simply not a formula that was going to work with so many other more interesting alternatives on the grounds. Entertainment options in Manhattan too during the spring, especially an amazing collection of Broadway shows (*A Funny Thing Happened on the Way to the Forum* at the Alvin, *Barefoot in the Park* at the Biltmore, *Funny Girl* at the Winter Garden,

*Hello Dolly* at the St. James, *How to Succeed in Business Without Really Trying* at the Forty-sixth Street Theater, *Oliver!* at the Imperial, *What Makes Sammy Run?* at the Fifty-fourth Street Theater, and *Who's Afraid of Virginia Woolf?* at the Billy Rose), further made the Lake Amusement Area at the Fair a losing proposition. *Time* perfectly described the problem a month into the first season: "The so-called Lake Amusement sector is merely a disaster area. Its trouble is simple: the amusements the area offers are almost all less amusing than the free shows of the industries. In 1939 this amusement area was four times as large, and there were nudes there. This time there are a few trained porpoises and the flume ride."[49]

Alarmed at the thin crowds, Fair staffers quickly added new signs on the grounds to try to direct visitors to the Lake Amusement Area, thinking that fairgoers perhaps just could not find it. One did have to cross a bridge to get to the area, enough of a deterrent to the already foot weary. Another strategy to boost attendance was to offer discounts to the area for a week to the city's 42,000 cab drivers, hoping they and their families would enjoy the experience and start spreading the news to their fares. However, many cabbies were, as feared, reluctant to take passengers to the Fair, in part because fairgoers were widely acknowledged to be the worst tippers in New York City, except perhaps for "women who lunch" and major league baseball players, both of whom were widely and notoriously considered cheaper than cheap. (Politicians, gamblers, jockeys, and, of course, waiters were considered the biggest "sports.")[50]

The taxi-driver strategy not working, the next idea was to install $100,000 worth of floodlights to the area in the hope it would incite more visitors to come in the evening.[51] None of these cosmetic fixes, however, could remedy the fundamental issue with the Lake Amusement Area—it was not amusing. Proprietors of shows and rides in the area were fuming, thinking Moses had left them in the lurch, and the WFC president's refusal to meet with them to discuss ways to increase business did not help matters.

Just a couple of months into the first season, many of the area's features began to fold. The plug on the 250-cast-member "Wonder World" extravaganza (which was performed on the same site as Billy Rose's very popular "Aquacade" show in the 1939–40 fair) was pulled on July 5, as there were often more people in the show than watching it. The "Wonder World" exhibitor filed a bankruptcy petition in June, making a pledge for a new and improved format the next season.[52] With the Lake Amusement Area turning into the black hole at the Fair, Moses conceded that the sector was indeed experiencing some difficulties but added that its problems were "grossly exaggerated"—damage control for his stubborn refusal to consider other entertainment options for the area years earlier. The press was quick to jump on Moses's blunder. "Visitors are more entertained by the nine Sinclair Fiberglass dinosaurs which don't bat an eye than the overblown, celebrity-less, and pricey extravaganzas [in the area]," a reporter for *Newsweek* observed.[53] Not just in the Lake Amusement Area but across the Fair, staffers and exhibitors had misjudged that visitors would pay extra admission prices when there was already too much to take in that was free. Six hundred forty-six acres of supply, to put it simply, was exceeding the demand.

The Lake Amusement Area was not the only part of the Fair in trouble early on. Still unfinished, the Louisiana Pavilion in the Federal and State Area was a particular mess, something that no doubt delighted the civil rights activists who had demonstrated there on opening day. There were understandably few seat takers at the pavilion's minstrel show "America Be Seated," with audiences apparently not seeing it as the satirical antibigotry revue it was intended to be. Considering the racially charged atmosphere, Broadway and Hollywood producer Michael Todd's "America Be Seated" was clearly the winner of the "what-were-they-thinking?" award at the Fair, and the show was shut down on May 10 after taking in a total of $300 during its run, which consisted of two days.[54] Operators of the Louisiana Pavilion soon had to file bankruptcy when they could not pay most of the $2 million construction tab. Surprisingly, however, the WFC decided to lend the Louisianans $150,000 to complete their building, going against its own policy to avoid being in the risky construction business.[55] Just a few days later, however, a private company, Pavilion Property, bought the building's assets and assumed its debts, its executives thinking that they could turn the operation into a moneymaking venture. Governor John J. McKeithen severed all ties with the Fair and withdrew his state's sanction of the pavilion, leaving it a completely private enterprise that was renamed "Bourbon Street."[56]

Other state-sponsored pavilions started to drop like flies in the July heat, as construction costs and operating expenses exceeded revenues from extra admission fees, merchandise, and food. The director of the West Virginia Pavilion resigned because of financial difficulties, while operators of the Florida Pavilion decided to drop the extra admission fee except for the Everglades area that offered alligator wrestling and what was unfortunately described as "Seminole Indian and reptile acts."[57] The governor of Florida, Farris Bryant, knowing that the failure of his state's pavilion was a lost opportunity for future tourism dollars, had the rare honor to sit down with Moses a number of times to try to figure out ways to get more visitors to come see the showcase for the Sunshine State. Farris wanted Moses to provide free transportation from the main gate to the Lake Amusement Area, but with such a service supposedly costing the WFC $3 million for the Fair's full run, it wasn't going to happen. Montana too was in the red, so much so that its operators would soon be spending the cold winter brainstorming ways to pay off their debt so that the pavilion could open for the 1965 season.[58]

Also in July, producers of the "To Broadway with Love" show at the Texas Pavilion were cutting performances to save money and fill their house. One can see how the show, with music by Berlin, Bernstein, Gershwin, Kern, Porter, Rodgers, and the title theme and original material from Broadway pros Jerry Bock and Sheldon Harnick, would look like a hit on paper. But with reserved seats costing

$2 to $4.80 and set against the rest of the Texas Pavilion (which included the Old West–themed Frontier Palace as well as NASA, cattle industry, and petroleum exhibits), "To Broadway with Love" was a Texas-sized bomb.[59] When reducing the number of performances failed to fill the house, producers then, rather sadly, asked patrons to pay only if they had enjoyed the show. Predictably, the show closed a few days later, no doubt leaving some to wonder why a show called "To Broadway with Love" was held in the Texas Pavilion in the first place. The president of the pavilion, Angus G. Wynne Jr. (creator of the recently opened Six Flags Over Texas amusement park), soon filed for bankruptcy, but things took an even worse turn when Wynne's nephew, Angus Wynne III, was arrested for trespassing, assaulting police, and resisting arrest. Wynne the younger, the director of the Texas Pavilion and just twenty years old, had tried to reenter the building after the Fair had closed, something even a pavilion operator was not allowed to do. The case got even more bizarre when two of Wynne's buddies showed up at the precinct station where he was being booked in an attempt to break him out of jail. The two cowboys, apparently forgetting that Queens was a long way from the Wild West, promptly joined their friend in the clink.[60]

Besides the bad judgment regarding what visitors did or did not consider entertaining, the significant number of pavilion failures was largely a result of too much competition for the fairgoer's limited time and dollar. Seventy-five percent of the exhibits were free after paying the admission fee, but some of the better exhibits, not to mention food and souvenirs, were not. "Watch out for Hawaii," *Newsweek* warned. "A visit to the islands might be cheaper." In these days when an automatic teller machine could not be found on every corner and even credit cards were relatively uncommon, the WFC and many exhibitors had clearly overestimated how much money visitors would bring to and spend at the Fair. *Time* wrote, "One of the most common sights at the fair is of grown men wandering dazedly, holding their trouser pockets inside out in the timeless gesture of bankruptcy. People who have just rounded their first million sometimes go there to celebrate and are paupers by nightfall. No complaint is more frequently heard at the fair than the cries of the nouveau broke."[61]

The decision by the WFC to allow certain better exhibits to charge visitors a special admission fare was having the unexpected and undesirable effect of leaving visitors with little money for food, something concessionaires were not happy about. The most expensive restaurants, whose managers believed people in New York would pay high prices for food (even in Queens), were especially suffering. With its $8 steaks, the Top of the Fair restaurant was forced to throw in the towel in August, a victim of visitors' thrift when it came to food.[62] Midpriced eating places, which tended to be off the beaten track but a good compromise between gourmet fare and a hot dog from a Brass Rail snack bar kiosk, often had long lines. Especially popular was the $3.40 all-you-can-eat buffet at the Schaefer Center, an even better bargain because the first beer was free. The Schaefer Center also threw in some entertainment value, a display model of the original Schaefer brewery that showed how beer was made in the mid-nineteenth century. The first glass of beer was also on the house at Rheingold's tavern, the centerpiece of its "Little Old New York" exhibit that re-created the city circa 1904 complete with cobblestone streets and gas lamps. Another very popular bargain was Chun King's Chinese Inn where, for just 99 cents, a hungry fairgoer got a seven-course Chinese dinner. The inn, which had been a big hit at the Seattle fair, also offered a "Hong Kong Burger" whose ingredients—a double-decker hamburger, cheese, lettuce, special sauce, and bean sprouts—foreshadowed Ray Kroc's Big Mac, albeit with an Asian twist.[63] Although it was plain to all that many of the Fair's restaurants were too highly priced for the average visitor—something difficult to appreciate now when an $8 steak would cause suspicion because of its cheapness—WFC officials were reluctant to admit that there was such a problem. When asked about it in May, vice president for operations Stuart Constable claimed that only twenty of the first million visitors to the Fair had officially filed complaints for any problem whatsoever, and Moses too claimed that "out of the first 200 letters, 198 were wildly enthusiastic." In fact, some of the busier restaurants, such as the ones at the Danish Pavilion and the Frontier Palace, were planning to raise their prices to cover their own high operating expenses, making more fairgoers opt to dine al fresco out of the brown bags they had brought.[64]

## Spring Fever

Adding to the woes of exhibitors was a less than gung-ho workforce. Some of the four thousand college students quickly became homesick (it was the first trip north for many southerners), while others were more interested in the considerable dating opportunities than the work itself.[65] As early as just two weeks into the Fair's run, some employees were grumbling about being bored at their jobs. Fanny Chow, a New Yorker who worked at the Chinese Pavilion, thought her job at the Fair was about as interesting as her last one as a cashier in a restaurant. "At first I spent my time for dinner in visiting and looking," she said, "but now I sit and rest." Peter Lyle, a nineteen-year-old cashier at one of the Brass Rail snack stands, was spending his downtime reading four volumes of Winston Churchill's *History of the English-Speaking Peoples.* Gerald Weber, a guard at GM's Futurama, had the Sartrean misfortune of having to listen to the same part of the audio portion of the ride as cars passed him every few seconds. "Now you are coming into the land of ice twice the size of the United States," he heard thousands of times a day, an experience that understandably got old very fast.[66] By September, some Fair workers had begun to find creative ways to make their repetitive jobs more interesting. At the New York State Pavilion, a couple of elevator operators had taken to asking passengers to walk backward out of the elevators going up to the sky-high outdoor observation platform "because of the unusual air currents and air pressure prevailing tonight."

More often than not, puzzled passengers agreed to the strange request, only to be greeted at the top by laughing previous victims of the prank.[67]

A few guides at the Ford Pavilion, meanwhile, when they were not telling people who had been waiting patiently for an hour or two to take the the Magic Skyway ride that the building was "closed for lunch," which was, of course, untrue, were plucking couples out of the line to notify the woman that she was the exhibit's "two millionth visitor." The couple was then introduced to the crowd, escorted on a private tour, and asked to pose for a photograph, never knowing that the entire event was staged purely for the guides' own amusement.[68] Some male Ford employees were also fond of asking young women to remove their blazers before getting on the ride because of potential "overheating." And at the Coca-Cola Pavilion, an employee had started to pose as a Disney animatronic, amazing crowds as a colleague pressed a button to supposedly make her smile and another to get her to take a drink from a bottle of Coke. "That's the most lifelike figure I've seen at any of the exhibits," one delighted visitor exclaimed.[69]

Because of the assembly line–like working conditions and low pay, employee turnover was very high at the Fair. GM's Futurama was experiencing a 30 percent turnover rate the first couple of months of season one, no doubt because of the existential nightmare its guards and guides had to endure.[70] Burnout was also high—25 percent—at the Brass Rail restaurants, where hosts and hostesses made $2 to $2.50 an hour. Many workers hired at the various Brass Rail restaurants were university students from the South for whom a summer job in New York City at a world's fair must have seemed like a dream come true. Brass Rail employees had a rude wake-up call in May when, after flipping burgers and hot dogs for the first two weeks of the Fair, they had yet to be paid. Angry employees showed up at the company's headquarters demanding their paychecks, with mistakes in computer forms blamed for the overdue pay (another ironic twist to the Fair's worship of technology).[71] Although hundreds of litter picker-uppers were being laid off in the spring because there were fewer visitors and thus less garbage than anticipated, the Brass Rail could not get (and keep) enough workers, adding five hundred more college students over the Memorial Day weekend as it prepared for the summer crowds. Another food and beverage concessionaire, the Lowenbrau Gardens, had a different hiring strategy, bringing over eleven young, titled women to work as barmaids in its replica of an eighteenth-century Bavarian hamlet complete with Alpine chalets. The nine baronesses and two countesses from Munich, some of whose families dated back to the ninth century, hauled beer steins to thirsty commoners in the open-air café, proud to serve as cultural ambassadors before returning home to their privileged lives.[72]

Also serving as proud cultural ambassadors were the eight religious pavilions on the fairground. Moses's decision to make religion a visible presence at the Fair was a bold one, fraught with potential risk. With each religious organization—Billy Graham's Evangelistic Association, the Christian Scientists,

Vatican, Protestant and Orthodox Center, Russian Orthodox Greek Catholic Church, Mormon Church, Christian Life Convention, and American-Israel Pavilion—promoting its particular brand of spirituality, there was ample opportunity for misunderstanding and conflict. Although pavilion staffers and visitors lived together remarkably happily in Moses's peaceable kingdom, the sensitive subject of religion did create a few sparks during the first season. The response to *Parable,* the film showing at the Protestant and Orthodox Center, was just as controversial as expected, proving to be a source of passion in more ways than one. The film, a passion play set in a circus setting where Christ, as a mime or clown, was crucified in a Punch and Judy show, was still showing, but some audience members and critics were having trouble decoding the complex imagery and thematic elements ("It's fine, but I can't understand it," said one viewer).[73] Interestingly, the New York Protestant Council decided to charge 50 cents' admission to the previously free film and drop the offering at the end of each showing, thinking it would deter those individuals more likely to react negatively. Attendance actually rose, however, as "people apparently felt that a film that was being shown with a 50-cent admission charge must be more worthwhile than a film that was shown without charge," as Dr. G. Barrett Rich, program director of the Protestant and Orthodox Center, put it. Another film showing at the center, *The Runaway Bus,* was also stirring things up with its appeal that parochial-school buses should

*6. One of the twenty-five Brass Rail "refreshment centers" on the grounds that, with their afford-able fare, were a welcome sight to often cash-poor visitors. Photo © Bill Cotter.*

receive state aid.[74] Considering how tight a ship Moses was running when it came to exhibits that he himself found offensive, significant leeway was being given to religious pavilions and their controversial presentations. For example, "Summer Time Revue," a rock-and-roll show, was allowed to run just three weeks in July before it was shut down by Moses for being in bad taste. Moses claimed he closed the show because he feared Catholics would complain, but, much more likely, it was more a victim of his own holier-than-thou morality.[75]

A couple of other flare-ups illustrated how sensitive an issue religion was even within the Fair's focus on peace through understanding. In June, a rabbi charged that the Reverend B. Haynie, a Baptist minister and head of the American Board of Missions to the Jews exhibit in the Hall of Education, had tried to convert a twelve-year-old Jewish boy by steering him away from his classmates and mother and bringing him to the Billy Graham's Pavilion to see the film *Man in the Fifth Dimension*. Even though the minister apologized ("I admit I made a mistake but the lad was so eager, so full of questions," he explained), and the boy still appeared to be Jewish, the WFC took the matter seriously, demanding a full investigation. In another case of rabid rabbis, Rabbi Joachim Prinz, who served as president of the American Jewish Congress, complained to Moses about the date set for a party for Fair employees, September 7, which was the second day of Rosh Hashana. Moses, who was Jewish but always insisted he was not, reluctantly canceled the party.[76]

These incidents were nothing, however, compared to what happened after officials from the American-Israel Pavilion wandered over to take a look at what its Jordanian neighbors were offering fairgoers. Besides its Holy Land exhibit, Cradle of Civilization exhibit, and Dead Sea Scrolls, Jordan's pavilion included a "Mural of a Refugee" exhibit depicting a displaced mother and child. The mural's poem told how Palestinians lived "in peaceful harmony" for centuries "until strangers from abroad, professing one thing, but underneath, another, began buying up land and stirring up the people," appealing for worldwide empathy and aid for a homeland of their own.[77] American and Israeli Jews considered the mural of the Arab refugees to be propagandist, politically motivated, and offensive and, because it was "not in the spirit of the Fair," demanded it be removed. The Jordanians, however, led by none other than King Hussein himself, refused to take it down. Through the spring of 1964, the mural would prove to be a bitter battleground as a host of characters including Moses, Mayor Wagner, Rabbi Prinz, Israel premier Levi Eshkol, and a litany of organizations such as the New York City Council, New York State Human Rights Commission, American Friends of the Middle East, B'nai B'rith Anti-Defamation League, and American-Arab Relations Committee all weighed in on the issue. The case wound up in the New York State Supreme Court, which, though sympathetic to the Jews' cause, ruled that there was no legal basis to have the mural removed. Seeing the literal writing on the wall, American-Israeli officials decided to put up a reproduction of the mural in their own pavilion along with a poem calling for world peace (and, for good measure, a Davidka mortar used in a battle with the Arabs).[78] With the Six-Day War just a few years out and Palestinians still fighting for a homeland, anything but peace through understanding was in store for these neighbors in the International Area and the Mideast.

## Put on a Happy Face

Despite the abundant reasons for concern, most of all lower-than-expected attendance, Fair officials remained optimistic as summer approached. In June, the WFC's controller, Erwin Witt, reported that the corporation would finish in the black in 1964 and be able to pay off $30 million in debt when it was due in 1966.[79] Because of the tremendous advance ticket sale, Witt claimed, the WFC had a large surplus, making the corporation financially fit as a fiddle. As a sign of its fiscal health, the WFC even announced it would prepay one-quarter of its debt—$7.5 million—on August 1, a full two years before it was due (the corporation would later regret this decision).[80] Although this rosy scenario could have been a public relations strategy to keep critics at bay while the Fair hit its stride, Moses and his people did have some cause for hope.[81] Daily average attendance remained below forecast, but it was indeed rising as summer approached. In July, the WFC again announced that the Fair was making money and would be able to pay off its loans, a retort to critics and to anyone perhaps getting a little worried that the city may have a bad debt on its hands.[82]

Judging from the long lines at some of the more popular exhibits, especially at GM's Futurama (whose 15 million visitors the first season would beat out the Vatican's 13 million), however, it was hard to believe that the Fair was losing money.[83] In fact, seeing just two of the big industrial exhibits often took the better part of a day, causing some visitors to come up with creative strategies—almost all of them futile—to get into exhibits without standing in line. Visitors routinely told hosts or hostesses they "were a big shareholder in the company" or "had a pregnant wife," thinking this excuse would give them preferential treatment, but were proved wrong by the workers who had heard it all before. "Journalists" by the hundreds, saying they were writing articles about the Fair, too showed up daily at the popular pavilions, to no avail. Less subtle approaches to skip the line, such as trying to slip a host or hostess a $20 bill, were also common, and more than a few visitors dressed up as nuns to avoid a wait (hosts were on to the latter immediately, knowing that nuns were among the most patient in a queue).[84] The long lines, hard-luck stories, and gate-crashing were all positive signs that the Fair was, as the showbiz saying went, "givin' 'em what they want," the foundation for good word-of-mouth and repeat business.

There was good news too outside the fairgrounds. Traffic to and from the Fair was flowing nicely, with few of the horrendous tie-ups that plagued commuters during the years of highway construction and improvement. Hotels in

Manhattan were filled to the gills (83 percent occupancy versus 64 percent during the 1939–40 fair), largely a result of a record number of conventions being held in the city during the run of the Fair. Not just businesspeople but also conventioneers from fraternities and sororities, clubs, and other organizations had in fact invaded the city, making the managers of high-end hotels (about $25 for a double room with bath) such as the Waldorf-Astoria, Americana, Savoy Hilton, and Drake very happy, and the managers of low-end ones (about $15 for the same) like the New Yorker, Piccadilly, and Henry Hudson equally so.[85] Many midtown hotels that had overbooked their reservations, planning on a high number of no-shows, were now hosting ugly scenes in their lobbies as angry guests were turned away. Garage operators too were packing cars in like sardines (and occasionally price gauging the unsuspecting out-of-towner), and unoccupied taxis were as scare as on a rainy day. Both expensive restaurants such as the Four Seasons and chain restaurants like Horn and Hardart were doing gangbusters business, and a number of major stores had decided to stay open late on Saturdays during the summer because of the influx of tourists.[86]

Other New York City institutions too seized the Fair day during the summer of '64. Managers of department stores such as Lord and Taylor, Bloomingdale's, and F. A. O. Schwartz, eager to sell peanuts when the circus was in town, opened their doors on Saturdays through July and August, abandoning their normal five-day week during summers. Retailers were also offering special services to Fair visitors as a way to keep them coming and spending. In one part of the World's Fair Room on the sixth floor of Gimbel's ("the world's largest guest room," the store proudly claimed) in June, Eartha Kitt regaled guests with stories, while in another part guests took the store up on its offer for free massages. Discount tickets, free writing paper, and the chance to win theater tickets were other perks to keep Gimbel's shoppers from heading over to Macy's. Other retailers such as Abraham and Strauss, B. Altman, Lane Bryant, Sak's Fifth Avenue, and Sterns set up information booths, giving away free maps to tourists to help them get around town and telling them what there was to see.[87]

Institutions of "high" culture in Manhattan too were tying into the event in Flushing Meadows to capitalize on both New Yorkers' and out-of-towners' interest in this and previous world's fairs. The Metropolitan Museum of Art was exhibiting World's Fairs: The Architecture of Fantasy; the New-York Historical Society had on display Crystal Palace, 1853–1858; the New York Public Library offered Treasures for the '64 Fair; the Pierpont Morgan Library was featuring Important Acquisitions since the Last New York World's Fair (1939–1964); and the Cooper Union Museum was showing World's Fairs of Yesterday.[88] New York State had even issued 1964 "World's Fair" license plates, turning tens of thousands of cars into promotional vehicles for the event.

Another good sign was that both the WFC and some exhibitors were taking active steps to improve their products. Additions and renovations were already being publicly discussed by WFC staff as early as late May, in fact, and exhibitors too had many improvements in mind to try to draw more visitors.[89] By late June, an advertising campaign was in the works to try to offset the adverse publicity the Fair was getting and show those individuals hesitant to come out to Flushing Meadows that the ones who did had a good time there. The WFC's advertising agency, J. Walter Thompson, was placing ads in New York City newspapers that included quotes from people who had a good time at the Fair and was also sending out hundreds of thousands of a sixteen-page pamphlet called *Fair Answers to Some Fair Questions* to newspaper editors and travel agents that answered questions like, "Does it cost an arm and a leg to eat at the fair?" and "Is the wait in exhibit lines very long?"[90] Exhibitors too joined the accentuate-the-positive, eliminate-the-negative chorus by agreeing to end their public complaining about high labor and maintenance costs by keeping the tiffs "within the family."[91]

Despite the positive momentum, however, an intense heat wave around July 4 dampened officials' and exhibitors' hopes that the holiday would be an attendance bonanza and perhaps even set an upbeat tone for the rest of the summer.[92] A few days later, a city councilman urged that the Fair cut its admission prices to increase attendance, anathema, of course, to Moses who did not even want to offer a discount to schoolchildren.[93] Adding to everyone's concern was that New York City's notoriously high crime rate and, especially, reports of rioting were deterring would-be visitors from coming to town. Fifty percent of Fair visitors to date lived in the New York metropolitan area, in fact, evidence perhaps that out-of-towners were indeed afraid to come to the city (and putting a dent in the enterprise being a "world's" fair, much less the ultimate one). Moses reassured out-of-towners that the city's crime problem was highly exaggerated, while Mayor Wagner urged non–New Yorkers not to cancel plans to visit the Fair because of what the *New York Times* referred to as "racial disorders" in Harlem and Bedford-Stuyvesant.[94] Almost 500 hotel reservations were canceled in mid-July as a result of violence between blacks and police in Manhattan and Brooklyn (no doubt making those visitors told there was no room at the inn very happy), and other out-of-towners were on the fence about coming to the city. One man from Alabama called the city's Convention and Visitors Bureau asking if his family would be safe in their automobile that bore their home state's name, while Moses felt the need to personally assure a Minnesota family that reports of violence were mostly media hype. A group of 150,000 Shriners and their families who came to town in late July was comforted to hear that the rioting took place "miles away from the downtown area," as the Masonic group's leaders told them, with "not a single Shriner" involved in the civil disobedience. Black Africans working at the Fair were especially shocked at the riots, although their relative support for African Americans' struggle for civil rights varied significantly.[95]

At least publicly, Moses remained upbeat about his Fair's success despite the disappointing attendance numbers and the rash of show closings. On August 4,

Fair officials honored its 20 millionth visitor, something it had hoped it would have done weeks earlier at the midpoint of the first season. The WFC's William Berns, vice president of communications and public relations, showered the Brown family—Robert, Betty, and their four kids—from Bedford, Indiana, with gifts and promised them a blimp ride over the city.[96]

August proved to be a great month for the Fair, its attendance of 5.8 million the highest of any month to date and a whopping 800,000 over July, buoying staffers' and exhibitors' hopes that the first season was going to finish with a bang.[97] The August bonanza turned out to be just a blip, however, as post–Labor Day attendance dropped precipitously, just as it had in 1939. There was even no waiting at GM's Futurama, something that had not occurred since May during a bout of bad weather. A combination of factors—the Jewish holidays, reopening of many area schools, and disappearance of many tourists—was blamed for the steep decline.[98]

Clearly frustrated as it became clear to all that he would miss his first-season attendance forecast of 40 million by a country mile, Moses lashed out at the press and other critics of the Fair at a meeting of the New York State Publishing Association in mid-September. "We have been listening too much to the raving hyenas, scavengers, jackals, parrots and vultures who should be kept behind moats in the Bronx Zoo," he scolded 250 newspaper publishers from upstate New York.[99] At a board meeting in July, Moses had similarly aired his displeasure at the "captious criticism" of "professional detractors" who he believed were jealous of the Fair's success and were responsible for discouraging millions of people from coming out to Flushing Meadows.[100] About a week before the Fair closed, Moses took his criticism of the media to a new level, blaming a "small but influential segment of the local press" for the less-than-great attendance. In a special address to the officers and directors of the Fair, Moses had demoted the press along the evolutionary scale to "ants" who reported only the bad news to the public. Even reporters from *Life* and *Fortune* were "wicked little gremlins and leprechauns" bent on bringing down the Fair because of journalistic tricks designed only to provoke and create sensation. Moses, sounding more and more like Captain Queeg, also blamed "race riots," difficulties with transportation and hotel accommodations, and New Yorkers in general for the lackluster first season. Later that day, the seventy-four-year-old Moses hopped on a plane to Tokyo to take in the Olympics, perhaps to pick up some tips on how to turn his "Olympics of progress" into an unqualified hit.[101]

## Closing Time

With surprisingly little fanfare, at least compared to the opening-day festivities, the first season of the 1964–65 New York World's Fair closed on October 21. The last day's crowd of 200,000 scooped up bargains galore, as exhibitors slashed their prices on merchandise. Employees gathered at their pavilions for bittersweet good-bye parties, exchanging addresses and taking photos, and workers from the International Area lowered the flags of both their native and their host nations. The entire WFC police force was mobilized in case of a surprise appearance by hordes of picketers or if genuine fears of rampant looting or vandalism by un-named entities were realized. The trusty paddy wagon, however, remained put. Moses, still in Tokyo, recorded a message that was broadcast over loudspeakers at the closing ceremonies, calling the Fair a success and inviting the crowd back in 1965. With the lights not yet even out, however, there were disturbing signs that the Fair was turning out to be something very different from a success, at least financially. As Moses's taped voice echoed over the grounds, Thomas Deegan, chairman of the Fair's executive committee, was on the radio announcing that the Fair's projected profit was going to fall well short of the $53 million forecasted in 1961, a figure that had not budged for nearly three and a half years. "If I had to guess I would say it will be $30 million," Deegan told listeners.[102]

Indeed, an interim financial report filed just a few days before confirmed the bad news. A profit of just $12.6 million for the first season of the Fair was expected, which, if projected to the second season, would not be even half of the $53 million everyone had been counting on. Twenty-four million dollars of the mythical $53 million was to repay the city for improvements made to the site, with the remaining $29 million to go to Moses's chain of parks or Beame's litany of educational needs.[103] It appeared now that the Fair was going to barely break even after paying the city back, and the various interests fighting over the ephemeral profits were counting chickens before they hatched. Moses, however, the eternal optimist, remained confident that attendance would be, in his words, "considerably larger" the second season, which would result in higher profits.[104] The always trusty "word-of-mouth advertising" would bail the WFC out of the hole it was beginning to appear it had dug in the former garbage dump in Queens, although this prediction contradicted global exposition history. Moses himself, having been directly involved in the 1939–40 fair, was sure to have known that attendance for the second season of two-year exhibitions was typically lower than the first season. WFC officials themselves, of course, had forecasted a drop in attendance for the second season, with 40 million expected to come the first year and 30 million the next, a ratio consistent with past fairs. On a much more positive financial note, the New York Convention and Visitors Bureau was reporting that the Fair had pumped a whopping $400 million into the local economy. Twice the number of people as usual visited the Empire State Building's observation deck, and Radio City did its best summer business in its thirty-two-year history.[105] As well, the Triborough Bridge and Tunnel Authority reported that 10 million passenger cars went over its roads and bridges to and from the Fair, adding an extra $2.4 million to its coffers.[106] Everyone except the WFC had made some money, it appeared, with the Fair acting in retail terms like a giant loss leader or promotional vehicle to build traffic across the city.

Even before the leaves of the trees on the newly landscaped grounds could fall, a host of ideas on how to improve the Fair's second season was circulating in the air of Flushing Meadows. Although it was pretty clear by now that WFC forecasts could hardly be trusted, in mid-November Deegan told members of a Rotary Club that he expected a paid attendance of 37.5 million for the 1965 season, adding that overall the Fair was "in good shape." Fixing the problematic Lake Amusement Area was clearly the number-one priority for the WFC between seasons. Deegan told a group of "advertising men" a few days later that a "sportsmen's show" was in the works where visitors could enjoy fly casting and bowling, a joint venture with American Machine and Foundry (AMF), which made fishing and bowling equipment. Another idea on the drawing boards for the area was a Great American Barnyard exhibit, this one a partnership with the National 4-H Club and the Department of Agriculture. The WFC was aggressively pursuing its strategy to forge partnerships with companies or organizations in order to share costs, something that would turn the Fair into even more of a commercial enterprise. No new buildings would go up, Deegan told reporters that same month, but there would be many changes in existing ones and about a dozen new restaurants. He was quick to add that there was "no possibility" for a third season of the Fair, a response to a proposal a city councilman had recently made, thinking an extension could be a way to generate the funds for education that appeared to have evaporated.[107]

As Thanksgiving approached and officials took a closer look at the results from the first season, it was becoming clearer and clearer that Moses and New York City would have less to be thankful for in 1964. Moses sent a letter to Beame telling him that the WFC would possibly not be able to pay back the $24 million it had borrowed from the city for improvements to the grounds, a new revelation in the continually worsening financial accounting of the first season. Upon hearing the news, Mayor Wagner announced he was not counting on any of the money due the city from the WFC for the 1965–66 budget, ruefully admitting, "You can only count on something you are sure is going to be there."[108]

Because of its disappointing numbers and the cloud of conflict that continually hovered over the grounds, it would be easy, as many have done, to judge the Fair's first season (and the enterprise as a whole) as a dismal failure. For those people who mattered most—visitors and exhibitors—however, the 1964 season was a major success. Nearly all exhibitors remained committed to the second season, even if they had lost money, a clear sign that they still believed it was important to be represented at this Fair. As well, more people attended the Fair's first season than in any other held in the United States, with the overwhelming majority of the 27 million paying customers more than glad they had come.[109]

It would take, however, some local high school students to remind everyone— Robert Moses, local politicians, members of CORE, the Jordanians and the Jews, the "gremlins" and "leprechauns," and even General Motors, the U.S. government, and the Vatican—what the 1964–65 New York World's Fair was all about. In November 1964, Consolidated Edison, the New York City energy company, held an essay contest on what the Fair meant. The winner of the contest, Jo Ann Fargo, a seventeen-year-old senior at the Academy of St. Aloysius in Jersey City, wrote that the Fair was not so much about "peace through understanding" as "peace through people." Fourth-prize winner Robert Gardner, a fifteen-year-old senior at Flushing High School in Queens, saw the Fair as an attempt to bring together "the inhabitants of all the major continents" to combat ignorance, the world's major evil. And third-prize winner Joanne Weintraub, a fourteen-year-old ninth grader at South Woods Junior High School in Syosset, Long Island, believed that the Fair was simply about being "a citizen of a large, worldwide community."[110] Rather fittingly, the original idea for the Fair as articulated by Robert Kopple in 1958—to teach children about other people, especially people from other countries—was being realized by those it was intended for. The stuff of real life—money, politics, social inequities, differences in opinions and taste, and the pursuit of personal dreams—had obscured the simple vision shared by a father and some friends, but another season awaited for the Fair to fulfill its noble aims.

# 3  Second Time Around

*It has been good business nevertheless.*
　　　—Robert Moses, speaking of the Fair,
　　　　　in his self-published booklet, The Saga of Flushing Meadow

ONE DAY DURING THE WINTER OF 1964–65, the mayor of New York City found himself driving along the Long Island Expressway. Passing the deserted fairgrounds, Mayor Wagner found the site rather depressing, as debris swirled around what he later likened to "some ghost town on Mars."[1] The Unisphere was capped with ice, another reminder that the first season of the world's fair seemed like a very long time ago. During what could reasonably described as this winter of discontent, however, given the lingering turmoil of the 1964 season, hundreds if not thousands of people were already at work to make the second and final season of the Fair a complete success. Fair officials and exhibitors had another chance to turn the 1964–65 New York World's Fair into a profit-making venture and, who knows, maybe even into the greatest event in history some believed it could and would be.

Everyone knew that the key to a financially successful 1965 season resided in one thing: increased attendance. One did not have to be city controller Beame to know that the Fair had lost money because revenues from attendance fell significantly short of the huge costs it took to operate the Fair, at least the way that the WFC was operating it. Moses may have saved the corporation money on construction costs but was more than making up for it by spending like a drunken sailor on things like security, promotion, and travel and entertainment. The WFC's business model was based on the assumption that 40 million people would come to the Fair the first season and 30 million the next, a lofty but achievable goal based on what it believed were sound forecasting principles. Although getting 27 million folks to pass through any particular set of gates over a period of six months, an average of 150,000 per day, could be considered an amazing feat on many levels—historical, cultural, social—it was, from a financial perspective, simply a losing proposition.

As the 646 acres in Flushing Meadows took their long winter nap, Robert Moses and his army of soldiers huddled to learn from the financial mistakes and misfortunes of 1964 and figure out how to get 30 million or even more people out to the former garbage dump in Queens from April to October. The year 1965 was not only an opportunity for redemption, Moses believed, but another chance to fulfill his dream of a final, lasting legacy for the city he had remade.

## Beating the Drums

To have any chance of increasing attendance the second season over 1964's tally, it became clear to the WFC that it would have to take a much more targeted and efficient approach to marketing than it did before and during the first season. The WFC's primary marketing technique to date was to use public relations campaigns developed by Thomas Deegan's firm, the T. J. Deegan Company, one of a few firms chosen or approved by Moses without allowing for competitive bidding, which was (and remains) standard business practice. In January, however, Deegan was forced to withdraw his firm from the WFC's operations, as it became known from an internal audit of the 1964 season that his company had received a whopping $300,000 in fees every year going back to the Fair's early planning stages, totally more than $1.2 million.[2] As the press went to town on this previously undisclosed windfall, it became suddenly obvious to all that an executive vice president hiring his own firm for public relations was without question a conflict of interest, and the T. J. Deegan Company was promptly replaced by another firm. This cat out of Moses's bag, increasing attention began to be paid to the carte blanche lucrative contracts awarded by the WFC and to the power broker's long-standing business practice of "You pat my back and I'll pat yours" (or, perhaps, "You pat my back or else I'll crush yours").

Besides the unplanned midseason switching of public relations firms, both the WFC and exhibitors agreed that more than shotgunlike press releases and media events were necessary to persuade more people to come to the Fair. Much like its Big 3 automotive exhibitors, the WFC decided to use market-segmentation techniques to pitch its new 1965 model. One strategy was to target New Yorkers, a reversal of the WFC's previous position that the Fair already had too much local representation. Many New Yorkers approached the Fair much like any tourist attraction in the city and stayed away in droves, especially mid-1960s hipsters who considered the event in Queens totally Squaresville. "New Yorkers murdered us," said one exhibitor. "It became very fashionable around town to make fun of the fair, even if you really enjoyed it," he explained, adding, "In any other city we would have been boffo." Despite this lack of civic pride, a major share of Fair visitors over the course of the first season—40 percent—had been New Yorkers, incentive enough for the WFC to want more locals to see what they had missed on the first go-round.[3] In January 1965, officials were reportedly considering a "family rate" ticket to get more budget-minded New Yorkers to come out, something rather difficult to believe given that discounts of any kind made Moses's blood pressure rise almost as much as critics. In fact, just as the "family rate" was being discussed, the WFC announced that the regular admission rate for adults would increase from $2 to $2.50 because of "increased operating costs."[4] This rationale too was hogwash, given that the WFC planned to slash its huge budget and thus decrease its operating costs in 1965 to get closer to profitability. Drastically reducing the WFC's staff, which had ballooned to gigantic proportions, was a major way to get the Fair into the black. By February 1, rather incredibly, Moses had let go 3,000 people on the WFC payroll.[5]

Although common business sense suggested that raising the price of a product or service would be the last thing one would want to do to increase its usage, as some noted at the time, common business sense seemed to be an alien concept to Robert Moses and his staff. Under pressure to make back some of the losses from 1964, Moses was gambling that not only would more people come to the Fair the second season but at a 25 percent premium. Moses later essentially admitted that the extra 50 cents per ticket was purely a means to generate additional revenue, believing that the Fair was underpriced in 1964. "If people can spend $2.50 to line up to see a movie like *Goldfinger*," Moses said, "they can pay $2.50 to come to the fair." Moses also justified the price hike by citing the case in which Thomas E. Dewey, then governor of New York, ordered an increased admission fee to Jones Beach against Moses's wishes. Attendance actually rose, according to Moses, and, if history was correct, it would similarly rise in Flushing Meadows.[6] This forecast again contradicted world's fair history, however, as no exposition in the past hundred years had generated higher attendance the second season than the first. In fact, the admission rate at the 1939–40 fair was lowered from 75 cents to 50 cents, and attendance still dropped 25 percent.[7]

To attract more tourists, the WFC had a number of ideas up its sleeve in early 1965. One idea was to recruit city employees to suggest to out-of-towners to come out to the Fair throughout the second season, a smart (and free) use of New York's thousands of civil service employees. Wanting to make it easier for tourists without cars to get to the Fair by mass transportation, the corporation asked the NYCTA to put subway directions to the Fair on its new pocket maps and the IRT to add an express run from Times Square to Flushing Meadows, to which they each agreed. The New York Convention and Visitors Bureau also agreed to plug the Fair, bringing back its 1964 theme, "New York Is a World's Fair and a Summer Festival, Too!" in 1965.[8]

Although word-of-mouth advertising and tourism promotion would no doubt help spread the Fair gospel and easier mass transit would reduce the traffic and parking problems of the first season, the WFC had high hopes that a new film it had commissioned, *To the Fair*, would be the thing that would pull in hordes of visitors from across the country. The corporation had put $240,000 into the 26.5-minute film produced by Francis Thompson, the man responsible for *To Be Alive*, one of the big hits of the 1964 season. Officials believed Thompson could spin the same magic he had spun in his film that had not only packed them in at the Johnson Wax Pavilion but also perfectly reflected the Fair's theme of Peace Through Understanding.[9] *To the Fair*, which was shot during the summer of 1964, took viewers on a tour of the grounds and selected exhibits by following around a disparate group of people—an American family, two "spinster" teachers, an Indian engineer and his sari-clad wife, two college boys pursuing two girls, and Boy Scout Troop 295 of the Bronx—as they enjoyed a typical day at the Fair. The film did not use the innovative multiscreen technology Thompson used in *To Be Alive* but did have much of the same joie de vivre as his previous film, exactly how the WFC wanted to position the critically maligned Fair. It was clear that even before the start of the second season, Moses and his staff were fully aware there were effectively two fairs taking place in Flushing Meadows, one the popular event enjoyed by visitors and another the financial mess that was getting messier every day. Wanting more Americans to focus on the former, the WFC distributed *To the Fair* to movie theaters, private organizations, service clubs, and schools but was also hoping to air it on both network and local television should a sponsor be found. The film was also shown on airlines before in-flight movies, aligning the World's Fair with the glamorous, ring-a-ding-ding jet-travel experience of the mid-1960s.[10]

In addition to *To the Fair*, the WFC was distributing a million posters and six million brochures to travel agents, airlines, railroads, hotels, resort areas, and the media to get more out-of-towners to come to Flushing Meadows. The brochures focused on the affordability of the Fair to counter the nearly universal opinion that even a one-day visit, especially for a family, would put a major dent in one's wallet or pocketbook. One brochure, *Family Fun at the Fair*, explained how a family of four could spend a day there for just $7.46 (excluding admission), while another, *What's Free at the Fair*, emphasized that 85 percent of the attractions would be free (versus 75 percent in 1964).[11]

Though appreciative that the WFC was making more of an effort to promote the Fair to boost attendance the second season, many exhibitors decided to launch their own campaigns as well. By January 1965, about thirty exhibitors had in fact created their own promotion films, typically touting not just the Fair but their particular pavilions as well. By March, twenty-six exhibitors, including such heavyweights as GE, Du Pont, and Ford, had also banded together to launch a $75 million drive to promote the 1965 season via speaker kits, traveling exhibits, and other forms of publicity.[12] Corporate America was committed to protecting its huge investment, and not about to let this great opportunity to make a favorable impression among a global audience of consumers slip away.

## New and Improved

The sixth months of breathing room between the end of the first season and the beginning of the new one was a much needed period for both the WFC and exhibitors to take a close look at what they had offered visitors and think about what they could possibly do better so that the Fair could make money. The WFC had decided not only to market the Fair much like the carmakers exhibiting there but also, like them, to retool and redesign last year's product for 1965. The 1964 model of the Fair was no 1958 Edsel, but clear changes to both the mechanics and the finish were necessary for any chance of profitability in 1965. "We've had six months to study fairgoers' preferences, tastes and spending habits and to make additions and improvements keyed to them," explained William Berns, now the WFC's director of radio, television, and film publicity, in classic postwar marketing-speak.[13]

Besides a new and improved Lake Amusement Area, much hope was riding on the Belgian Village completed the day before the close of the first season. Eliminating long lines at the more popular exhibits and restaurants too was deemed essential, a tricky feat considering that Fair staffers were doing everything they could to increase overall attendance, of course, not decrease it. The WFC persuaded bigger exhibitors to shorten lines by opening earlier, closing later, taking advance reservations for seats, increasing the number of seats (especially GE), and speeding things up with extra building doors (notably Ford). The WFC announced that 198 restaurants would be spread out over the fairgrounds in 1965, 87 more than last season when angry fairgoers lost precious time waiting to get food.[14] Also, 62 additional color-coded Greyhound Glide-a-Ride trains and buses would replace the expensive, clunky three-wheeled Escorters used by those visitors in a hurry (or with tired dogs) to get around the Fair.[15] Above all, the WFC wanted to avoid having the second season appear like a tired, unwanted encore performance, something that some previous world's fairs had been guilty of.

Just as they decided to go beyond what the WFC was doing to attract more visitors in 1965 through advertising and promotion, many exhibitors were taking it upon themselves to improve their product offerings and, ultimately, draw more people to their own pavilions. For some exhibitors who charged an additional fee, increasing attendance was a matter of survival, with eleven major ones and three affiliates filing for bankruptcy by mid-February 1965 (and owing a collective thirty-seven million dollars, most of which could not and would never be paid back).[16] For the many more whose exhibits were free, more people meant a higher return on their investment in the Fair. Exhibitors would, by opening day of the second season, spend five million dollars for new shows and another two million dollars to refurbish existing ones.[17] Du Pont, for example, was revamping its musical review, whereas Eastman Kodak was creating a new version of its film *The Searching Eye.* GE had asked Walt Disney to go back to his workshop to make the figures in the Carousel of Progress more realistic than ever, and, not wanting last year's model of animatronic figures for its Magic Skyway ride, Ford made a similar request. The car company was naturally replacing its 1964 Ford and Mercury models in the ride with fresh-off-the-assembly-line 1965s, and GM was making improvements to its already immensely popular Futurama. Chrysler's

*7. One of Greyhound's Glide-a-Rides, a welcome sight for foot-weary fairgoers. Photo © Bill Cotter.*

popular Bill Baird puppet show would be all new in 1965, with music and lyrics developed by Burt Shevelove and Larry Gelbart, coauthors of the recent Broadway smash *A Funny Thing Happened on the Way to the Forum*.[18] The much criticized House of Good Taste was thankfully undergoing a total makeover, whereas the Schaefer Center had decided to go the celebrity route in 1965 by bringing in big-time sports heroes such as Y. A. Tittle, Joe Louis, Johnny Unitas, and Rocky Graziano, a surefire way to attract beer-guzzling fans.[19]

Especially exciting was the news that no fewer than nine new discotheques would be on the grounds in 1965, as Moses, seeing his post-Fair plans for the site evaporate, loosened up a bit.[20] Soon, cooler cats would be doing the twist and the frug in Flushing Meadows as the Pavilion of Paris, Bourbon Street, the Hollywood, USA Pavilion, and other exhibitors added dance floors. Even the Underground House was putting in a discotheque, a comforting sign that an apocalypse was no reason to stop mamboing. (For more traditional swingers, free dancing could be found in the Tiparillo Band Pavilion adjacent to General Cigar's Hall of Magic, with Guy Lombardo, Moses's favorite bandleader, on the stand.) Perhaps the best news of all, however, was that Chun King Inn not only planned to still offer its seven-course Chinese meal for ninety-nine cents, but was going to replace its table service with a double buffet line that would serve no fewer than eight hundred hungry fairgoers an hour (and, to top it off, no need to tip!).[21]

8. *Guy Lombardo and his Royal Canadians, a personal favorite of Robert Moses, symbolized the decidedly "square" entertainment offerings at the Fair. Photo © Bill Cotter.*

Many states and international exhibitors too were thinking long and hard about how to make the upcoming season's fairgoers put their pavilions on their short list. Minnesota decided to bring its Kensington rune stone (said to have been left in what would be the land of ten thousand lakes by early Viking explorers in 1362) to its pavilion in April, whereas the Vatican planned to add not only a Gutenberg Bible but Pope Paul VI's jeweled tiara once it returned from its tour across the United States.[22]

No part of the Fair would look more different in 1965, however, than the disastrous Lake Amusement Area. Expensive to produce and attend extravaganzas would be gone, much of their space gobbled up by Florida and its Citrus Commission. The state decided to make admission to its pavilion's offerings, including the aqua show (featuring six porpoises who sang "Dixie" and danced) and a new water ski show completely free, as Governor Bryant realized that it was much smarter to use its space as tourism bait and to promote oranges (a Minute Maid exhibit was conveniently located at the base of Florida's Citrus Tower). Not wanting "anyone to think that amusement is confined to just one area," as one Fair official explained it (or maybe just conceding that the section would still be less than truly amusing), the WFC decided to rename the Lake Amusement Area simply the Lake Area. (It was hoped this name would stick; exhibitors and concessionaires often referred to the deserted area by alternative names during

*9. Like other states vying for fairgoers' difficult-to-get attention, Minnesota showed off a giant Viking and historically questionable rune stone. Photo © Bill Cotter.*

the 1964 season: "Siberia" and "Death Valley.") Hawaii, which had drawn two million paid spectators to its exhibit in the area in 1964 (more than three times the state's population!), was adding more performers to its "Fashion Fantasy" and "Hawaiian Village Show," as well as planning to offer a new show featuring Polynesian singing and dancing in its Aloha Theater. These improvements, combined with the pavilion's existing twelve-course luau and "5 Volcanoes Rum Punch" (an all-one-can-drink available in the Lava Pit Bar), almost guaranteed that Hawaii would have a smash season.[23]

In a significant display of what the Fair was intended to be and what visitors wanted to get out of it, managers of the U.S. government's Federal Pavilion were planning to overhaul their Challenge to Greatness exhibit and, in the process, turn

10. *Fairgoers mill around the Challenges to Freedom section of the Challenge to Greatness exhibit in the Federal Pavilion, one of very few references at the Fair to the nation's major social problems. Photo © Bill Cotter.*

the event into even more of a sanctuary from the real, less-than-perfect world. The exhibit was one of the precious few at the Fair to address America's social problems of slums, lack of civil rights, and violence, something that reportedly made some visitors uncomfortable. Although this reaction was, of course, precisely the point, "A lot of people thought we played up the problems too much," a spokesman for the pavilion explained.[24] Instead, the 1965 version to Challenge to Greatness would focus less on the challenges, more on the greatness, featuring achievements in such areas as space exploration and "urban development."[25] It was clear that fairgoers, American ones at least, came to Flushing Meadows not for a civics lesson but to have pride in their nation's past, present, and future at a time when it was most needed, and both the WFC and exhibitors were more than happy to oblige. Later world's fairs would begin to ask serious questions about society's challenges but not this one, which served as one last hurrah for an innocence that was rapidly fading.

## Sinking Ship

Although the marketing of the second season, with its more aggressive advertising and promotion of what promised to be an improved product, was certainly good news to all, the Fair's dire financial straits of 1964 quickly began to become what could only be called a nightmare in early 1965. The first major blow came in mid-January when a group of leading bank executives, including David Rockefeller, president of Chase Manhattan, resigned from the WFC's finance advisory committee after Moses refused to provide detailed data on the Fair's finances. The chairman of the committee was George Moore, who beseeched Moses to get the Fair's financial house in order. One of their increasingly heated conversations, as reported by an anonymous onlooker, went as follows:

> MOORE: Bob, we've found bills of six and seven figures that weren't booked. We just can't continue without reliable information.
> MOSES: George, your figures are wrong. You don't know what you're talking about.
> MOORE: Bob, I've been in the banking business all my life and if there's one thing I know it's a column of figures.

Moses ended a later conversation with Moore by saying, "If you don't like it, you can get the hell out," and, following Moore's response, Moses replied, "You're a son of a bitch."[26]

After city controller Abe Beame too pressured Moses to provide more numbers, the latter released twenty documents (along with a statement criticizing the bankers who had abandoned ship).[27] Although Moses included some impressive cost-cutting measures in his report, few certainly expected to hear his news that the Fair would need $3.5 million by opening day if there was to be a second season.[28] The following day, Manhattan Democratic city councilman Paul O'Dwyer urged a probe into the Fair's financial "shenanigans," especially regarding a $750,000 loan the WFC had made to an exhibitor deep in debt, sensing that there might be much more to the story.[29] "How many more instances like that went on behind closed doors in the board of directors is what I'd like to know," O'Dwyer said in a news conference aired on radio station WABC.[30]

Indeed there was more to the story. Moses soon announced that the WFC would be unable to repay the city any of the $24 million it had loaned the corporation for improvements to the site, and, with no money to pay the city back, it appeared certain that there would be no surplus funds for any post-Fair projects, great park included. The WFC's internally audited financial report revealed a deficit of more than $17 million at the end of 1964 with cash reserves of only $600,000—not enough to open a world's fair in April. The corporation had made bad loans to pavilions that went belly up and, even worse, had spent more than $23 million of 1965 revenue from unused advance admission tickets in 1964.[31] Interestingly, newspapers had received the financial report by messenger but not Beame, a silly and petty insult by Moses since the controller would of course eventually get to see Moses's internal audit.

In learning about the finances of the Fair, many New Yorkers became irate about how their tax dollars were being spent, and a lawsuit was quickly in the works to force an independent audit of the WFC's books. Going further, Brooklyn Republican city councilman Angelo J. Arculeo suggested that the city take over the Fair operation in order "to protect the taxpayers' investment," although it was unclear specifically who would want to try to keep this rapidly sinking ship afloat.[32]

As concern about the Fair's finances turned into alarm, Beame ordered his own audit of the WFC's books, smelling something rotten in Flushing Meadows. Moses told Beame he would have the WFC's auditors provide the report, but Beame insisted his office do the audit, writing a letter to Moses that it would "be in the best interests of the city as well as the fair."[33] Knowing Moses would not budge, however, Beame requested a subpoena for the WFC's books and got it the next day. Moses then tried to block the subpoena, triggering a four-month court battle over whether the controller had the right to inspect the numbers from the first season. Beame would eventually win this round, and his suspicions, interested parties would soon learn, were literally right on the money.

Despite the continually worsening news about the Fair's finances, Moses was not completely ready to concede that his future park was a lost cause. After Mayor Wagner said that the WFC had no legal obligation to pay back the $24 million, that it was, in his words, simply a "gentlemen's agreement" and a "contribution" versus an investment, Moses went back on the offensive to rescue the park from returning to a valley of ashes.[34] In mid-February, Moses announced on *Ladies of the Press*, a television program, that the restoration of Flushing Meadows Park should receive priority over paying the city back, clearly contradicting his earlier statement that repayment of bank loans was the first obligation of the WFC and repayment of the holders of the Fair's notes the second obligation. Despite the Fair's deep financial troubles, Moses had revived his intention to "deliver a park a great deal better than what we inherited" to the city.[35]

Right after the show, Moses flew off to Madrid to present a gold medal to Generalissimo Francisco Franco in recognition of the great building the Spaniards had put up in Flushing Meadows, obviously a boondoggle to escape the tremendous criticism he was facing in New York. "Everyone has begun to suspect but almost no one dares to say that the New York World's Fair is sinking into a sea of insolvency with a good deal more speed if considerably less splendor than Venice is sinking into the Adriatic," wrote Murray Kempton in the *New Republic* in February.[36] Just a week after returning from Spain, Moses again got out of Dodge, heading to the Caribbean along with his daughter Jane (nepotistically appointed deputy chairman of the WFC's hospitality committee), the personal guests of Robert Blum, a vice president of the Abraham and Straus department store.

The fallout from the mess in Flushing Meadows was hardly over. George V. McLaughlin, now chairman of the WFC's finance committee's revolving door, resigned in late February, charging that Moses was now planning to use $6.4 million in Triborough Bridge and Transit Authority funds to restore the park after the Fair closed. McLaughlin had been one of Moses's closest allies for some forty years but felt obligated to send him a four-page telegram announcing his resignation after he saw a confidential memo in which Moses made his intention clear. Such an act, many agreed, would be a misapplication and misappropriation of funds, as the TBTA was a state agency completely separate from the WFC, which was, as it had argued itself, a private corporation. This manipulation, like the awarding of contracts with no opportunity for competitive bidding, was the classic Moses MO, moving money around from different pots to pursue his particular agendas. Hearing about Moses's plan, the Automobile Club of New York chimed in, calling such an idea "morally improper," as there was "no connection between Flushing Meadow [sic] Park and the function of the TBTA."[37]

Just as this controversy swirled around, the WFC executive committee was meeting to decide if Moses should stay on as president of the corporation. Such a meeting was necessary to respond to calls from state and city politicians that Moses be removed from his official duties as president because of mismanagement and instead be "elevated" to an honorary or emeritus position. Moses had no intention of stepping down, forcing the executive committee to take a vote of confidence. Moses, who did not participate in the meeting, did receive a vote of confidence, although support for him to keep his job was hardly unanimous. Moses received votes from twelve members of the committee, but another nine members abstained (including Moses himself and, interestingly, his right-hand man, Thomas Deegan), hardly an enthusiastic outpouring of support for the once omnipotent power broker.[38]

This vote was the first public sign of the growing rift between Moses and Deegan that, it was later disclosed, had started in October during the final days of the opening season. While Moses was enjoying the Olympics in Tokyo, Deegan fired ninety-five employees in the WFC's press publicity division, either as a cost-cutting measure or as a way for his public relations firm to pick up even more business.[39] Whatever the reason, Moses was furious that Deegan had made such a decision without his approval. At a news conference, Deegan said that their falling-out was over Moses's recent decision to withhold the corporation's financial statements from the bankers and to raise the adult admission price to $2.50, each against Deegan's own advice. "I'm Irish enough to have an opinion and he's contrary enough to be Irish," Deegan's shorthand explanation went.[40] It appeared to be every man for himself as the WFC's ship started to go down.

Soon Moses and city officials too would be going at it, as the tension enveloping the world's fair between the two planned seasons strained formerly warm relationships and signaled a revolution in the palace. "In recent months the dialogue between Moses and City Hall has crackled with the asperity of divorce proceedings," quipped *Business Week*, "and there has even been City Council pressure to lock Moses out of the apartment." In early March, Moses accused Mayor Wagner of not fully supporting the Fair, specifically that the latter "ran out on his promises" that he had made when he met with President Eisenhower's commission to determine the best site for a world's fair. Wagner immediately denied the accusation, reminding Moses that his administration had forked over the $24 million necessary to make the site capable of hosting the Fair. It was also revealed that the two men had held a "secret conference" in early February, with Moses asking Wagner to issue a joint statement calling for all citizens of New York to support the Fair. With the Fair's operations in such turmoil, Wagner had to refuse so as not to do serious damage to his political career and further distanced himself from his former ally by appointing John A. Coleman, former chairman of the New York Stock Exchange, as his "personal emissary" to investigate the murky doings surrounding the WFC's books.[41]

During this maelstrom, representatives from fifty-three industry exhibitors, including U.S. Steel, Chrysler, IBM, and Coca-Cola, met to see what they could do to avoid a disastrous second season because of all the bad press the Fair was getting. The group came up with the idea for a "Fair Festival Week" to hype the exposition a week before opening day with a parade up Fifth Avenue and other events, agreeing to develop the event without consulting Moses, who clearly had other things on his mind.[42] Local hoteliers too were getting nervous that the second season would not turn out to be as profitable as the first. It was no wonder that the hotel people were concerned; a new American Automobile Association survey revealed that New York City hotels had upped their rates 44 percent in 1964, a clear case of price gauging.[43]

If there was any good news during the tumultuous first quarter of 1965, it was came in March when two banks loaned the WFC $1 million as a short-term loan, all it actually needed to ensure there would indeed be a second season. The WFC had found some unused funds that had been reserved for executive salaries (to ensure the top dogs would get paid whether the Fair made money or not), and some creditors had agreed to defer the corporation's debt until cash started to roll in, making it unnecessary to borrow the additional $2.5 million it claimed it would need.[44] For better or worse, there would definitely be a world's fair in New York City in 1965.

## Take Two

On April 21, the second half of the 1964–65 New York World's Fair kicked off with almost as much fanfare as it had a year earlier. More than 150,000 people showed up for the second opening day—more than three times the number in 1964 when rainy, cool weather and anxiousness about the civil rights protests kept many away.[45] Vice President Hubert Humphrey ably filled in for his boss, joining in the formal opening ceremony held again in the Singer Bowl by Governor Rockefeller,

Mayor Wagner, Willy Brandt (the mayor of West Berlin), Supreme Court Chief Justice Earl Warren, and Robert Moses. Sarah Churchill, the daughter of the former prime minister, too was on the grounds, inspecting the new Winston Churchill Center that was not yet open to the public. (The Churchill memorial, celebrating the achievements of the man who had died in early 1965, was another attempt by Moses to get more people to come to the Fair the second season.) CORE had planned to stage a protest to show its discontent with Mayor Wagner's integration program for the city's workforce, but the organization was, much to the delight of Fair officials and the politicians, a no-show. Humphrey's debut visit to the Fair ("I was very busy last year," he explained) turned out to be a huge hit, with throngs of fairgoers following him, Justice Warren, and John T. Connor, secretary of the interior, around as they toured the grounds accompanied by the Secret Service.[46] The obligatory parade rivaled the diversity of the last one, with cancan girls (daringly new at the Fair this season), a Viking ship, two dinosaurs, Mickey Mouse, two Great Danes, and no fewer than twenty-one floats filled with bathing beauties, including Miss America, marching through the grounds. The highlight of the festivities was the arrival of Abebe Bikila, the Ethiopian winner of the 1960 and 1964 Olympic marathons, who had run to the fairgrounds from midtown Manhattan, carrying a rolled parchment scroll on his thirteen-mile jaunt offering the greetings of Emperor Haile Selassie.[47]

Soon the parade of notable personalities visiting the Fair would again attract the attention of the media and public. Caroline Kennedy made a return visit on day 4 of the second season, this time leaving her mom at home but taking along her kid brother, John. The children, who were accompanied by their cousins Antony and Anna Christina Radziwill had already become rather savvy at avoiding the paparazzi. Caroline, the *New York Times* noted, deftly used the Radziwills to screen her from photographers, whereas John had learned the art of hiding underneath the overcoat of a Secret Service man when cameras were pointed his way.[48] Princess Grace of Monaco and her eight-year-old daughter, Caroline, went out to Flushing Meadows a couple of weeks later, taking a formal tour of the Vatican Pavilion to see the *Pietà* and then making an unscheduled stop to see another genius's tour de force, Walt Disney's robotic Abraham Lincoln in the Illinois Pavilion. General Eisenhower inspected the grounds two days later, taking in the Churchill exhibit and getting the chance to revisit a jacket and some memorabilia he had lent to the Federal Pavilion's Hall of Presidents.[49]

Another personality whose presence on the fairgrounds was not overlooked was Gail Gordon, a twenty-four-year-old stripper. While holding court at the Balcony, a downstairs club within the Bourbon Street complex (go-go dancers were also doing their thing at the Gay New Orleans Club in the pavilion), Miss Gordon quickly captured the attention of Fair officials, who had heard about the performer's act. At her early show one night in May, she removed her gloves, shoes, one stocking, and her dress to the tune of "Tea for Two," which apparently was as much clothing as one could take off in Flushing Meadows. By the end of her second performance at 11:25 P.M., she was left wearing just an oversized bikini, cause enough for a couple of Pinkerton guards and a Fair staffer in the house to ensure there would be no late show. In Gordon's defense, the manager of the Balcony believed that "the strip was going to be O.K. at the fair" because he had heard a rumor that Sherry Britton, a more renowned professional stripper, was taking it off over at "Dancing Waters" in the Lake Area. The truth, however, was that the producer of "Dancing Waters," Harold Steinman, had simply asked Fair officials to preview Miss Britton's performance, as regulations required for all shows. The officials initially refused but then accepted, only to have Miss Britton then refuse to perform just for them, wanting to have some impartial viewers "like the press" to also watch her act.[50] The officials declined her request, putting an end to all stripteasing at the world's fair for good.

Even though the prudish Moses had relaxed his ban on any kind of sexuality at the Fair (and the fact that Miss Britton's performance was, according to Steinman, "full of class" and when it concluded she "had more left on than [dancers in] most Broadway musicals"), such doings violated what the former considered "an intellectual picnic." Moses, in fact, occasionally referred to the Fair as "Flushing Meadow [sic] University," once claiming that visitors would "get a well-rounded education for the entrance price of second rate movies." As he argued to critics who thought the Fair was low-brow and pure fluff, "This is the opportunity of millions to obtain wisdom without pain." It was obvious to all that the Fair desperately needed more business in the evening if it was going to turn a profit, but nearly naked women was apparently not the answer.[51]

Another, certainly less sexy, idea to boost attendance proposed by Mayor Wagner, other city officials, and exhibitors in the International Area was for a reduced admission fee. Wagner and the others thought that Moses's decision to raise the price of the regular adult admission fee the second season from $2 to $2.50 was a mistake and urged the WFC's executive committee to consider offering an evening fare of $1.50. Moses had declined the same request made by the exhibitors but, with Wagner's support behind them, agreed to have the committee consider the idea. A few weeks later, the committee (led by Moses, of course) said no to the $1.50 nighttime admission, triggering an avalanche of criticism from the foreign exhibitors. Some pavilion managers in the International Area threatened to close for a few days per week to try to stay profitable, but ultimately decided against it.[52] A few days later, Republican-Liberal mayoral candidate John Lindsay visited the Fair and picked up some votes by announcing that he was in favor of the price cut. Not to be outdone, city council members and Senator Jacob Javits were soon pleading for an even lower evening fare—$1—to get New Yorkers to come to the Fair after work and on weekend nights, but the WFC would not budge.[53] There was little doubt that a clear divide had been created between New York politicians and the WFC, with each group thinking it knew best how to manage the Fair for its remaining run.

The battle over a discounted nighttime fare was a direct result of the disappointing attendance figures for the first few weeks of the second season. Attendance the first twenty days was in fact 22 percent lower than the first twenty days of the first season, hardly the direction the Fair had to go if 1965 was going to bail the WFC out of its red ink.[54] New Yorkers, like people in other parts of the country, seemed to be somewhat distracted by a revival double bill of the James Bond movies *Dr. No* and *From Russia, with Love.* Lines snaked around the theaters playing the films every night in late May and into June, making the lines at the Fair seem downright puny. Bond fans who did get out to Flushing Meadows were no doubt delighted to find 007's Aston-Martin from *Goldfinger,* complete with seat ejector and fog dispenser, on display at the Fair.

Besides tying into pop-culture phenomena such as James Bond mania, Moses had another idea how to increase traffic at the Fair: have the Weather Bureau take a more "positive" approach in its forecasts for the area. Rather than saying there was a "20 per cent chance of precipitation," Moses asked Anthony F. Tancreto, head of the New York division of the bureau, in a letter, why not say there was an "80 per cent chance of fair weather"?[55] Amazingly, and as a testament to the power Moses wielded, the bureau agreed to use the phrase "variable sunshine" in place of "variable cloudiness."[56] The God-like Moses could, it appeared, even change the weather.

Season two was beginning to look a lot like season one beyond the disappointing early attendance figures. Even before opening day, the Jews and Arabs had picked up much from where they had left off in the fall of 1964. In early April, Rabbi Joachim Prinz and ten of his American Jewish Congress colleagues filed a suit for a permit to picket at the mural of the Jordanian Pavilion, and, by the second day of the Fair, the organization was stationing one or two people outside the pavilion to hand out leaflets claiming the mural was anti-Semitic.[57] Within a few days, the American-Arab Relations Action Committee was picketing the American-Israel Pavilion and distributing its own leaflets, and, rather predictably, a member from each organization was soon scuffling with the other in the middle of the fairgrounds.[58] Rather than "peace through understanding," the tit-for-tat gamesmanship between the Jews and the Arabs was resulting in violence, a small-scale foreshadowing of the Six-Day War just two years away. In response to the Arabs' handing out of leaflets urging visitors to not buy "Israel war bonds," the Jews one day set up a table near them offering kosher bologna sandwiches and Israeli beer.[59] The Arabs did not take the Jews up on the free lunch.

Although CORE had decided to skip opening day of the second season, one hundred members of the group did show up a few days later, picketing at the New York City Pavilion. Surprisingly, members of a pseudo organization, the Society for the Prevention of Negroes Getting Everything (SPONGE), also showed up, resulting in some scuffling between the two groups. SPONGE consisted of some high school students from East New York who wore Confederate caps and carried signs of support for Alabama governor George Wallace, vivid proof that blacks still had a long way to go in their fight for equal rights. Other signs of racism could be found at the Fair in 1965. The NAACP was not pleased to see and hear Chrysler's new puppet show, "The Show Go Round," which included a song called "Dem Parts." In the number, four purple puppets sang how a Chrysler was built in a theatrical representation of the car company's assembly line. To the tune of "Dem Bones" (a well-known minstrel song), the lyrics went:

> Dem nuts, dem bolts, dem pistons;
> Dem rings, dem rods, dem gaskets;
> Dem plugs, dem lugs, dem clutch plates
> All of dem made of steel.

Although it was obvious that the song had a clear racial component and that minstrel references had little place in 1965, Chrysler insisted that the number was color free. "There's no reference at all to human beings or to race," a company spokesman insisted, but the NAACP disagreed, threatening demonstrations at the pavilion and a boycott against Chrysler dealerships in the New York City area if the song was not changed or dropped. If that did not work, the organization planned to take the matter to its upcoming national convention in Denver and move for a coast-to-coast boycott of the car company's products. Just two days later, Chrysler not only agreed to change all mentions of "dem" to "them" and any "de" to "the" but also agreed to change the color of the puppets from purple to yellow.[60]

The NAACP victory was not the first time that racism at the Fair was quashed. Right before opening day, the owner of an employment agency, Mrs. Claire Gaber, had placed a newspaper ad seeking "blue-eyed blondes" to work at the Fair. Gaber soon found herself before the New York State Human Rights Commission, explaining that no racial bias was intended and apologizing for any misunderstanding. She also promised to revise the ad to appeal to persons of "all races and creeds," but the agency intended to look further into her company's recruiting and hiring practices.[61]

African Americans, Jews, and Arabs were not the only groups to use the world's fair as an ideal stage to voice their particular cause the second season. In June, four representatives of the Student Peace Union protested the administration's involvement in Vietnam by distributing pamphlets outside the Federal Pavilion. The organization had sought permission to demonstrate on the grounds but was, as the Fair's rules made clear, turned down by the WFC's director of security. A worker at the Wisconsin Pavilion, nineteen-year-old Michael Cohen, apparently didn't get the memo, however, arriving at the Fair's gates with a bunch of signs with slogans like "All Hands Off Vietnam." Cohen was stopped by Pinkerton guards and his permanent pass taken away, with a report of the incident to be sent to his employer. Undeterred, Cohen paid the $2.50 regular admission fee and went to work.[62]

One group that did get the very rare permission to demonstrate at the Fair was Women Strike for Peace. In August, four hundred members of the organization, all dressed in black, marched in silence around the Unisphere pool and then near the Japanese Pavilion to mark the twentieth anniversary of the dropping of the first atomic bomb on Hiroshima and to call for a cease-fire in Vietnam. As for the Student Peace Union, the WFC had denied the group's request to demonstrate, but Queens district attorney (and, in a couple of years, candidate for governor) Frank O'Connor intervened and persuaded the director of security to allow it. The women were careful to abide by the WFC's terms calling for the protestors to remain quiet so as not to disturb fairgoers and cause too much of a scene. "Silently, ladies, please," Mrs. Alice Miller of Great Neck, a leader of the organization, reminded her colleagues, knowing that a team of the Fair's pool of fifteen hundred Pinkerton guards would arrest them should the demonstration get too rowdy.[63]

## Home Stretch

Although some of its shine seemed to have rubbed off—Russell Lynes of *Harper's* thought it had taken on a "bruised and weary look"—the World's Fair kept rolling through the spring and summer of 1965, albeit with a few speed bumps.[64] The first and only murder occurred on the grounds in May when a teenager was killed by two others in a dispute over money, an unfortunate but not totally unexpected event given the millions of people at the Fair over the course of twelve months. With only 117 arrests, the first season was remarkably crime free, again considering that 27 million people—what would be by far the biggest city in the world—had been on the grounds from morning till night.[65] In June 1965, two dinosaurs worth $10,000 went missing from Sinclair's Dinoland, with no explanation forthcoming from the nineteen year old who had swiped them why or how he got the fiberglass models off the grounds, and in August a melee erupted at the Belgian Village when an after-hours party got decidedly out of control, resulting in a number of arrests.[66]

Less dramatic but much more disturbing was that attendance remained below the first season's, surprising to those individuals who believed the new and improved version of the Fair would result in boffo box office. Palisades Amusement Park in New Jersey, which had been around for sixty-eight years, was occasionally outdrawing the Fair, a real embarrassment. The lagging attendance even prompted a billboard company in Des Moines to jokingly suggest on one of its signs that tourists get some peace and quiet by vacationing at Flushing Meadows. "Get away from the crowd," the sign read. "Visit the New York World's Fair."[67]

The WFC would soon have other problems with billboards. In early September, Henry Barnes, the city's traffic commissioner, ordered the corporation to take down six large signs it had placed alongside highways leading to the Fair. Moses had put up the signs without permission from Barnes, all the more illegal because the WFC was a private corporation. Moreover, the signs were ridiculously wordy, posing a clear safety hazard as drivers slowed down and took their eyes off the road to try to read them. The longest read, "By October 17 more than 50 million people will have visited the New York World's Fair; more than visited any similar event in world history. Few days are left. Come before it is too late. The fair ends October 17." Moses's posting of the billboards was particularly ironic given his long history of opposing highway advertising signs. He had often blocked advertisers from placing billboards near the highways he built, thinking they marred the beauty of the roads and detracted from the driving experience. In fact, as parks commissioner, Moses had made Billy Rose take down a sign he had put up to promote his "Aquacade" show for the 1939–40 world's fair, the location of which was just three hundred yards away from one of Moses's own signs. Barnes gave Moses forty-eight hours to take down the signs, threatening to have them removed himself if Moses did not. After Moses naturally refused to take down the signs, Barnes decided not to have them removed, knowing full well what happened to the careers of most who got into a one-on-one brawl with the man.[68]

These pesky problems would prove, however, to be the proverbial calm before the storm, as once again the management of the Fair came under attack by elected officials. On September 1, Abraham Beame, now not just the city's controller but one of four Democratic candidates for mayor, issued his interim audit of the Fair. The report was damning, with Beame charging the WFC with "fiscal mismanagement on a broad scale." The corporation, it was disclosed, did not seek competitive bids for security and maintenance (Moses called it "a waste of time"); loaned exhibitors millions of dollars, most of which was now not collectible; and made "improper payments," such as paying for the same item three times. Many WFC executives had taken their wives along on all-expenses-paid trips to Europe and Asia to recruit foreign exhibitors, something few other corporations would have allowed.[69]

Queens district attorney Frank O'Connor soon ordered a probe for possible "illegal acts" in the Fair's management, while city councilman O'Dwyer, now another Democratic candidate for mayor, urged that the city take over the Fair by "condemnation proceedings if necessary" and open it free to the public for a month after the scheduled closing date. O'Dwyer thought that although the Fair was "a fine educational experience for the well-heeled," many other New Yorkers had not gone out to Flushing Meadows because they simply could not afford to spend a day there. Adding to the damaging evidence was when the executive director of the Illinois Pavilion confirmed that the WFC had paid Disney Enterprises $250,000 of the cost of the Great Moments with Mr. Lincoln exhibit, money it had no obligations to or intentions of paying back.[70]

Nonplussed, Moses immediately discounted Beame's audit as an "inter-rupt[ion]" of the second season of the Fair and as a political ploy to curry favor among angry New Yorkers. Borrowing from his recent stint as a billboard copy-writer, Moses claimed that "the Fair had done more for New York than any com-parable event in history anywhere" and that "its lessons and memories will last a long time." Although it would be hard to dispute the veracity of Beame's indepen-dent audit (he was not running against Moses, after all), the Fair's biggest cham-pion was 100 percent correct. Completely separate from all the ugliness outside the grounds, inside remained an enchanted land that most visitors found delight-ful. As well, many if not most exhibitors were glad they had invested in the event despite their frustrations with the WFC, and there was no doubt that the Fair was responsible for contributing a boatload of money into the local economy—much more than the $24 million the city had loaned (actually given) the WFC to get it off the ground. Best-guess estimates were that the city's restaurant business increased 6 percent to 8 percent during the two seasons, and retail trade in midtown was up 4 percent, each translating into millions of dollars.[71] Moses was also right that both the lessons and the memories of his Fair would be remembered for quite a long time, much longer in fact than the results of a controller's audit.

Despite the critical, even shocking findings contained in Beame's audit, Moses continued to pursue his plan to use TBTA money to turn what was left of the Fair into a park, albeit a more modest one than what he originally wanted. Since the WFC would have no money to create the park in Queens, Moses had every inten-tion of finding funds from another budget he controlled to plant the seed there and hope that the city would one day create his real Promised Land—the elabo-rate corridor system connecting six parks in the center of the borough to serve its two million residents. By using an obscure clause in his TBTA contract that gave him the legal right to "build parks and recreational facilities along access property to highways or bridges of the Triborough Bridge and Tunnel Authority," Moses had an ace in the hole to plant that seed.[72] Moses viewed the idea of a big, beautiful cluster of parks in Queens from a long-term, historical perspective, almost as if it was destiny that it would one day materialize. The Fair, he once said, would be "great and wonderful, but our park . . . even greater."[73] He remembered Flush-ing Meadows from his youth as a rat-infested swampland run by a "garbage czar" named "Fishhooks" McCarthy who ruled over the area under the mis-leadingly pleasant-sounding name of the Brooklyn Ash Removal Company. Seemingly obsessed with the incredible dirtiness of the place, it was Moses's lifelong dream to sanitize the area by locating immense projects directly on the site. "I prepared Flushing Meadow [sic], then a foul dump, for the World's Fair of 1939–40," he reminded people after Beame's audit was published, leaving the site after that Fair "in intimately better shape" than how he had found it.[74] Now, some twenty-five years later, the seventy-six-year-old man was determined to finish scrubbing up the place.

Although he was by far the most enthusiastic proponent for a park, Moses was not alone in believing that, after the Fair, the grounds should be "rehabilitated" for public use. In late August, city councilman Edward Sadowsky proposed that Mayor Wagner set up a Flushing Meadows–Corona Park Development Commission to restore the grounds after the Fair, and mayoral candidate John Lindsay too called on Wagner "to tap the best brains available" to develop an "imaginative and creative park."[75] In fact, Mayor Wagner had already created a Committee on Flushing Meadows's Future back in January 1965 to determine which buildings should be preserved for a future park.[76] Moses initially wanted everything but Philip Johnson's New York State Pavilion and possibly the Federal Pavilion demolished, although he also thought the Singer Bowl might make a nice site for outdoor concerts (something the Metropolitan Opera was also thinking). By July, the committee was thinking that the New York State and Federal Pavilions were not worth saving but did think the Unisphere, Singer Bowl, Hall of Science, stone wall of the Japanese Pavilion, U.S. Rubber Ferris wheel, and New York City building (a remnant of the 1939–40 fair) were.[77]

As the committee and others pondered which buildings to save, a colossal yard sale was soon under way, with pavilion managers unloading everything they could not or did not want to carry out with them come mid-October. The sell-off, taking place via both auctions and set prices and listed in an eighty-page catalog, was nothing less than the largest sale of surplus goods since the end of World War II when huge supplies of military equipment were auctioned off.[78] The variety of things (and creatures) for sale was startling, reflecting the almost psychedelic experience that was the Fair. The New York Roman Catholic Archdiocese, a little oddly, got dibs on the RCA color TVs scattered around the Fair.[79] Borden, the dairy company, was pleased as punch to score the world's largest cheese (cheddar, weighing it at 34,591 pounds and 14.5 feet long), from the Wisconsin Pavilion, which would soon be the star of a traveling "cheesemobile" show. The Spaniards were hawking a sixteenth-century painted wood sculpture of the Virgin Mary for $11,590, while the Filipinos were auctioning twelve hand-carved acacia-wood panels depicting the history of their country, something that had taken thirty workers more than a year to construct. Guinea was looking to unload its voodoo tom-toms, native spears, and, somewhat anachronistically, a forty-ton air conditioner, while Florida was asking $50,000 for its trained porpoise, Smokey, who could not only play basketball but also extinguish fires by spitting. Montana had some interesting items up for grabs—a 300-foot-long boardwalk, 56-foot-long bathroom, and three live elk ($500 per, corral extra), as did Mississippi, which was trying to find a new home for its $7,000 paddle wheeler. A Beatles fan in Cleveland had grabbed the Fab Four replicas from the Fair's wax museum for $6,000, with the equally lifelike Charles de Gaulle headed to the big-time, Ripley's Believe It or Not on Broadway. Caroline Kennedy, who adored the Fair on both of her two visits, was going to be the lucky recipient of Coca-Cola's electronically croaking bullfrog courtesy of the company. Walt Disney's robotic dog from GE's Carousel of Progress, which Caroline also loved, was going to—where else?—Disneyland, along with its animatronic kin: Illinois's Abe Lincoln, Ford's cavemen, and, of course, Pepsi's "It's a Small World" puppets.[80]

With costs to demolish larger buildings running from $100,000 to $300,000, most exhibitors were offering their buildings to anyone who would pay for the cost of moving them and restoring the grounds they sat on. U.S. Rubber offered its giant tire Ferris wheel to the city, adding that it would give it away to the first taker if the city did not want it. By August, some inquiries had been made for specific items, but no one seemed to be in the market for a whole building, except for the Spanish Pavilion, the crown jewel of the architecture at the Fair. Mobile, Alabama, was interested in the pavilion, as was the New York State Arts Council and the New York Trade Board, the latter wanting to keep the building on the present site. No one really knew what to do with AMF's seven-car, dual-track Monorail that had carried so many happy (and air-conditioned) fairgoers over the grounds. Clearly, the most innovative proposal for it came from Councilman O'Dwyer, who suggested that the city take the thing and use it as a form of mass transit running crosstown at both Forty-second and Thirty-fourth Streets. Rumor was that the Monorail, which had cost $5.5 million to build, could be scooped up by the first taker for just a million bucks.[81]

As the Fair entered its final six weeks, some of the steam would be taken out of Beame's preliminary report, increasing the odds that Moses would be allowed to do whatever he wanted to in Flushing Meadows. After a total of ten and a half months over the course of two seasons in which lighter-than-expected attendance was the rule, the New York World's Fair seemed to finally hit its stride. Like a horse that was saving its kick for the home stretch, the Fair peaked during the Labor Day weekend of 1965, setting a single-day attendance record of 317,310 on September 5. With parking lots filled and the traffic on the highways ringing the Fair jammed, some drivers on the way to it simply turned around and went home. Jones Beach—another Moses project—and Coney Island were comparatively deserted, as hordes of people waited three hours to get into the Johnson Wax Pavilion and two and a half to get inside IBM's. Most of the tickets presented at the gate, however, had been purchased in advance before the first season at the rock-bottom price of $1.35 (proceeds the WFC had already long spent).[82] With time running out, people were rushing to use up their tickets before they became collectibles.

The boom continued through September and into October, as shirtsleeved, camera-toting throngs heeded Moses's billboard warning to "come before it is too late."[83] As in the beginning of the Fair, Manhattan was a hotbed of entertainment (*Carousel, Fiddler on the Roof, The Odd Couple,* and *The Owl and the Pussycat* on Broadway; *My Fair Lady* and *The Sound of Music* at Radio City), but the Fair was more than holding its own against all comers. The final week of the Fair was simply a madhouse, so much so that some worn-out exhibit managers were elated when it rained. Dads who had promised to take their kids to Flushing Meadows over the past couple of years now had to come up with the goods, accounting for a large number of exhausted middle-aged men being led around by groups of peppy children.[84] As the Fair surged past the 50 million mark its last week, restaurants that had been in the red for almost two full seasons suddenly had a chance to climb into the black as they operated at peak capacity. Rather ironically, more people attended the Fair on its final day, October 17, than any other, with 446,953 passing through the turnstiles. Total attendance came in at 51,607,037, a record attendance for international fairs, and more than a quarter of the entire U.S. population. The 1964–65 Fair had surpassed the 44,932,978 who went to the 1939–40 New York Fair, the 41,454,412 who visited the one-season Brussels Exposition in 1958, the 39,052,236 who were at the 1933–34 Chicago Century of Progress, and the attendance of all previous world's fairs.[85] During the first season, 27,148,280 had come to Flushing Meadows, and 24,458,757 came the second, relatively proportionate for two-season fairs. The most popular pavilion was General Motors, which drew 29,002,186, with the Vatican not too far behind at 27,020,857, proving Moses right in his claim that these two institutions would be vital to the success of the Fair.[86]

As darkness fell on the Fair on its last day, emotions ran strong among employees who had spent so much time on the grounds for its twelve-month run. "There's a sadness here now," noted Emmett Kelly Jr., clown extraordinaire, as he sat in his closet-size dressing room in the Kodak Pavilion where he had performed both seasons. College students would soon be returning to school and foreign exhibitors going back to their home countries, with some hoping for a miracle that Moses and the city would decide to extend the Fair. Some employees would remember the Fair more for social than professional reasons. "There's been a lot of inter-fair dating," explained twenty-three-year-old John Gilsenan, an ambulance driver. Some employees (and quite a number of visitors) who had met at the Fair were engaged, marking the event with extraspecial memories. Others were less wistful. "I'm sick of it," said a Greyhound hostess. "I'm sick of stupid questions and I'm sick of this job." Yiennis Voyistzis of the Greek Pavilion thought the first season was better than the second. "Last year it was prettier, more music, more art. This year there are so many hamburger and hot dog stands."[87]

Despite the hundreds of extra security personnel assigned to the grounds on the final day, a significant number of visitors were determined to take home a literal piece of the Fair. Flowers and shrubbery—including the chrysanthemums that had just been planted for the new park—were ripped up and countless souvenirs taken, even the black plastic "You Are Here" tags on the outdoor maps. Vandals too struck the fairgrounds, with signs torn down from buildings and trash cans dumped into fountains.[88] More than a few tipsy men wandered into the Unisphere pool, too good of a photo op to miss out on as anarchy reigned. Flags were taken from the United Nations Pavilion and, somehow, a few twenty-foot flagpoles. Booty accumulated at the Fair's gates, as guards took away visitors' pickin's.[89] Adding to the chaos of the last day was when two cars of a train ride at the Long Island Rail Road Pavilion toppled over, sending three adults and four children to the ground's Atomedic hospital. *Time* described the last day's happenings as a "scene straight out of a Federico Fellini film," bookending the chaos of the first day. The Fair was going out just like it came in.[90]

The controversy and chaos blanketing both seasons of the 1964–65 Fair did not go unnoticed by organizers of Expo 67, who were determined to go to school on New York to avoid many of its problems. Meeting in Montreal, the site of the upcoming event, just a week after the New York Fair had closed, 160 commissioners and foreign representatives agreed that, first and foremost, Expo 67 would have to be officially endorsed by the Bureau of International Exhibitions. Sixty-eight nations—including New York no-shows such as Britain and the Soviet Union—had in fact already signed up for the event that, despite not even calling itself a "world's fair," planned to focus on internationalism versus commerce. Part of this change was by default, as many corporate exhibitors, having overspent their budgets at Flushing Meadows, decided to sit this one out.[91] The official theme of the exhibition, Man and His World, may have been less ambitious than New York's theme of Peace Through Understanding, but it was certainly more achievable. Expo 67 might not turn out to be as exciting as the New York World's Fair, its organizers must have thought, and that was okay with them. To help plan its pavilion for Expo 67, the province of Ontario commissioned a firm called the Analytical Research Institute, which found that the New York Fair was too big and unwieldy and, as if there were any doubt, that the New York Fair lacked a "personal touch."[92]

An executive of another proposed upcoming international exposition, Hemis-Fair '68 in San Antonio, also planned for his event to be much different from the Wild West that was New York's. Ewen C. Dingwall, who had been director of the successful, human-scale fair in Seattle, thought the New York Fair was overbuilt, poorly managed, and confusing to the visitor, citing the actual possibility for one to tour the Hall of Education and then go upstairs and play a game of pool. Compounding the many problems, Dingwall stated, was "the self-evident antipathy of New York's top management to listen to or to take advantage of independent professional advice." On cue, Moses went on the record to say that he was not interested in Dingwall's opinion.[93]

## Going, Going, Gone

One day after the Fair locked its gates, wreckers had already started taking down the Ford and RCA Pavilions, a vivid reminder that the clock was ticking on all the other buildings on the grounds. Pavilion operators had ninety days after the Fair closed to get their buildings off the site one way or another, their contracts with the WFC specified. With at least a baker's dozen exhibitors having gone belly up, however, it looked like the WFC or the city was going to have to pick up some of the demolition tab.[94] There was no doubt the much praised Spanish Pavilion would survive, with St. Louis mayor A. J. Cervantes keen on locating it on a bank of the Mississippi River near the recently completed Gateway Arch and sports stadium. The $2.7 million needed to move the building was being raised from private sources, although Mobile (like St. Louis ruled by Spain for a time in the late eighteenth century, hence its interest in it) was not giving up on its bid. St. Louis, partly because it had hosted the 1904 World's Fair, won the prize, however. Mayor Cervantes, whose Hispanic heritage certainly didn't hurt in swaying the Spaniards, toured the pavilion with a delegation of no fewer than ninety-two people in January 1966 before it was dismantled, shipped, and reconstructed in the Gateway City, where it remains today as the lobby of the Marriott Pavilion Hotel. Councilman O'Dwyer's proposal to move the Monorail to midtown Manhattan was apparently a little too ahead of its time, with the airborne people mover purchased by a wrecking company that was now trying to unload the thing, noting in its advertising that it was "used just two summer seasons."[95]

Some other pavilions were able to avoid the wrecking ball by finding a good home somewhere in the world. A ski resort in Jamestown, New York, bought the Austrian Pavilion for use as a lodge for just $3,000, whereas Japan's Pavilion, stone wall and all, was given to Manhattanville College of the Sacred Heart in Purchase, New York, for use as an Asian studies center. Indonesia was packing up its pagoda-style building and taking it back to Jakarta, whereas the Danish Pavilion's next home would be in a Westport, Connecticut, shopping center as the "Danish House," a Danish-themed store and restaurant. Although the price of the pavilion was a bargain at $40,000 given that the building originally cost more than $1 million, it cost another $500,000 to dismantle, truck, and rebuild it. The Christian Science Pavilion was headed to Poway, California, via the Panama Canal, to be born again as a church, a real steal at $79,000, and the Mormon Pavilion still serves the faithful as a church in Plainview, Long Island. Wreckers took down the Vatican Pavilion but not before the *Pietà* and *Good Shepherd* statues were carefully packed up and shipped back to Rome. Thankfully, there was no need to cash in the $6 million insurance policy on the *Pietà*, which arrived safely back home at St. Peter's Basilica in November, unlikely to ever leave again.[96]

Some corporate pavilions or parts of them made it out of Flushing Meadows in one piece. After the city approved the acquisition of the New York State Pavilion but rejected the U.S. Rubber Ferris wheel, the company planned to move the giant tire to its Allen Park, Michigan, headquarters, but it ended up being bought by a Lake George, New York, amusement park operator (who also snagged a few of the fifty-four-passenger Greyhound Glide-a-Ride trams).[97] The Johnson Wax Pavilion did return to its corporate headquarters in Racine, Wisconsin, where it now functions as S. C. Johnson's Golden Rondelle Theater, whereas Coca-Cola's carillon now chimes for visitors to Stone Mountain Park near Atlanta. Thailand's eighteenth-century Buddhist shrine was taken apart for reassembly in Montreal at Expo 67, and in March, U.S. Steel donated $100,000 to make its Unisphere a permanent part of Flushing Meadows Park. The Unisphere lives on not just as the primary architectural symbol of the Fair but, along with the Brooklyn Bridge, Guggenheim Museum, and Washington Square Arch, as one of what can be considered second-tier New York City icons. It may be less recognizable than the city's Big 3—the Empire State Building, Chrysler Building, and Statue of Liberty—but it is at least as durable, ensuring its long-term survival as a cultural icon. A couple of other corporate pavilions were converted into mobile exhibits after the Fair by marketers wanting to get more bang from their promotional buck. Clairol put a smaller, transportable version of its Color Carousel on the road in March 1966, wanting to leverage the popularity of the pavilion that had drawn two million women over the two seasons. Retrofitted into two huge vans, the Carousel stopped at shopping centers in eighteen cities across the country, where four thousand women a day got personal consultations from the company's color advisers. Knowing the publicity mileage it got when its huge plastic dinosaurs floated to the fairgrounds on a barge down the Hudson River, Sinclair also sent a scaled-down version of its exhibit on a shopping center tour from New York that ended with a five-day prehistoric stand in Miami.[98]

Wrecking of the grounds and salvage operations continued throughout 1966, with Moses hoping to turn the refurbished park over to the city by the end of that year. Although his Fair had lost versus made millions, Moses still had designs to, as he put it in March, "make the post-fair park the greatest park in the center of the greatest city." Moses was now going to use $3 million in TBTA funds—less than half of what he had originally planned—to convert the grounds for public use, justifying the controversial expenditure by claiming that the Fair was leaving a legacy of $225 million in permanent improvements, including roads, remaining structures, and park amenities.[99] The physical legacy of the Fair would indeed stretch significantly beyond the 646-acre site itself because of the new and improved highways that Moses had built to handle the expected traffic. Just as following the 1939–40 fair, in fact, there was an increased demand for housing in Queens, as residents of both the city and Long Island "discovered" the borough and its great roads. Knowing many commuters would love the location, location, location, builders again rushed to construct new housing near the grounds, with homes and apartment complexes squeezed into already fairly dense bedroom communities like Bayside and Douglaston. "Say what you will about the fair," gushed one builder, Skee Taubin of the aptly named Trylon Realty Corporation, "it left us with a terrific highway system."[100]

Wanting to be sure that he was credited with the transformation of Flushing Meadows that he had committed so much time and energy to, Moses published a twenty-page brochure, *The Saga of Flushing Meadow* [sic], under the auspices of the TBTA in April 1966. Fifteen hundred copies of the brochure, which traced the history of the area from as far back as 1645, were sent to city, county, and state officials. The brochure was, of course, Moses's way to be recognized for the leading role he had played in using both the 1939–40 fair and the recently completed one to redeem the site from its shame as a valley of ashes. "We believe it is no exaggeration to say that two World's Fairs have ushered in, at the very geographical and population center of New York, on the scene of a notorious ash dump, one of the very great municipal parks of our country," Moses wrote. Moses saw the 1964–65 Fair as nothing short of wondrous, if not the greatest event in history, then something pretty darn close, "We rivaled the Seven Wonders of the Ancient World. We evolved [sic] Renaissance, Louis XIV, Tudor, Jacobian, Jeffersonian, Victorian, General Grant, Bogart, Sanford White, Nervi, Bauhaus, Lloyd Wright, Baroque, Rococo, Igloo, Ankhor Wat, Animated Typewriters, Frozen Music and the ecstasies of Viennese pastry cooks."[101]

If Moses was still wondering if all the troubles of the Fair were worth it, all doubts surely disappeared in August 1966 when he broke ground for a zoo on the site, something he had been lobbying for since his planning days for the 1939–40 fair. By diverting another $2 million from the TBTA budget, Moses got the go-ahead to build the eighteen-acre zoo that was scheduled for completion in the fall of 1967. At the groundbreaking ceremony, Moses ably played the role of the returning hero claiming the spoils of victory. An admiring crowd of five thousand watched Moses toss the first shovel of dirt, also drawn by free hot dogs and the music of a rather famous local resident, Louis Armstrong. Autograph seekers hounded Moses, while others said "God bless you" to him. One woman actually kissed Moses's hand as if he were royalty.[102] Despite his fall from grace and tarnished reputation, many New Yorkers did indeed still consider Robert Moses a king, the man who during his almost half-century reign had not only rebuilt a city as perhaps no other single individual in the history of the world had but also delivered a magical, unforgettable Fair to the people.

To his many critics, however, it appeared that the emperor wore no clothes, especially when the final report on the Fair's fiscal operations was issued at the end of 1965. The WFC had defaulted on 60 percent of the $30 million in bonds it had borrowed from four hundred individuals and corporations to get the Fair up and running and was able to pay back none of the $24 million (more than 10 percent of the city's budget for education) it had borrowed from the city to prepare the site.[103] Despite all the precautions Moses had taken to make his enterprise a profitable one, this Fair's balance sheet looked a lot like the one of the last fair in New York. The Fair had lost $20 million its first season, the audit showed, and said, more generally, that "controls necessary for good management were lacking." Very surprising was the disclosure that Moses would receive a total of $1,080,625 as Fair president, the result of a $15,000 "annuity contract" for each year of his tenure—seven years and seven and a half months to be precise. Anyone else responsible for losing that many millions of dollars would have been fired if not sent to jail for reporting the Fair's first season's deficit of $17.2 million as a surplus of $12.6 million, but Moses was going to get a $200,000 bonus.[104] When the final report was released, Moses was unavailable for comment, attending a meeting of the Nassau-Suffolk Planning Board to promote his next project—a bridge across Long Island Sound.

On its editorial page on October 17, 1965, the final day of the exposition, the *New York Times* captured the event's fundamental contradiction that persists to this day: the gap between the Fair's official and unofficial memories. "It is unfortunate . . . that recriminations over the mistakes the fair's management kept making will probably continue to overshadow its very real contributions," the editor astutely observed. Because of its backroom trials and tribulations, the editor already seemed to know, the 1964–65 New York World's Fair would be officially remembered as a bloated mess, the world's fair to end all world's fairs. The newspaper also recognized, however, that the popular memory of the Fair would be much different, an experience that truly enriched peoples' lives. Like the World of Tomorrow, which had also lost money but deeply shaped how millions of people saw the world twenty-five years earlier, this New York fair too would be permanently etched into the minds of an entire generation. "Those old enough to recall the 1939–40 fair will be encouraged to hope that intangible things—the sights and sounds and artistry and magic—will linger in memory when the harsh accusations are forgotten," the editor wrote.[105] It is precisely these lingering memories, set against the backdrop of a now long-lost innocence, that should and will live on as the Fair's most enduring legacy.

# PART TWO

# ✦ Tomorrow Begins Today

# 4  The House of Good Taste

*The greatest good for the greatest number means, in its material sense,*
*the greatest goods for the greatest number, which, in turn, means the greatest*
*productivity per worker.*
　　　—Inscription on the Hall of Free Enterprise

ON MAY 1, 1964, more than two hundred dignitaries gathered at the World's Fair to pay homage to America's free-enterprise system. The occasion was the dedication of the Hall of Free Enterprise in the International Area, highlighted by the lighting of the "Torch of Truth" on top of the pavilion. The irony of it being May Day was likely not missed on those individuals in attendance, some of whom seized the event as an ideal opportunity to promote the American way of life grounded in consumer capitalism. John Davis Lodge, president of Junior Achievement (and former governor of Connecticut and ambassador to Spain), delivered a feisty attack against "Russian Communist imperialist aggression," while Mayor Wagner praised the pavilion as "a most valuable endeavor to explain in practical terms . . . the daily economic benefits inherent to our free enterprise system." Messages of congratulation came from President Johnson, former president Herbert Hoover, FBI director J. Edgar Hoover, and David J. McDonald, president of the United Steelworkers Union, who spoke of the close, symbiotic relationship between free enterprise and "free labor."[1] The main feature of the Hall of Free Enterprise was "Mr. Both Comes to Town," a seventeen-minute animated show sponsored by the American Economic Foundation illustrating the basics of economics by depicting individuals as both producers and consumers in a small town. The exhibit included a revolving tree in which a machine printed out the answer to any of 120 predetermined questions on economics asked by visitors. As coup de grâce, the Hall of Free Enterprise allowed franchise businesses to advertise opportunities for budding entrepreneurs and, rather amazingly, offered a free two-week postgraduate course given by the Adelphi University Business Institute called Enterprise Economics, with students earning credit toward a master's degree.[2]

Although the Hall of Free Enterprise elevated laissez-faire capitalism to a nearly spiritual plane, organizers of the 1964–65 New York World's Fair were simply following a long tradition in which global expositions and commerce were virtually synonymous. The very first world's fair, in fact, the Crystal Palace Exhibition in London 1851, was essentially a large international version of the trade and industrial exhibits common in Europe since the mid-1700s. The fair was a giant display case for the Industrial Revolution and, more specifically, an unprecedented opportunity to prove to the rest of the world that Britain was producing and using the most technologically advanced machinery in existence. With the rise of American consumer culture in the early twentieth century, world's fairs switched their economic focus from machines for the farm and factory to products for the home and road. As well, American marketers eagerly seized world's fairs as a valuable promotional and public relations tool, using them to introduce new products to and create corporate goodwill among a large global audience.[3]

In the 1930s, with capitalism in crisis, world's fairs were assigned the grander cultural role to shore up Americans' faith in a consumer-based society. The 1933–34 Century of Progress exposition in Chicago not only reminded Americans of our past accomplishments but also sent a strong message that the popular value of thrift was not in the best long-term interests of either the nation or the individual. Although President Roosevelt backed the Century of Progress as a form of economic (and psychological) recovery, private corporations, most notably General Motors and Ford, championed the somewhat damaged idea that spending money was the essence of the American way. Other American fairs of the 1930s, that is, San Diego (1935–36), Dallas (1936), Cleveland (1936–37), and San Francisco (1939–40), carried similar ideological themes, but it was the 1939–40 New York World's Fair that most enthusiastically celebrated the American way of life steeped in consumerism and rebutted the pessimism of the Great Depression. Tubular chairs, nylon, and television all made their debut in 1939 in New York, just a few of the "products of tomorrow" that would lead us to a better, happier future. With a board of directors dominated by business leaders and an all-star team of industrial designers including Walter Dorwin Teague, Norman Bel Geddes, Raymond Loewy, and Henry Dreyfus, commerce was clearly at the core of the 1939–40 fair. All the major carmakers and an assortment of other large companies, including AT&T, Kodak, RCA, U.S. Steel, and Westinghouse, exhibited at the fair, a re–coming out of sorts for big business that had been largely blamed for the Depression. GM's Futurama ride, designed by Geddes, not only offered visitors a peek into a utopian world of 1960 but also correctly predicted that much of tomorrow would be brought to us by corporate America.[4]

It was thus virtually inevitable that the 1964–65 New York World's Fair would not just continue along this trajectory of consumerism but, given the postwar American experience, exponentially advance it. The Fair was grounded in commerce from the get-go, dependent on the blessings of local businessmen for it to move from idea to reality. This Fair, even more than previous ones, would embrace the promise of science and technology to make our lives easier and more fulfilling. The commercial nature of the Fair trickled down from its leader, Robert Moses, who, viewing the event as a business opportunity for the city, filled his board of directors with men of industry. From Moses's perspective, it was also essential that the Fair itself be profitable in order for the WFC to pay back the bonds it had borrowed, to silence the many critics, and, most important, to pave the way for the realization of his ultimate dream—a world-class park in Queens, perhaps even carrying his name. Business, not political differences or social inequities, would define the 1964–65 New York World's Fair, offering both visitors and exhibitors a strong sense of comfort surrounded by the familiar and friendly ideology of American free enterprise and the fruits of the marketplace.

## The Pool of Industry

Long before opening day, it was already apparent that commerce at the Fair would crush almost everything else in its path. As soon as the WFC moved into its head-quarters in the Empire State Building, in fact, critics came out of the journalistic woodwork to voice their concerns about the Fair becoming a yearlong advertise-ment for exhibitors and for the idea of business itself. Some were simply concerned that the commercial aspects of the Fair would make the event less than an enter-taining affair. A full four years before opening day, for example, Robert Fontaine of *Atlantic Monthly* predicted, "The place will be cluttered with the latest color TV sets, the newest in prefabricated houses, the finest dynamos available, and, quite possibly, a machine that can take all the available statistics and come out with an answer to the effect that these are precisely the things the fair should have exhibited." Fontaine also anticipated that the typical fairgoer would be exiting the grounds "haggard and bored, his arms weighed down with pamphlets and brightly printed books of statistics."[5]

By late 1963, it was quite clear that the type of scenario Fontaine imagined was not too much of an exaggeration. Even some Fair officials had been taken aback by the overt commercialism of the event as it took shape. "We have to crack down on this," one staffer observed as it became clear that corporate pavilions would dominate the Fair's landscape. "It's beginning to look like a bazaar." Writing for the *Nation* in November of that year, C. Gervin Hayden described the Fair that was rapidly taking shape as "646 acres of mammoth ads, corporate images and soft-sell" and "the biggest array of wallet-tempting sales messages of the decade." Hayden added, "U.S. industry has seized upon the New York Fair as a rare mar-keting opportunity, masquerading as a public-service endeavor [but] becom[ing] a hard-nosed, profit-oriented business operation." Other journalists were struck by the Fair's evolution as a pure, unadulterated exercise in marketing. "The fair offers an unmatched opportunity for on-the-spot consumer research and product exposure, and the business exhibitors are making the most of it," a writer for *Business Week* observed a month before opening day. True to form, Ford was doing consumer research at the Fair even before it opened, hiring four hundred people to try out its Magic Skyway to make sure it was up to snuff.[6]

Hard proof that business ruled the Fair roost were the swank, exclusive executive lounges hidden in most of the corporate pavilions. Filled with wall-to-wall deep-pile carpet, recessed lighting, station wagon–size stereophonic cabinetry, and more martinis than in a James Bond movie, executive lounges at the Fair resembled bachelor pads for men in gray flannel suits. Ford had three such hideaways, including one ultraplush lounge just for company officers and directors and their guests featuring Ford vinyl-coated fabrics on the furnishings and a chef imported from the Four Seasons in New York. The Tower of Light Pavilion, which represented 150 private utility companies, had two lounges that separated employees like military clubs did for officers and noncoms. For company brass and VIPs there was the Kite and Key Club, equipped with rosewood paneling, dining and bar facilities, and a one-way mirror to view the hoi polloi on the outside. In their lounge, however, utility-company worker bees were treated to not much more than a soft-drink vending machine. Although they ranged in amenities and appointments, companies kept hush-hush about these rooms because they contradicted the democratic spirit of the Fair, symbols of the vast inequalities and discrimination across class, racial, and gender lines in business and virtually every other sphere of life around the world. Interestingly, executive lounges at the 1939–40 New York World's Fair were even bigger and more ornate, as there was no central private club for entertaining as there was at the 1964–65 Fair. Corporate members and individuals gained access to the exclusive Terrace Club for $3,750 to $12,500 and $1,250, respectively, a pricey but affordable option for those sponsors wanting to do some private entertaining at the Fair.[7]

One did not have to have access to or even know about the private executive lounges to realize that the Fair was a multimillion-dollar salute to business. As visitors walked through the main gate, they typically entered the Industrial Area, at more than 3.5-million square feet the largest of the Fair's five sections. There they walked along either the Avenue of Progress or the Avenue of Commerce, both of which looked directly out at the Pool of Industry. The Pool of Industry was a focal point of the Fair, with fairgoers gathering 'round its Fountain of the Planets every night at nine to hear symphonic music and see a "tone poem" of water patterns, rainbow-colored lights, and fireworks explode above them.[8] The pool was not just a celebration of the Fair but a tribute to commerce, an audiovisual spectacle symbolizing the awesome power of American business. Further inside the grounds were the exhibits of some three hundred corporations, about three dozen of them in their own custom-built pavilions and the remainder in leased space in one of four multiexhibit buildings.[9]

11. *"The Fountain of the Fairs," one of no fewer than eight water gushers on the grounds. Photo © Bill Cotter.*

Critics were quick to attack the Fair's shameless tutorial in capitalism, especially those critics who leaned left. Writing for the *Nation* in July 1964, for example, Max Kozloff mused that the Fair was as sophisticated a form of propaganda as was possible: "In fairs on the scale of the present one at Flushing Meadows, the free-enterprise system mirrors itself as flatteringly and seductively as it knows how. Neither permanence nor restraint hobbles a project whose aim is an artful fantasy in which individual products are not nearly so important as the spectacular packaging of the business idea itself." Robert Hughes, who in 1964 was serving as an Australian-based art critic for the *Nation* when he was not painting, was especially vitriolic about all the selling at the Fair: "From the moment you enter Flushing Meadow [*sic*], you become a fetus in the bulging womb of commerce, suspended in an amniotic fluid of ballyhoo and gimmickry. You are disoriented and cushioned, and thus made porous to the seepage of advertising copy which is the sole reason for the fair. . . . The fair is only nominally a gathering of nations. In fact it is a promotional orgy for American business." Hughes went further in his analysis of the Fair, seeing it as a watershed moment of the nation's cultural history. The Fair, he argued, "implies the passing of `the Kennedy style,' with all its attendant complexities of humanism, and heralds a return to the Philistine simplicities that Calvin Coolidge summed up: `Business is America's business.'"[10]

America indeed appeared to have turned a corner, with large corporations taking the charge in defining our national identity and social values as charismatic, visionary political leadership waned. Continental Insurance's Great Moments of the American Revolution pavilion at the Fair was certainly a prime example of how business traded on American mythologies as a powerful marketing tool. Using the Continental soldier (the company's trademark) as a starting point, the pavilion brought the American Revolution to life in cartoons, dioramas, paintings, and song, further endowing its brand identity with iconography of the nation's proud past. A twenty-minute animated *Parade of Heroes* film in the pavilion's Cinema '76 movie theater told the stories of various Revolutionary war heroes, with information about Continental Insurance's operations displayed alongside such other exhibits as a life-size tableau of *The Spirit of '76*, thirteen battle flags of the American Revolution, and patriotic paintings commissioned by the company.[11] Continental's strategy was an effective one, although the exact relationship between insurance—a product steeped in the values of practicality, prudence, and caution—and "revolution" was not explained in any detail.

Other criticism of the Fair focused on its designed disposability, that little would be left after the show closed in a year and a half. The idea that most of the Fair buildings be permanent so that they could be used after the event was tossed around in the initial planning stages, a way to justify or amortize the tremendous construction costs. One idea was that the grounds be used as the campus for an international university after the event, but Moses rejected this idea ("hogwash" was his exact response), arguing instead that a science museum be built for the Fair and then turned into a permanent fixture of his planned park.[12] Another proposal led by Bill Shea, who would successfully champion the construction of a new sports stadium next to the fairgrounds, was for the city to bid for the 1968 Olympics and, if successful, use the Fair site for the games.[13] Although the fairgrounds would end up hosting the rowing, track, and some other trials for the 1964 Games, it was clear by 1963 that Flushing Meadows would not be the site of the 1968 Olympics or any permanent institution except perhaps Moses's science museum.[14] Horace Sutton of the *Saturday Review* was particularly disturbed that the Fair would be "knock[ed] down and discard[ed] like a used Kleenex" and that the city and nation were missing an opportunity to leave something valuable and enduring. "The glittering show astride Grand Central Parkway," Sutton continued, "is a reflection not so much of the American penchant for conspicuous consumption as for conspicuous waste. What mammoth something or other, something useful to mankind might have risen there on the Flushing flats—what library, research center, medical complex, university, might all that money have bought?"[15] Of course, Moses had considered all of these ideas and many more but had rejected them all, unwilling or unable to imagine anything on the site except a park to rival all others. This Fair, like virtually all past ones, would be almost entirely disposable.

Many other less elitist observers too could not help but conclude that the Fair was first and foremost about selling. "From nations to corporations," a reporter from *Time* noted about six weeks after opening day, "everybody is there to hawk and horn-blow." *Ebony* believed that Fair planners realized that a successful event had to not only "satisfy visitors' curiosity about foreign lands and peoples" but also "encourage visitors to want and buy and own the latest in consumer products and creature comforts" and "stir in fair goers a desire to have the newest kinds of housing and household gadgets, the latest automobiles and clothes." The *Ebony* reporter concluded, "Most of those who have seen the fair agree that it does just that and does it as no fair has done before."[16] One visitor from Albany, New York, however, was more critical, considering the Fair to be steeped in "crass commercialism." "The pretty show cases containing overpriced products and hack commercials in the form of vapid ditties and sterile exhibits do not, I hope, portray our future for the next 25 years," he griped. Another observer simply thought it was odd and a little disturbing that the Fair "omitted Russia, all central Europe and most of Asia, while including Clairol, General Cigar, Mastro Pizza, Johnson's Wax and Seven-Up."[17]

With commerce the common denominator or Esperanto of the Fair, national pavilions tended to take on the appearance of corporations and vice versa. Because the exhibits of the Big 3 automakers dwarfed the displays of many nations, in fact, *Time* referred to their pavilions as "the sovereign republics of Ford, Chrysler, and General Motors." International pavilions could be easily mistaken for corporate exhibitors because most of them were in fact sponsored by the foreign equivalent to Chambers of Commerce, which, in turn, leased space to private exporters. It was not only a way for foreign exhibitors who wanted a presence at the Fair to get around the BIE's ban but also a way for them to recover some or all of the high rental costs and, perhaps, even make a profit. It was thus not surprising that Fair literature often described foreign pavilions in business terms. At the Central America Pavilion, for example, "the culture and commerce of five countries [were] linked in a common market," whereas at India's pavilion, "displays and recordings show how a once-backward nation is now able to make aircraft engines and automobiles, and exploit the peaceful uses of atomic power."[18] Ironically, religious and state exhibits had been actively sought to lessen the grounds' resemblance to the world's largest shopping center, but, as some noted at the time, these exhibitors too were much about selling.

The Lake Amusement Area was also intended to serve as a way to balance out the heavy representation of industry at the Fair. Because little actual amusement could be found in the area, however, a result of Moses's insistence that everything at the Fair be as inoffensive as his billboard-free parkways, corporations took on the role as lead entertainer. *Time* considered the Fair to be "a showcase of entertainment mounted by America's most sophisticated and free-spending entertainers—its captains of industry." The magazine concluded, "Showmanship has become the respected and well-paid partner of industry."[19] It was no coincidence then that industry's most powerful marketing tool—television—would heavily shape fairgoers' experience. Almost twenty years of television had forever changed how entertainment, and thus world's fairs, would be presented and consumed (just as a fair of today would be inscribed by the medium du jour, the Internet). Much of the televisual nature of the Fair could be credited to (or blamed on) Martin Stone, president of a company called Media Enterprises, the nation's leading television production firm. Stone was hired by Moses in 1961 to sell exhibit space to companies, receiving a cool 5 percent of the rental revenues for his efforts. Having sold the rights to such big names as Jackie Gleason, Howdy Doody, and Lassie, Stone not surprisingly approached corporations considering a presence at the Fair through a television-like lens, namely, the opportunity to present products and services to consumers via a controlled, contained visual experience. "TV has oriented [businesspeople] toward entertainment as a way of selling products," Stone said in the fall of 1963, pitching a televisual model—visual entertainment to a captive audience within a defined period of time—to advertisers like the Bell System, GE, Du Pont, RCA, IBM, and Johnson's Wax.[20]

With one of the world's leading television executives the primary liaison to corporate customers, movement and action became the keys to a good pavilion experience versus the pre-TV model of static displays. As important to the entertainment component was the ability to control how long visitors stayed in a pavilion, with exhibitors appropriating fairgoers' inclination to move around at their own pace. A typical visitor's experience thus consisted of watching some form of presentation for eight to thirty minutes and then being summarily ejected from the building.[21] "Once he commences a ride or tour, he is systematically fed an entertaining, and hopefully convincing, sales message," the *Nation* observed, with visitors traveling through time and space by conveyer belts and hydraulic lifts and then deposited near the exit, cogs in a literal entertainment machine.[22] The impact of television—arguably the most important technological innovation of the second half of the twentieth century—on the Fair experience could be rivaled only by the most important technological innovation of the first half of the century: Henry Ford's assembly line.

## Hard Sell

As the 1964–65 New York World's Fair took shape as the ultimate trade show, American businesses spent a huge amount of money—a total of three hundred million dollars—on their exhibits. "We couldn't afford *not* to spend," one executive remarked. "You can't look cheap."[23] Cheap was the last thing some corporations looked. GM's exhibit cost more than fifty million dollars, Ford's thirty million, GE's fifteen million, AT&T's fifteen million, Chrysler's twelve million, NCR's three million, and Singer's two million—all when a million dollars was a million dollars.[24] Executives recognized, however, that their huge investment was long-term, their goal to build goodwill among a large number of potential consumers versus gain an immediate payback to their bottom line. Besides the prestige factor, businesses looked to the Fair as an opportunity to build better relations with dealers and their own employees. Having a presence at the Fair not only suggested that a company was forward thinking, research oriented, and public minded but also represented a rare chance to relate to consumers when they were in a festive mood. "Where else could we get the undivided attention of a captive audience of 74 million people?" asked Steven Van Voorbis, manager of GE's Progressland. The answer was nowhere, making the company's big outlay appear to be a hard-to-quantify but strategically sound use of its marketing budget. The right to add the tagline "As shown at the World's Fair" to print and TV ads was a bonus incentive to invest in the Fair. The net effect was, as *U.S. News and World Report* succinctly put it a few days after the Fair's opening, "It is U.S. industry that steals the show."[25]

Although American businesses spent freely on their exhibits—a full 60 percent of total Fair costs—what they built was not universally admired. The WFC's decision to allow exhibitors the freedom to build their own pavilions pleased corporations immensely but angered the many designers who understandably thought Moses was putting business interests instead of aesthetics. The WFC's decision to rent space versus construct buildings turned the fairgrounds into a patchwork quilt of architectural styles, just as the Fair's original design committee had predicted. Criticism of the architecture of corporate pavilions came fast and furious. One critic referred to the inside-out architecture of the General Electric pavilion as *"tripes à la mode de G.E.,"* whereas IBM's consisted of a "50-ton egg on a nest of plastic in the tops of metal trees." This same observer thought Bell Telephone's 400-foot fiberglass flying-wing portion of its building looked more like a "big hunk of sedimentary rock than an airfoil" and that the ten-story tail fin of GM's fifty million–dollar building "may be good as advertising but is ridiculous as architecture." (One could argue that, as an icon of 1950s versus mid-1960s automobile culture, the tail fin wasn't even good advertising.) Another critic agreed that both Bell Telephone's and GM's pavilions were less than inspiring. "A long wait in front of the mammoth whateveritis that houses the Bell Telephone hall of communicative wonderment might well set a telephone subscriber to wondering just why his phone bills are so high," he sneered of the former. Of the latter he quipped, "If this is Futurama architecture, many a sensitive youth of today may flatly refuse to take the trip into the twenty-first century."[26]

The Fair's primary symbol, the Unisphere, was, appropriately enough, also a 140-foot corporate logo. A two million–dollar "gift" to the Fair, U.S. Steel insisted that anytime the Unisphere was depicted, a line saying "Presented by United States Steel" had to be included. For the same amount of money, the company could have sponsored five sixty-minute television shows or about forty full-page ads in *Life*.

Executives realized, however, that a major presence at the Fair extended into a plethora of licensed products would deliver more than a billion "impressions" (ad-talk for exposures), far more than any traditional advertising plan. Although it was without a doubt a marketing coup, the Unisphere too was less than warmly received by architectural critics, especially when compared to the Atomium of the 1958 Brussels fair, the Space Needle at Seattle in 1961, or, for that matter, Sir Joseph Paxton's Crystal Palace in London in 1851 or Alexandre-Gustave Eiffel's tower in Paris in 1889. "The Unisphere is a bore," said Horace Sutton, "and a commercial bore at that."[27]

The idea for the Unisphere—a tip of the hat to another giant sphere, the Perisphere, which stood in the same spot twenty-five years earlier—is credited to Gilmore D. Clarke of Clarke and Rapuano, the engineering and architectural firm that developed the Fair's site plan (Clarke had also been a member of the 1939–40 fair's Board of Design). Not happy with the ideas that had been submitted to date in 1960 (including Walter Dorwin Teague's Journey to the Stars, a 170-foot metal spiral that looked not unlike a giant Slinky), Robert Moses asked Clarke to "give some thought" to what might serve as the Fair's principal symbol. On an airplane between Cleveland and New York in September of that year, Clarke doodled an armillary sphere—a globe constructed out of metal ribs—and the Unisphere was instantly born. In just a few more hours, Clarke had added to his design the latitudinal and longitudinal rings, the man-made satellite rings, the continents, and even the lights of major capitals. Moses immediately approved an architectural sketch, and then came the hard part, figuring out how to make it.[28]

A team of people was soon busy making the giant corporate symbol and Fair icon a reality. Borrowing his four-year-old son's rubber ball, Peter Martecchini, an engineer who worked for Clarke, constructed a working model of the sphere. Martecchini wanted the globe to revolve, but Roger M. Blough, chairman of U.S. Steel, rejected the idea, realizing his company would have enough of a challenge building a 384-ton version of earth whose continents behaved "like a giant sail," more than a minor concern given New York's occasional nor'easter. Blough is also credited with determining the Unisphere's height, this decision made by less than scientific methods. Looking out his window one day, he saw a twelve-story redbrick building and decided on the spot that that was how tall the globe should be. Blough assigned the structural engineering to the American Bridge Company, a subsidiary of U.S. Steel, which used computers to balance the biggest globe ever built.[29] Like all architectural symbols of world's fairs since 1889, the Unisphere aspired to match the grandeur of Alexandre-Gustave Eiffel's tower, a losing proposition but one that fair presidents, including Moses, could not resist. The grandson of Eiffel was even invited to attend the Unisphere's pedestal ceremony, an attempt to try to link the two icons, but few then or now likely confused the one in Paris for the one in Queens, despite the latter's use of the most advanced technology available.[30]

Other giant corporate symbols included Sinclair Oil's Dinoland, where the company's nine life-size fiberglass dinosaurs stood next to a diorama on the origins of oil, apparently not realizing they would soon become extinct and ultimately turned into fuel for combustible engines. One certainly couldn't miss U.S. Rubber's exhibit featuring a Ferris wheel in the shape of an automobile tire with twenty-four gondolas seating four people each. The company, the maker of U.S. Royal tires and Keds sneakers, charged visitors fifty cents for a ride on the wheel not so much to cover its costs as to control the crowds on what was, at 80 feet, the largest replica of an automobile tire ever made.[31] With its huge red umbrella roof, Travelers Insurance too went for sheer size, although many if not most visitors mistook the company's corporate logo for a disturbingly large clamshell. Under the big red umbrella was "The Triumph of Man," a ten-vignette diorama of "man's struggle and growth against untold odds to reach his stature of today."[32]

With image marketers' primary reason to invest in the Fair, some exhibitors were happy to give away free products or services as a cheap way to promote their brands. A free Polaroid picture was available at the Dynamic Maturity Pavilion, as was a free "powered buffer" shoe shine courtesy of Johnson's Wax at its pavilion. Travelers Insurance gave out free (and, of course, red) 45-rpm records of the company's exhibition soundtrack, "The Triumph of Man." At the Parker

12. A Brontosaurus looms in Sinclair's Dinoland, one of nine fiberglass, "life-size" dinosaurs in the exhibit. Photo © Bill Cotter.

13. *U.S. Rubber's gargantuan, immensely popular tire was a twentieth-century version of the famed 1893 World's Columbian Exposition Ferris wheel. Photo © Bill Cotter.*

Pen Pavilion, visitors completed a form listing their age, interests, and talents and in seconds were matched up by computer with pen pals from around the world with similar backgrounds. Guests were then given a free postcard with their new friend's name and address on it and sat down to drop them a line at one of ninety writing desks, supervised by multilingual hostesses. The company's goal was to launch a million friendships, nicely echoing the Fair's theme of Peace Through Understanding. At the Socony Mobil Pavilion, one could test his or her driving skill and receive a free rating of one's ability. Most popular among teenagers itching for their real driving licenses, thirty-six guests seated at auto controls in front of a map competed against each other for economy and safety as various hazards appeared on the small individual screens facing them. Contestants "traveled" the route of the Mobil Economy Runs across America, trying to minimize fuel consumption and not crash into too many things or other cars. An electronic device recorded the amount of gasoline that would be used under actual conditions, with the winner receiving a certificate.

*14. The decidedly clamlike Travelers Insurance Pavilion. Photo © Bill Cotter.*

In addition to its Enchanted Forest, where woodland creatures told visitors the story of how paper moved from tree to finished goods amid a pine-scented, tree-shaded garden, Scott Paper provided free facilities for changing diapers (one of the products they made, naturally). Kodak offered a plethora of free services including on-site experts and repairmen to set and fix cameras and a day-by-day guide to the Fair's most photogenic goings-on. Expecting the Fair to be the most photographed event ever to be held—quite an expectation, given the coverage of World War II—the company also had what was perhaps the best photo op on the grounds, its "Magic Carpet Roof," which supposedly resembled the moon's landscape.[33]

In addition to giving fairgoers various freebies to build goodwill, corporations were paying big money to get their brands seen while consumers were in a "festive mood." Chrysler paid fifty thousand dollars to park two of its cars in the garage in the House of Good Taste, whereas Ford forked out twenty thousand to have a Mustang and Thunderbird play supporting roles in Dick Button's short-lived Ice-Travaganza. A street scene in the ill-fated "Wonder World" show included signs for Ballantine beer, Coca-Cola, Sealtest, SAS, Yamaha, and Compari,

15. *Kodak's "Magic Carpet Roof," or "moondeck," was designed to be an ideal spot to take photos of the fairgrounds. Photo © Bill Cotter.*

with each company paying fifteen thousand dollars for its advertisement-as-prop. The onstage refrigerator in GE's Progressland was well stocked with Coca-Cola, a side deal made by a GE board member who also happened to sit on Coke's board. Sometimes this anything-for-a-price policy exceeded the boundaries of logic. The rathskeller at the Belgian Village became the "Ballantine Rathskeller" when the makers of the brew—popular with working-class New Yorkers and completely alien to any beer-drinking Belgian—loaned the pavilion's owner a pile of money. Even odder, Revlon paid five thousand dollars to be allowed to scent the New York City Theater, making one wonder what possible connection there was among fragrance, theater, and New York City.[34]

Although many of the goods to be found in the International Area were readily available in American department stores and gift shops, foreign exhibitors believed that their elaborate displays in exotic settings would make them especially attractive. At Denmark's pavilion, for example, a wooden picnic basket for two containing butter, bread, and Danish herring was displayed alongside a *Meet the Danes* phonograph record (also for sale). Sweden and Austria offered ski sweaters, Greece served up olive oil and giant olives, Thailand sold teak elephant carvings, and the Philippines hawked wood carvings of monkeys.[35] Given this global sales-a-thon, many visitors could not help but notice that some foreign pavilions did not, as the *New York Times* put it, "represent the character of the nations whose names they take and that they are, in fact, little more than merchandise bazaars." After taking in the Caribbean Pavilion, which featured steel bands, calypso singers, and a varied assortment of touristy souvenirs for sale like bottles of rum and straw hats, one visitor remarked, "It has about as much to do with the Caribbean as any old nightclub with a Latin flavor."[36] Still, it would be hard to find in many parts of the country (and thirty years before e-commerce) a real fez from Morocco or a second-century stone sculpture from India, each an item one could pick up at the Fair. At the Hong Kong Pavilion, one could have a custom-made tweed or brocade suit, jacket, or dress measured, sewn, and delivered in twenty-four hours, something Macy's or Gimbel's sure couldn't do.[37]

*16. International pavilions like Thailand's may have been criticized for their merchandising but architecturally speaking looked like they could have been plucked right out of Bangkok. Photo © Bill Cotter.*

## Heaven on Wheels

Although all industrial exhibitors clamored for fairgoers' attention and dollars, General Motors and Ford would lay claim as the undisputed marketing heavy-weights of the Fair, just as they had in the New York fair twenty-five years earlier and at the Chicago exposition six years before that. These automakers naturally wanted to extend the phenomenal run they had enjoyed over the past twenty years as postwar Americans hit the road in record numbers. Little did GM and Ford know that their dominance of the American car market was about to hit a major speed bump as Japanese and European companies capitalized on the growing demand for smaller, more fuel-efficient vehicles. Volkswagens, the poster child for this new market segment, were already popping up on U.S. streets in increasing numbers, soon to become an icon of American youth culture. Ralph Nader's *Unsafe at Any Speed*, published in 1965, was another sign of the bumpy road ahead for American car companies.

For GM and Ford, however, it was big business as usual. "Manned by combat teams of admen and public relations experts," C. Gervin Hayden suspected a year before the Fair opened, "their pavilions will spearhead high-pressure, national sales campaigns." Knowing where his bread was buttered (Robert Caro called Moses "probably the world's most vocal, effective and prestigious apologist for the automobile"), Moses not only used the Fair as an opportunity to expand the city's highway system but used his position to show favoritism to automobile exhibitors from the very beginning. (Moses had also won an award of twenty-five thousand dollars from GM in 1953, Caro reported, for the best essay in a nationwide contest, "How to Plan and Pay for Better Highways.") When ten large corporations quickly filed applications for the largest exhibition space available (two acres) in 1960, Moses decided to reduce the maximum allotment to a little more than an acre, reportedly concerned that there would be a space shortage.[38] Despite this restriction, however, Ford soon was somehow able to reserve a seven-acre site, as was General Motors, a clear sign that Moses recognized that these two car companies were instrumental to the Fair's financial future (as well as his own).[39]

Although Ford gave General Motors a run for its money, GM won honors for the biggest, most expensive corporate pavilion. A couple of weeks before opening day, GM previewed its new and improved Futurama exhibit to about six hundred VIPs, proving that it was the richest, most powerful company on earth, just in case there was any doubt. Guests dined on chateaubriand and were served four different wines while swinging to the sounds of Lester Lanin, the famous society bandleader. When the gala ended, departing guests hopped into sixty-seven brand-new Cadillacs waiting outside to take them wherever they wanted to go. The very next night, the company played host to some five thousand New York City civic leaders, a clear attempt to reinforce the 1960s tenet that, as GM goes, so

17. *GM's Jet Age pavilion pointed the way to a virtually limitless transportation future.*
*Photo © Bill Cotter.*

goes the country. Not to be outdone, however, Ford invited twenty-three hundred VIPs for cocktails and a tour of its pavilion, throwing in a personal handshake with both Henry Ford II and Walt Disney for each and every guest. Ford then countered GM's appeal to local politicians by inviting twenty-four hundred members of the press along with their families for a guided tour of its thirty million–dollar tour de force, the Magic Skyway.[40] Fifteen million people would end up taking Ford's ride, traveling the equivalent of sixty-eight trips around the world over the course of the two seasons.[41]

An updated version of its classic ride at the 1939–40 fair, GM's Futurama was, as it was then, the most popular exhibit in both the 1964 and the 1965 seasons. While sitting in contoured seats equipped with speakers, visitors were offered a vision of "the not-too-distant" future in which man tamed or conquered everything that nature could dish out. Futuramans took a trip to the moon, relaxed under the ocean at an aquatic resort, visited a jungle in which trees were knocked down like toothpicks, and cruised through a desert where crops thrived in soil irrigated by desalted seawater and machines planted and harvested crops by remote control. No matter the terrain, visitors learned, technology created by man (and presumably GM) would be there to put it back in its place. GM's greatest challenge in re-creating Futurama was to imagine a world that was significantly different from the one of 1964 in order to make the exhibit interesting but not so different as to make the future appear alien and scary. Designers of the 1939 Futurama played it a bit too safe, many felt, with some of the exhibit's forecasts soon realized.[42] Futurama would, in retrospect, also play it relatively safe on some things on the technology horizon (manned "lunar crawlers," commuter space stations, real-time weather forecasts via satellites) but took quite the leap on others (underwater motels have yet to become a popular travel option).

Though entertaining, Futurama's world of technological wonders like oxygen-equipped aqua scooters, laser timber cutters, and automated superfarms forgot to include one thing—people. Its City of Tomorrow, which channeled Le Corbusier's Radiant City, was all about transportation (midtown airports amid superskyscrapers, high-speed bus-trains, moving sidewalks, underground freight-conveyor belts), a utopian metropolis with no slums or parking problems. Despite correctly anticipating one innovation now in development—an "autoline" that will electronically steer, brake, and regulate the speed of each car in an automatic lane—Futurama was a fantasy world that completely ignored the real, escalating problems of urban culture. As in the 1939 Fair, however, visitors to Futurama proudly wore "I have seen the Future" buttons on their lapels, yet another way GM could get mileage from their promotional bucks and take further ownership of the world of tomorrow. In fact, GM opened Futurama at special times for stockholders and visitors from cities where the company had

*18. Futurama's "City of Tomorrow" was neat, efficient, and, rather disturbingly, largely peopleless. Photo © Bill Cotter.*

*19. Futurama's home of the future—one part Le Corbusier, one part The Jetsons. Photo © Bill Cotter.*

plants, such as Anderson, Indiana, and Flint, Michigan, using the exhibit to buddy up to key constituents.[43]

Knowing GM would bring back a new and improved Futurama, Ford reached out to the only man alive who could possibly trump its archrival. Walt Disney had contributed a Circarama (360-degree) movie to the 1958 Brussels fair and designed most of the landscaping for the 1961–62 fair in Seattle, but they were small potatoes compared to what he would create for 1964.[44] By the mid-1960s, Disney, who was nearing the end of his career (and life), was a media empire unto himself, churning out television shows, hit films, educational films, and books published in twenty-two languages.[45] It was thus inevitable that corporate America would look to Walt Disney to embed promotion of their brands within an entertainment format, that is, to cloak consumer culture as popular culture as a persuasive selling technique. For this fair, Disney would team up with no fewer than four sponsors—Ford, Pepsi-Cola, GE, and the State of Illinois—introducing his "audio-animatronic" technology at each. Disney's mechanical Lincoln in the Illinois Pavilion especially wowed crowds with its lifelike facial features (taken from Honest Abe's death mask) and ability to recite excerpts from his most famous speeches while using as many as 250,000 combinations of actions.[46] Such technological feats earned Disney honors as the Fair's "presiding genius" and further established him as the definitive showman of the twentieth century.

With the exception of GM's Futurama and the Vatican's exhibit, Disney-created pavilions turned out to be the most popular at the Fair, with often a two or more hour wait to get into any of them. Disney's "It's a Small World" ride at Pepsi-Cola's pavilion was a particular crowd favorite, of course, taking visitors along a global boat ride past such icons as the Eiffel Tower, a Dutch windmill, and the Taj Mahal while 350 doll-size animatronic figures winked, blinked, and sang of world peace. Some of the ninety-five-cent admission price for the twelve-minute ride went to UNICEF, making visitors feel a little better about the extra expense (almost half of the Fair's first season two-dollar adult ticket). Largely because of the great success of "It's a Small World," Disney made a stab at turning Flushing Meadows into a permanent theme park after the Fair, but naturally Moses refused to give up the site as the planned future home of his great public park. Disney packed up his ride along with his animatronic Lincoln and Carousel of Progress and shipped them to Anaheim, his company ultimately creating replicas of all three for Disney World, which opened in 1971.[47]

20. The "It's a Small World" ride that, after the Fair, would become a seminal Disney-land experience was part of Pepsi's pavilion, but it was its creator—Walt Disney—who got star billing. Photo © Bill Cotter.

Disney's Magic Skyway, a free extravaganza in the company's "Wonder Rotunda" pavilion, was an equally exceptional piece of propaganda for Ford, building consumer goodwill through state-of-the-art entertainment. "We don't want
[visitors] to come out thinking Disney," confessed Ford executive John Sattler.
"We want them to come out thinking Ford." Although the ride lasted just twelve
minutes, the lines were so long for the Magic Skyway that one critic joked that
it appeared "as if the company were giving away Fords."[48] Sitting in brand-new,
track-guided Mustang and Thunderbird convertibles, visitors took a trip through
time (the ride's working title had in fact been Trip Through Time), witnessing
the evolution or progress of man through seminal discoveries or inventions
in history—fire, the wheel, and the first Ford (a wagon driven by, no kidding,
"wife-power"). The cars' radios provided the narrative for the ride, available in
various languages with the push of a button ("Je m'appelle Henry Ford," began the French version).[49] Visitors were carried along a track on the rotunda's
exterior, then on to scenes in the main exhibit hall including prehistoric earth
where life-size animatronic cavemen tried to hold their own against battling
dinosaurs, soaring primeval birds, and erupting volcanoes. From there, visitors
slipstreamed into the space age, gliding on a superskyway over their own City
of Tomorrow where, as Ford described it, "tomorrow begins today." Although
the ride was entertainment at its best circa 1964, Ford's vision of the future in
its Space City was, much like GM's Futurama, eerily absent of people and a too-
close-for-comfort depiction of Robert Moses's seeming present-day preference
for vehicles over people.

Other car marketers too joined the Fair fray, countering GM's and Ford's big-
budget presentations with cheap thrills or technical details. Thirty "Hell-Driv-
ers" performed feats on wheels at Dodge's "Auto Thrill Show," whereas Chrysler's
"Autofare" exhibit offered a full-size replica of one of its factory's assembly lines
in action. "Autofare," like GM's Futurama, was a reprise from 1939, when Chrysler
showed a ten-minute film in Polaroid's brand-new 3-D technology, taking viewers through the production of a car (and alarming many visitors in the process
with the amazing special effects). For 1964, Chrysler made its exhibit even more
interactive, allowing gearheads and others to walk through a giant car featuring a
fifty-five-foot, "one-million horsepower" engine and a crankshaft with snapping,
dragonlike jaws. Visitors, seated in airborne car bodies, traveled through the various stages of an assembly line—production, styling, and operations—while mechanical men wielding huge instruments "checked" each auto for imperfections.
The company also had on hand its first car (from 1924), a futuristic "Turbine"
model and, for the kiddies, a puppet theater.[50]

Car rental companies, which were booming as more Americans decided to
fly long distances rather than drive, had a high profile at the Fair. In Avis's Pan
American Highway Ride, visitors drove miniature cars along a simulation of the
Pan American Highway "through" seventeen nations (Mexico to Argentina).

21. *Chrysler's larger-than-life walkthrough engine was an attempt to keep up with GM's spectacular Futurama and Ford's popular Magic Skyway. Photo © Bill Cotter.*

Less glamorous, more homespun was Avis's Antique Car Ride, where visitors (older than ten years old) could drive an open-topped vintage reproduction model car on a four-minute ride down an old-fashioned country lane for fifty-five cents (forty cents for kids) at a top speed of six miles per hour.[51] Walter Smith Jr., the consultant hired by Avis to create the ride, acknowledged that the company intentionally went against the futuristic stream of the Fair to attract visitors. "Recognizing some of the extremely ambitious efforts of other industrial, state and other exhibitors, and recognizing the fact that the majority will depict a futuristic life in futuristic surroundings in a 21st century flavor," said Smith at the exhibit's dedication day on November 18, 1963, "we thought we should try to be somewhat unique and turn the tables back to the horseless carriage era." Whereas Greyhound rented four-passenger carts to foot-weary adults (for a whopping nine to eleven dollars an hour) and sprinkled the fairgrounds with "taxiettes" (which played the opening bars of "Go Greyhound," a promotional tune for the company's bus service as they cruised along at three miles an hour), Hertz rented children's strollers that looked like model cars for two dollars a day. The company's popular 1960s advertising slogan was plastered on the one thousand strollers, instructing fairgoers to "Let Hertz Put You in the Driver's Seat."[52]

*22. One of the strollers Hertz rented for two dollars a day to put children in, as its popular ad slogan went, "the driver's seat." Photo © Bill Cotter.*

## Better Living

The freedom of the road was but one of the familiar, reassuring liberties embedded in the postwar "American way of life" ethic that coursed through many of the industrial exhibits at the Fair. Like most global expositions, this one would promise visitors that "better living" could be found in the products and services of today and tomorrow and that the pursuit of happiness guaranteed each American by the Constitution resided foremost within the realm of consumerism. No clearer was this idea articulated at the Fair than in the aptly named Better Living Center, a monument to the theory and practice of consumption. The Better Living Center, the third-largest building on the grounds, was specifically designed to serve the many exhibitors who wanted to take part in the Fair but could not (or would not) afford a multimillion-dollar pavilion of their own (analogous to the International Plaza for smaller countries). The Better Living Center encompassed six areas—fashion, home, health, security, food, and leisure—all of them aimed toward the bull's-eye of consumerism, the American family.[53] "The Better Living Center will be a family affair," noted the pavilion's graphic identification manual, "oriented to the family as the basis of a 'Full Life.'" In the pavilion's planning stage, however, Edward Burdick, president of the pavilion, made clear that the Better Living

Center was going to be much more than just an alternative retail outlet. "We will present . . . not a trade show, not a county fair with rows of Aunt Matilda's pickles," Burdick said at the building's groundbreaking on February 13, 1963, "but a pre-planned, coordinated free flow of major exhibits, visually showing the present and future keys to a productive and satisfying life." In the "Fair within the Fair," as it was often promoted, some 175 exhibitors displayed fashions, furnishings, and foods, and the center's hyperconsumerism, over the top even for the Fair, was not lost on critics. *Time,* one of the pavilion's harsher critics, considered the Better Living Center a "trap," where "predator salesmen claw for the jugular."[54]

Here was, however, a classic example of how critics' opinions, heavily influenced by a pervasive disdain for Robert Moses (especially those many journalists the man frequently insulted), differed greatly from the sentiments of the general public. Children and adults alike enjoyed their trip to the colossal Better Living Center, perhaps because it crossed high and low culture with such reckless abandon.[55] On the building's roof, for example, was the Hilton-run Marco Polo Club for VIPs (with radio and television news celebrity Lowell Thomas serving as host), five Hilton International Cafes, and the Women's Clubs of America hospitality suite, where blue bloods from across the country mixed and mingled (and were offered the services of a beauty salon).[56] In the building's lobby exhibit area, hordes of kids continually hovered around the world's largest model train set, while their parents kicked the tires of the new Ford Mustangs cleverly located right next to it. Famous cartoonists like Al Capp ("Li'l Abner"), Chester Gould ("Dick Tracy"), and Milton Caniff ("Flash Gordon") and others also held court in the center's lobby, drawing large versions of their characters for the many fans who considered these men superstars of the day. On the center's first floor was the full-scale, six-room, fully decorated Dorothy Draper Westinghouse Dream House and about twenty-five home-furnishings exhibitors. The second floor featured the Crystal Palace of Fashion, a daily fashion show sponsored by manufacturers, retailers, and magazines that, according to the center's promotional material, featured "the latest in clothing, accessories, and cosmetics." The Tetley Tea Salon was located next door to the fashion-show stage, with servers in black uniforms pouring cups for society and nonsociety types alike.[57]

Interestingly, the fashion industry had been, in the words of Eugenia Sheppard, women's feature editor of the *New York Herald Tribune,* "in a complete state of apathy about the Fair" until it finally got serious in late 1963. Through the fall of that year, the WFC chartered helicopters to whisk celebrities and models between Seventh Avenue and Flushing Meadows in an attempt to get the rag trade to participate. *Vogue* and other major representatives of the fashion business had exhibited at the Brussels fair in 1958, and the WFC was determined that the industry turn out in a big way on its home turf. By Thanksgiving, Lord and Taylor had booked a month of fashion shows at the Better Living Center, and *Mademoiselle, Glamour,* and *Seventeen* had all contracted to put on two-a-day shows, with many

*23. A fashion exhibit in the Better Living Center unapologetically pitched "the present and future keys to a productive and satisfying life" to fairgoers. Photo © Bill Cotter.*

more businesses and magazines to follow. "Like it or not," Sheppard sniffed, "the New York World's Fair is about to come true."[58]

It was the Better Living Center's third floor, however, that really drove critics crazy while making visitors pleased as punch.[59] Juxtaposed against the Four Centuries of American Masterpieces gallery, a gem of a collection featuring works by artists including John Singer Sargent, Edward Hopper, and Jackson Pollock, was an actual tractor-trailer truck filled with groceries, a ninety-day supply of food for the average family, to be precise. The Supermarket Institute was not surprisingly the sponsor of the semi, also exhibiting the behind-the-scenes working of a grocery store.[60] About forty other exhibitors promoted themselves on the center's amusement-park fun house of a third floor, one of them Borden, whose bell cow, Elsie, had made quite a splash at her debut at the 1939 fair. For this Fair, the bovine would be bigger and better than ever, chewing and mooing in a specially commissioned musical, *All about Elsie* (whose script was written by Joel Oliansky, the playwright in residence at Yale University). The star of the show was selected from a literal cattle call of Jerseys by a prestigious group of judges that included columnist Earl Wilson and actor Jose Ferrer, the latter's jurisdiction being "voice" and "acting ability."[61] "The search for Miss America is nothing to the search Borden has been conducting for the `personification of the Elsie image,'" commented Eugenia Sheppard. Playing to thirty packed houses a day, the show featured "a day in the life of Elsie," with the diva (reportedly discovered in Africa, of all places) re-peatedly chatting up the wonders of dairy foods in this lactose-friendly era when milk, butter, and cheese were considered the core of a healthy diet.[62]

Appeals for visitors to embrace the joys of better living were similarly pep-pered throughout the Fair outside the Better Living Center. At the Simmons Beautyrest Center, nicknamed "the Land of Enchantment," visitors could rent a bed in one of forty-six nine-foot-by-six-foot slumber rooms, or "rest alcoves," for a half-hour siesta for fifty cents. "Stroll through this delightful Wonderland of Sleep where saucy little Pixies and Elves frolic," Simmons tempted tired fairgo-ers, wooing them to its "newest sleeping aid," the Adjustable Beautyrest Bed. Be-sides disposable turquoise sheets, the beds had electric push buttons to raise and lower one's head or feet. As well, "Beautyrest Ladies" who talked in hushed tones were on-site to "check and gently awaken any guest who may have drifted from a light nap to a deep sleep."[63] "We're hoping for a birth," one Beautyrest Lady remarked, adding that "it would be good publicity."[64] The Beautyrest Ladies (all of them married to prevent anything but napping in the Land of Enchantment) were hardly the only hostesses at the Fair, with many pavilions hiring attractive women to meet and greet visitors. Female guides welcomed guests at corporate exhibits such as IBM's and Hertz's, at international pavilions such as Japan's and India's, and at state pavilions such as Texas's, reinforcing the nurturing caretaker role that many women were already beginning to reject as the feminism move-ment took shape (Betty Friedan's landmark book, *The Feminine Mystique,* was pub-lished just a year before the Beautyrest Ladies and other hostesses arrived at the Fair in 1964). One could convincingly argue that a stronger case for women's rights in world's fair history was made almost a hundred years earlier when, at the 1876 Centennial Exposition in Philadelphia, Susan B. Anthony and other suf-fragettes presented a "Declaration of the Rights of Women" to a shocked acting vice president Thomas W. Ferry.[65]

At least one pavilion at the Fair, Clairol's, was specifically designated "for women only." Outside the pavilion, women tried on colored wigs while their male companions more often than not were heard to say, "I'm going to General Electric," which was conveniently located next door.[66] Besides showing a film on beauty and exhibiting a Hairdressers Hall of Fame, Clairol encouraged ladies to peer into a mirrored device to see themselves in several different hairstyles and colors. Inside was the Color Carousel, a revolving turntable of forty private booths, taking women on a seven-minute ride during which they completed "personal information" cards and then got advice on what was their most flattering shade of hair coloring. Tele-phone booths were also provided—again, ladies only, please—where women could dial hair-color consultants for free. Beauty consultants in pastel dresses too were on hand to provide formulas for desired colors, also gratis.[67] The answer to Clairol's famous question, "Is it true blondes have more fun?" was apparently yes, as blonde was by far the most popular choice of hair coloring at the exhibit. One dissenter

24. *Ladies (only, please) waiting at the Clairol Pavilion for their free color analysis. Photo © Bill Cotter.*

was Mary Ellen Hudock of 245 East Nineteenth Street in New York City, a brunette. "I've been a blonde twice already," Miss Hudock told the Clairol beauty consultants. "You don't have any more fun."[68]

The idea of better living was also percolating next door at the hugely popular General Electric pavilion. GE's Carousel of Progress was quite the miracle of engineering, revolving six separate audiences in their seats in front of various tableaux from the 1890s, the 1920s, the 1940s, and the present day. In each vignette a Disney animatronic man surrounded by his family and household appliances spoke to the audience about the changes electricity had brought in American life while an equally robotic dog moved and barked on a nearby rug. (Caroline Kennedy reportedly loved the Disneyesque dog so much during her visit that she wanted to take him—or rather it—home.) While the family of the past struggled with yesterday's primitive technology—a gas lamp, a kitchen pump, an icebox, a flatiron— the family of the present rejoiced in the electrical wonders of 1964 in a bountiful Christmas scene. Throughout the ride, visitors heard (and heard and heard) GE's jingle, "There's a Great Big Beautiful Tomorrow," a comforting reminder that the consumer paradise embedded in the American Dream was still alive and well.[69] Most visitors were delighted by Disney's magic, but a reporter for *Time* was less impressed with the ride's technology, summing up the experience as "the general effect of a family under the influence of drugs."[70] With a clear hit on its hands, however, GE allocated an additional twenty million dollars in advertising and promotion to tie in with the Carousel of Progress, putting up banners and displays in retail outlets across the country to flaunt its enviable role in creating our great big beautiful tomorrow.[71]

Battling it out with electricity as America's leading energy source was the nation's gas industry that sponsored the Festival of Gas Pavilion. Designed by Walter Teague Associates, the pavilion offered cooking shows, recipes from famous chefs in the Theater of Food, a movie, and appliance displays, all showcasing the "limitless possibilities [of gas] which the scientists and technicians are developing." A giant elevated carousel carried visitors on a tour of the unfortunately named World of Gas, from the gaslit streets of the nineteenth century to a futuristic City of Tomorrow (at least the third interpretation of such at the Fair).[72] The Kitchen of Tomorrow featured appliances that would perhaps be produced in three to five years "if," according to the gas industry, "there is demand for it."[73] Tomorrow's appliances included a circular, rotating Norge refrigerator; a home dry-cleaning machine; and a Norge Dish Maker that ground dirty plastic dishes into pellets and then sent back a clean new plate made of thermoplastic film.[74] Apparently, consumers of the late 1960s preferred the Kitchen of Today versus the Kitchen of Tomorrow.

Fortunately, a more humanistic interpretation of better living illustrating experiences and emotions common to people all over the world rather than the latest consumer goods could be found at the Fair. Besides a Home Care Information Center where a computer answered questions on the proper care of floors and furniture, automobiles, and shoes and an international display of flooring materials, the Johnson Wax Pavilion offered visitors a refreshing break from the incessant commercialism of the Fair. The pavilion featured an eighteen-minute, three-screen documentary film called *To Be Alive!* that turned out to be the surprise hit of the first season, immensely pleasing company executives who, with nowhere near the budget of the Fair's corporate giants, knew they had to do something different. The film, which was free and shown thirty times a day, was made by Francis Thompson and Alexander Hammid and took eighteen months to complete. Shot in "Tri-Arc 335," the film simultaneously showed a joyful Italian wedding on one screen, children at play in Nigeria on another screen, and other scenes shot in the United States on a third. Each screen was eighteen feet wide, with a foot of space between them, creating a montage impression that allowed the viewer to complete the experience.[75] Audiences, rather surprisingly, did not have trouble following the action. (This film was in fact hardly the first multiscreen movie, with a ten-screen film having been shown in Paris as early as 1896). Even more interesting than the technology of the film was its subject. Johnson Wax originally asked Thompson to make a film based on what they referred to as the "new leisure in America," made possible in part by the company's time-saving products that, executives naturally expected, would be the star of the film. Amazingly, Thompson talked the suits out of this idea and, even more amazingly, got the go-ahead to make a completely noncommercial film based around the "joy of living." No Johnson Wax products would appear in the film, and the company agreed not to interfere with the project. In place of a waxy sell, Thompson viewed the film's message as a simple one: "While millions of people are frustrated and unhappy in this complex modern world of ours, there are millions of others who retain a sense of the underlying wonder of the world; who have a capacity for finding delight in normal, everyday experiences, and who realize . . . that there can be great joy in simply being alive." The two filmmakers were understandably nervous that this message would be lost among audiences at the Fair, but viewers enjoyed the film very much, even standing up and cheering after some showings. Usually jaded critics too loved the film, many of them considering it to be nothing less than the best thing at the Fair (it would later win the 1965 Oscar for best short documentary film). "Few films have ever conveyed more warmly what is implicit throughout the script—the basic oneness of people everywhere," glowed Arthur Knight of the *Saturday Review.*[76] *To Be Alive!* was a perfect example of the Fair's theme of Peace Through Understanding, exactly what the visionary Robert Kopple thought the Fair should be about.

## Home Sweet Home

Complementing the Fair's exploration of "better living" was its focus on the heart and hearth of American consumer culture—the home. The nation's postwar obsession with domestic life was on proud exhibit at the Fair, often a backward-looking perspective that presented the home as a self-contained bunker offering sanctuary from a dangerous world. Filled-to-the-gills model houses seemed to be everywhere one looked at the Fair, many of them described as utopian paradises or, in real estate lingo, dream homes. "American model houses at the World's Fair come in all shapes and sizes, above and below ground," noted the *New York Times,* all of them stocked with the stuff of the American Dream.[77] Six "space-saving" model rooms designed by *Better Homes and Gardens* were on display, as was the full-size, seven-room Westinghouse "Dream House," where predictions about the future of the kitchen were offered.[78] There were in fact no fewer than twenty-nine kitchen exhibits at the Fair, displaying what *Look* described as "the greatest concentration of take-home planning ideas ever presented."[79] Leading appliance manufacturers presented ranges, refrigerators, ovens, freezers, dishwashers, and sinks in pastel and primary colors and in a global potpourri of styles including early American, international modern, Oriental, and Latin American.[80] GM's exhibits included a Frigidaire Kitchen Idea Center, offering "clever decorating ideas from all over the world" as well as "revolutionary appliances" such as the Imperial refrigerator-freezer and the world's first Jet Action Washer.[81]

At the Fair's House of Good Taste pavilion, three more model homes—traditional, contemporary, and modern—presented "the latest ideas in comfortable living" under the slogan "The World of Tomorrow Today." The traditional house was an updated version of a New England farmhouse, complete with a white (and plastic) clapboard, sewing nook, fully equipped nursery, and indoor barbecue. Rooms in the Cleaveresque traditional house included a "Dining Room for Irenne Dunne" and "Study for Douglas Fairbanks Jr.," evoking the tastes of stars whose heydays were closer to the last New York fair than this one. The contemporary house, with its Asian-inspired decor, incorporated reflecting pools, sliding glass walls, and a skylight window in the living room. Rooms in the Bradyesque contemporary house included a "Family Room for Anita Bryant," she then known more as a singer than orange juice shill or homophobe, and a Finnish sauna. With privacy as its central theme, the modern house was "inward looking," best exemplified by its indoor garden under a big glass dome. Rooms in the modern house, "a house for the sophisticated and young at heart," included a "Kitchen for Joan Crawford" and "Dining Room for Kitty Carlisle," two other stars of yesteryear. As the names of its rooms perhaps suggested, the architects and designers for these model homes were not chosen by experts but by one Lady Malcolm Douglas-Hamilton, head of the aptly named American Institute of Approval, which organized the exhibit. Members of the Institute of Approval were women prominent in their communities, with no professional design experience required.[82]

Another literally big-as-a-house exhibit was the Formica World's Fair House, seven-room model home that made extensive use of plastics. Designed with an emphasis on "care-free" living, the Formica house would be the very first to use "wipe clean" laminated plastic for all interior and exterior walls.[83] A sweepstakes to win a complete fifty thousand–dollar (one hundred thousand–dollar in 1965) version of the house (lot included) to be built anywhere in the United States was offered, along with twenty-five hundred other prizes, including automobiles, stereos, and furniture.[84]

Not surprisingly, critics were less than impressed with the amateurs' choices. "By and large, the buildings are disappointing, and do not begin to indicate the current thinking and planning of American architects and interior and furniture designers," said one reporter for the *New York Times*. Another one from that newspaper added, "The House of Good Taste exhibit is in quiet good taste, which is to say it neither excites nor offends." The architectural critic concluded, "A wonderful opportunity to show the world what America is capable of in housing has been missed." A Swedish architect was less kind, thinking that "they all look about 20 years behind the times."[85] Critics were largely missing the point of the House of Taste (named by PR man Deegan), however. The purpose of the pavilion was not to display leading-edge architecture and design but to sell existing furnishings and appliances, all of which were readily available in stores across the country. The pavilion was sponsored by scores of building, decorating, and housewares companies, with manufacturers paying five thousand to a whopping one hundred thousand dollars to display their appliances and furnishings in the homes.

*25. The Formica House was a full-scale shrine to the miracle material of plastic.*
*Photo © Bill Cotter.*

One towel manufacturer gladly shelled out twenty thousand dollars to have its products in the bathrooms of the three homes, a good indication of how big a sales opportunity some companies viewed the House of Good Taste.[86]

The Pavilion of American Interiors, cosponsored by Du Pont and the American Institute of Interior Designers, was another blatantly commercial enterprise, with manufacturers also ponying up to show their wares. The four-story, two-wing pavilion stretched two city blocks, as more than 120 exhibitors displayed furniture, floor coverings, fabrics, tableware, paints, decorations, and lighting fixtures. In addition to a number of do-it-yourself exhibits, inside were fourteen model rooms, including two Leisurama houses.[87] In 1959, a prototype of the Leisurama house became a weapon in the cold war when it was shown off as a typical American home at a trade show in Moscow, sparking the famous "kitchen debate" between Vice President Nixon and Soviet leader Nikita Khrushchev. The most interesting space in the pavilion, however, was the "Moon Room," featuring a clear plastic table and chairs that floated in the air, suspended from the ceiling. Despite this bit of futuristic whimsy, *Time* considered the pavilion to be simply "a big furniture showroom that charges 50 cents admission." George O'Brien of the *New York Times* was especially critical of the pavilion's heavy representation of contemporary furnishings, considering "contemporary" to be "a polite word for anonymous design" and saying that the furniture would "probably look more at home in a motel." O'Brien was particularly disappointed that the Pavilion of American Interiors failed to show what the American home-furnishings industry was truly capable of, seeing it as nothing more than a "paid advertisement."[88] Visitors apparently agreed with O'Brien, the pavilion going bankrupt during the Fair's second season.

Unquestionably, the oddest model home at the Fair was the Underground World Home, an "ultramodern" ten-room house built fifteen feet below the earth's surface. The house and its patio were contained within a specially designed concrete shell under two million pounds of topsoil.[89] Windows looked out onto a mural of trees, grass, and sky, while in the garden lay a bed of plastic flowers. Not subject to the whims of nature, lighting could be set for daytime or nighttime (starry sky or glowing moonlight), offering the happy subterranean owner "summer in winter" and "midnight at noon." With its steel double door and "quadruply filtered" air, the home offered complete privacy, acoustical and climatic control, and protection from noise, pollution, inclement weather, and, oh by the way, radioactive fallout. Curiously, the house was positioned not as a fallout shelter but rather as "a way to save space above ground" (begging the question, "Was there a shortage?"). Underground living was presented by guides as less expensive, healthier, and "more fun" than aboveground, with a no-joke-intended side benefit of 100 percent security against Peeping Toms. The house's snack bar sold, appropriately enough, "crab burgers."[90]

The designer of the underground home, Jay Swayze, was clearly convinced that appealing to a mass market meant staying away from the unpleasantness associated with nuclear war. Swayze cited solid research to pitch his house to fairgoers, including a study he conducted showing that people did not look out their windows 80 percent of the time, and of the 20 percent of the time they did, half the time what they saw was "undesirable." "I aim to give people views that are equal to or better than what they see ordinarily," said Swayze, who lived with his family in such a house in Plainview, Texas, saying that they much preferred living underground. Although the designer preferred to focus on the superior quality of life of a molelike existence, some visitors could not help but view the home as a bunker, albeit a plush one. The *New Yorker* considered the home to be "the ultimate article in fallout shelters . . . combining the small, familiar pleasures of the hearth with the headier excitements of Doomsday." The only real flaw with the house seemed to be that there was no way to tell what was going on aboveground, that is, whether the radioactive smoke had cleared. The magazine, tongue in its cheek, recommended that Mr. Swayze add a "good working periscope, so that mistakes can be avoided" in this regard.[91]

As the smoke of the world's fair began to clear, it appeared that American business could have used a good working periscope before investing so heavily in its pavilions. This Fair turned out to be a much more costly venture than anticipated for industrial exhibitors, with many companies burned by construction and maintenance expenses that far exceeded their budgets. The actual cost to major exhibitors came in at $1 to $3 per person per pavilion visit, a number significantly higher than expected because of lower-than-forecasted attendance.[92] Many companies spent additional money on advertising plugging the Fair in an attempt to protect their original investment, another unplanned expense. "Our marketing team must ask itself if an investment of this size could not be better spent in another way," said an anonymous manager of one pavilion in June 1965, seeing the red ink on the wall. Many executives came to the conclusion that the days of investing in expositions could very well be over because the public no longer had "wide-eyed wonder" when it came to world's fairs. "They've seen it all on television," explained one exhibit manager. A reporter for the *New York Times* went further, correctly predicting, "World's fairs in the foreseeable future will not be the same as the result of the experience of the major industrial exhibitors."[93] As organizers of Expo 67, Montreal's planned fair, tried to attract American businesses as the second season of the New York Fair wound down, the Big 3 automakers passed on separate pavilions, opting instead to share a $1.5 million joint exhibition. Corporate executives estimated that it would be at least ten years before they invested heavily in a world's fair, if they ever did so again.[94]

Despite corporate executives' understandable immediate anger when all the bills came in, the Fair would ultimately deliver on its promise to pay off long-term dividends for the hundreds of companies that invested in it. For decades after the Fair, in fact, marketers continued to reap benefits from having a presence in Flushing Meadows, as millions of visitors fondly looked back at the event and the great time they had there. To this day even, consumers who had their hair-color analysis done at the Clairol Pavilion, rode in a Mustang for the first time at Ford, or saw *To Be Alive!* at Johnson Wax may very well be loyal to those brands because of their memories from the Fair. As for the event as a whole, it was and remains visitors' experiences, not bookkeepers' reports, that represent the true meaning and value of the 1964–65 New York World's Fair, experiences that still represent an important part of many people's lives.

# 5 Global Holiday

*It's a world of laughter, a world of tears*
*It's a world of hopes and a world of fears*
*There's so much that we share*
*That it's time we're aware*
*It's a small world after all.*
        —First verse of "It's a Small World"

HAD YOU BOARDED the Swiss Sky Ride in Flushing Meadows in 1964 or 1965, as millions of fairgoers did, consider the sights, sounds, and smells directly beneath you as you skimmed over the International Area and then the Federal and State Area. Look left during your seventy-five-cent, four-and-a-half-minute ride, and you may very well have observed a Chinese pagoda, Buddhist shrine, Japanese feudal shrine, Alpine chateau, and cluster of African thatched-roof huts. Look right and 115 feet below was a Little Old New York street circa 1890, a miniature version of the Tivoli amusement park, and an entire Flemish town of 134 buildings. Also from your bird's-eye view you might have noticed some Zulu and Watusi dancers, Burundi drummers, samurai sword warriors, and five Mexican men ascending and descending a 114-foot pole in a most alarming manner. If you brought your binoculars, you could have even made out some of the food people were eating, such as Tunisian pastry, fresh Sudanese dates, an Egyptian bean-cake sandwich, and something called a Hong Kong Burger, naturally being served by Japanese waitresses in kimonos on motorized rickshaws.[1]

Just this quick tour makes it clear that the International Area and the Federal and State Area—the two "geographic" parts of the Fair—brought together a disparate range of architectural styles, arts, and cuisine from the four corners of the earth, exactly as a world's fair should do. The 1964–65 New York World's Fair was truly a "global holiday," as the name of Coca-Cola's pavilion made clear, with the United States joined by twenty-three individual states and sixty-five foreign nations as a celebration of humankind's multiculturalism and diversity. The Fair's ambitious goal

124

of peace through understanding may not have been achieved, but the event exposed millions of people from around the world to ways of life they had never experienced before and, perhaps, never would again, just as Robert Kopple dreamed.

## The Spirit of '76

Smack in the middle of the grounds, presumably so no fairgoer could possibly miss it, was the Federal and State Area, home to the United States Pavilion and the "Avenue of States." The Federal and State Area was indeed considered the "home-site" of the Fair, proudly displaying, as the official guidebook put it, the "natural resources, recreational splendors, and productive might" of the nation.[2] Amazingly, it was hardly certain that the United States would have a pavilion at the 1964–65 New York World's Fair. Many senators were in fact opposed to the idea, remembering the pledge made by the New York delegation to Congress in 1959 that no federal funds be devoted to the Fair. Senator Frank Lausche (D-OH) was especially against it, believing that a U.S. pavilion would be a "breach of commitment" and claiming that the exposition would not even be a world's fair because it had not been officially sanctioned as one. Lausche had blocked passage of a bill in 1960 that would have provided $300,000 as seed money, and, a year later, he and Senator J. W. Fulbright (D-AR) were leading a fight to stop a federally sponsored pavilion in its tracks.[3] The belief that the Russians were going to exhibit was cause enough for others in Washington to support a U.S. pavilion; however, the idea that Communists would have a stage to promote their ideology without an American retort was incomprehensible. The *New York Times* agreed, stating in an editorial that it was important for Congress to "endorse the planning and construction of a showcase that will document before the world our way of life" and that "it would be unthinkable for the United States to go into this half-heartedly."[4]

Still, understandably alarmed at the prospect of the nation being a no-show at its own party, Moses and other officials petitioned President Kennedy in September 1961 to support federal participation.[5] Kennedy quickly jumped into the fray, asking Congress to appropriate $25 million for a pavilion, not coincidentally timing his support just when Mayor Wagner, a Democrat, needed it in his reelection campaign.[6] Some of the difficulty in getting the go-ahead for a U.S. pavilion may have been the result of lingering resentment of Eisenhower's awarding New York the winning bid for the Fair over Washington, D.C. Senator Jacob Javits, a Republican who was particularly peeved at JFK's apparent political maneuvering, believed that those individuals trying to block the United States from taking part viewed the Fair simply as "a New York promotion project." It was true that funding for the upcoming world's fair in Seattle and previous ones in Geneva, Brussels, and even Moscow sailed through Congress, leaving Javits to conclude that resistance from his colleagues was classic "anti–New York City phobia."[7] President Kennedy asked Congress again in March 1962 to come up with $25 million to fund a U.S. pavilion, now calling federal participation "essential." It was imperative, JFK stated, that America "present to the world not a boastful picture of our unparalleled progress but a picture of democracy—its opportunities, its problems, its inspirations, and its freedoms."[8] Rather grudgingly, a Senate appropriations subcommittee approved $17 million the following month, ensuring that the United States would indeed have a building in Flushing Meadows two years down the road.[9]

When it became time to fill the Charles Luckman–designed building (the largest world's fair exhibition hall the United States had ever sponsored), however, government officials in charge of the project found that they were short on cash. Of the $17 million, $10.5 million had gone to construction, with another $2.5 million needed to operate the pavilion for the run of the Fair, leaving just $4 million in the kitty for exhibits. Under pressure to put on a good show, Assistant Secretary of Commerce Hubert W. Klotz decided to make an appeal to other federal agencies, corporations, and private individuals for exhibits, furnishings, professional services, and hard cash and, luckily, found some takers.[10]

In the completed Federal Pavilion, visitors first viewed *Voyage to America*, a film shown in a six hundred–seat theater that traced the nation's story of immigration, and then moved to the Challenges to Greatness area featuring exhibits depicting some of the major problems facing the United States. Visitors then went upstairs for "The American Journey," which was by far the most popular part of the pavilion in 1964. The tunnel ride combined still photography, film, narration, and music, compressing 472 years of American history into 14 minutes. Fairgoers were ushered into grandstandlike cars that seated fifty-five people, equipped with individual headsets, and sent through the twelve hundred–foot tunnel as hundreds of images of seminal historic events—Ben Franklin's kite, Robert Fulton's steamboat, old-time movies—flashed before them. "Here is our past! Look at it," the narration began, as visitors embarked on the multimedia experience that also offered not just breathtaking scenes of purple mountain majesties and amber waves of grain but also, as the finale, an imaginary rocket flight into space. Written by Ray Bradbury, shot in Cinerama, and spoken by John McIntire (the voice of *Wagon Train*), *The American Journey* was a tour de force of equal parts patriotism and entertainment.[11]

For 1965, the Federal Pavilion complemented the razzle-dazzle of *The American Journey* with an outstanding collection of presidential memorabilia, filling up a football field–size storage space with mementos from thirteen presidents. The idea for what would be called the Hall of Presidents had actually come from President Kennedy, who approved the nearly final design just two days before his assassination. JFK reportedly had found an old typewriter in the White House that Woodrow Wilson had used to type his speeches and thought a collection of important presidential objects and documents could be inspirational to Americans. A panel of seventy-five historians was convened to determine "great" or "near-great" presidents, coming up with a list of eleven: George Washington, John Adams, Thomas Jefferson, Andrew Jackson, James K. Polk, Abraham Lincoln,

26. *A portion of the enormous United States or Federal Pavilion that included exhibits celebrating the nation's history and acknowledging the challenges to create a "great society." The National Tennis Center's Arthur Ashe Stadium sits on the spot today. Photo © Bill Cotter.*

Grover Cleveland, Theodore Roosevelt, Woodrow Wilson, Franklin D. Roosevelt, and Harry Truman. Kennedy's advisers insisted that Eisenhower be added to the list to avoid criticism that the exhibit was politically biased, and Kennedy himself was posthumously added by President Johnson. Representatives and curators from the Library of Congress, Smithsonian Institution, National Archives, White House, and National Park Services were assigned the mighty task of choosing which artifacts should be included in the exhibit (all of whom not surprisingly lobbied for items from their own collections).[12]

The Hall of Presidents turned out to be hugely popular, as both Americans and foreigners gawked at the papers and, even more so, the personal belongings of the thirteen presidents. Iconic artifacts like Washington's sword, Lincoln's stovepipe hat, Teddy Roosevelt's Rough Rider uniform, and JFK's rocking chair were on display, as were precious documents such as the Bill of Rights, the Emancipation Proclamation, Lincoln's Gettysburg Address, and all thirteen presidents' inaugural addresses. Other interesting items included a lock of Jackson's hair, Indian artifacts presented to Jefferson by Lewis and Clark, a microphone used by FDR for his "Fireside Chats," and Truman's "The Buck Stops Here" desk sign. Visitors to the hall included President Eisenhower, who wistfully observed he would never be able to fit into his World War II battle jacket that was on display, and eighty-five-year-old Jenny Phinney, great-granddaughter of James K. Polk, who, viewing a painting of the eleventh president, noted the "striking resemblance" between herself and her kin. Lynda Johnson, LBJ's twenty-one-year-old daughter, also stopped by, and was delighted to see on display the White House's copy of the Gettysburg Address, having wondered what had happened to it when it went missing from its usual spot in her home.[13] Extreme measures were naturally taken to protect what was the most comprehensive collection of presidential memora- bilia ever assembled. A group of "extremists" had recently tried to desecrate such national shrines as the Statue of Liberty and the Liberty Bell, cause for officials to be especially concerned about the safety of the collection. The items were trans- ported first by armored trucks and then by trains equipped with armed guards, with a special security force employed to protect them from harm at the Fair.[14] A stuffed marlin or a couple of dinosaur models might mysteriously disappear from the grounds, but there was no chance that a fairgoer was going to walk through the gates wearing Lincoln's stovepipe hat or carrying Washington's sword.

## O'er the Ramparts

Joining the United States in the Federal and State Area were the pavilions of nine- teen states along with New York City, the Long Island Rail Road, and Hollywood. (The Unisphere and the Westinghouse time capsule were also, rather oddly, located in the area.) Four other states—Texas, Florida, Hawaii, and Oregon (the latter a tim- berfest of tree climbing and chopping, log rolling and jousting, double-bladed-ax throwing, canoe tilting, and, shades of John Irving, a wrestling match between a man and a bear)—exhibited elsewhere.[15] As in the International Area, dedication ceremonies, groundbreakings, and the laying of cornerstones took place through- out 1963 in the Federal and State Area. Governors, secretaries of state, mayors, and other state VIPs were welcomed by Fair officials, most often General William E. Potter (executive vice president), Ambassador Richard C. Patterson Jr. (chief of pro- tocol), or Dr. Roberto de Mendoza (deputy chief of protocol). Moses too often made an appearance, and sometimes a religious leader would offer a convocation before the proceedings. Speeches recounted the proud history of each state and its prom- ising future, followed by the standard publicity photos and plunge into the Queens dirt with a shovel or bulldozer or both. Like the religious pavilions, individual states got into the Fair rent free, but construction and operating costs kept more than half away.

History was a major theme of many of the state's pavilions, offering a nostalgic escape from the increasingly tense mid-1960s and reinforcing classic American my- thologies, as, outside the grounds, the nation's postwar dreams began to crumble. Illinois's pavilion was a tribute to all things Lincoln, serving up not just Disney's ani- matronic version of Honest Abe but pretty much everything else state officials could find relating to the prairie president. With its eight-minute film *O'er the Ramparts We*

*Watched* (co-produced by U.S. Rubber and the U.S. Army), Maryland took visitors back through time to the Battle of Fort McEnroy during the War of 1812, the inspiration for Francis Scott Key writing the words to "The Star-Spangled Banner." Montana adopted the western frontier as its theme, its "Museum on Wheels" featuring works by two leading western artists of the nineteenth century, Charles M. Russell and Frederic Remington. The state also channeled the Wild West with its million-dollar pile of gold nuggets and dust and tribal dancing by Indians, the latter just one of many references to or performances by Native Americans at the Fair. (An entire Indian village, complete with tepees, was located in the Boy Scouts of America Pavilion.) New Mexico's pavilion consisted of a pueblo of five adobe buildings featuring Indian crafts, while three thirty-foot totem poles, originally carved by Indians for the St. Louis fair of 1904, stood in front of Alaska's white, igloo-shaped pavilion. Eskimo and Indian dances were staged behind the building, and various stuffed animals or parts of animals—bears, a walrus head, a seventy-four-pound salmon, a moose, and a caribou—added to the North Country effect.[16]

*27. A Native American happy to be part of New Mexico's re-creation of a "pueblo," which included a trading post that sold Indian pottery and blankets. New Mexico was one of many Native American references at the Fair, following a long world's fair tradition. Photo © Bill Cotter.*

Tourism too was a common theme in the Federal and State Area as exhibitors tried to persuade visitors to choose their state as their next vacation destination. New England's pavilion, a collaboration among six states in the region, laid out a big dollop of Yankee charm, re-creating a colonial town square complete with village green. A bit of the Down East could be found (and purchased) in the pavilion's country store, "where the potbellied stove, the cracker barrel and the candy jars are just as they were generations ago." New England also focused on its skiing business, having Vermont ski experts demonstrate techniques and even building a snow slope (made out of nylon) for visitors to test their skills. Hyperrealistic interpretations of real places, clearly inspired by Disneyland, turned the Federal and State Area into a dizzying mishmash of American iconography. Visitors could start on the northwest corner of the area by buying crab cakes and steamed clams from Maryland's fisherman's wharf and proceed to the southeast corner, where Bourbon Street, with its Dixieland jazz and Creole food, offered at least a hint of the atmosphere of the French Quarter ("Nightclubs offer music and dancing as well as other kinds of entertainment," as the Fair's official guide coyly described the area).

*28. With its jazz, bars, and go-go dancers, Bourbon Street was one of the very few places at the Fair that visitors could let down their hair. Photo © Bill Cotter.*

In between one could take in the biggest piece of cheese in the world (seven feet high, nine and a half feet in diameter), watch some expert fly casting, or actually do a little trout fishing at Wisconsin's pavilion, and then have lunch at Minnesota's North Star Viking Restaurant, which featured not just local delicacies like duck, venison, pheasant, and pike but also a one hundred–dish smorgasbord.[17]

Industry was the final theme individual states decided to center their pavilions around. Promoting natural resources and locally produced goods or services to a global audience was a staple of world's fairs, and some states, backed by a particular industry, seized the opportunity. West Virginia showed off both its glassblowing and coal industries, having six on-site glassblowers continually creating glass horses, fish, and ducks and taking visitors into a simulated coal mine. West Virginia also held a lottery for a lucky fairgoer to win a ten-acre mountaintop,

29. Inside Wisconsin's tepee-shaped pavilion was, at seventeen tons, the biggest cheese in the world. Photo © Bill Cotter.

*30. West Virginia's gift shop featured locally made handblown glass but, more important, served as advertising for the lucrative tourism market. Photo © Bill Cotter.*

complete with chalet (a "gift" of a local housing developer) as well as one to win a thoroughbred race horse (sired by Celtic Ash and dammed by Ambiorix), a clever way to promote the Tri-State Futurity, the state's biggest horse race. Missouri focused on its role in flight, displaying replicas of Charles Lindbergh's *Spirit of St. Louis* and two space capsules, the Gemini and the Mercury Friendship 7, each built by McDonnell Aircraft based in St. Louis. Though not representing a state, the Hollywood U.S.A. Pavilion was the most compelling presentation of California's (and America's) most famous industry. With its front facade reproduction of Grauman's Chinese Theater, Walk of Fame with celebrity hand- and footprints, and sets from famous movies such as *Cleopatra, The King and I,* and *West Side Story,* the pavilion was designed to give a boost to an industry still trying to recover from the breakup of the studio system and the popularity of television (and now facing the terrifying threat of color TV). The pavilion also housed a museum displaying costumes, jewelry, and props from classic motion pictures, giving visitors more reasons to say three cheers for Hollywood.[18]

## New York, New York

As the host of the party, New York—both the city and the state—was sure to have a sizable presence at its world's fair. The fact that Robert Moses, the man

31. *With its Hollywood U.S.A. Pavilion, the American movie industry tried to regain some of the glory days of its glamorous past. Photo © Bill Cotter.*

responsible for building much of the city's and a sizable chunk of the state's infrastructure, was in charge of the event made it all the more certain that New York would be generously represented in Flushing Meadows. Not only did the state and the city each have its own pavilion, but so did the Port Authority and the Long Island Rail Road, very familiar entities to local New Yorkers but most likely obscure to the out-of-towner and certainly the foreign visitor. New York State's $11.5 million pavilion, designed by Philip Johnson, included three observation towers, the tallest one the high spot of the Fair at 226 feet. For 50 cents, visitors could take the "Sky-Streak" capsule elevators that rode up the tallest building's sides and see, on a clear day, maybe not forever but New Jersey, Connecticut, the Atlantic Ocean, and a good piece of Long Island. Also part of the pavilion was the "Tent of Tomorrow" whose ceiling was the world's biggest suspension roof and whose floor was a giant terrazzo road map of the state (the latter built and sponsored by, not surprisingly, Texaco). In addition to a less-than-thrilling exhibit of the New York State Power Authority, visitors to the tent could walk along a state "highway," passing a conservation area, rose garden, and other attractions. The tent also included a fine arts museum, one collection featuring portraits of early colonists of the state and the other a collection of fifty Hudson River School paintings. Next to the Tent of Tomorrow was the Theaterama, a cylindrical movie theater (Johnson called it a "cheese box") featuring a 360-degree

32. *The three observation towers at the New York State Pavilion. The "Sky-Streak" elevator can be seen near the top of the tallest one in the foreground. The towers still stand but are in ruins, serving as a ghostly reminder of the Fair and as a setting for the occasional sci-fi movie. Photo © Bill Cotter.*

screen transporting viewers to Niagara Falls, Jones Beach, and other tourist spots in the state. Also inside Theaterama was Art in New York State, an exhibit of fifty paintings by New York–based artists, including Childe Hassam, George Bellows, Arthur Dove, Reginald Marsh, Edward Hopper, Frank Stella, John Marin, Georgia O'Keeffe, Willem de Kooning, and Jackson Pollock, which had been selected by Katherine Kuh, art critic of the *Saturday Review*.[19]

It was the outside of Theaterama, however, that got people talking at the Fair. The exterior of the building was decorated with "pop" art by ten contemporary, avant-garde artists (commissioned by Philip Johnson himself), a rather daring move by state and WFC officials who knew it would most likely generate controversy. Although one might first think it was a disconnect to see leading-edge art at, of all places, a world's fair, the populism-loving artists themselves relished

*33. The view from New York State's 226-foot observation tower was proof positive that, as Robert Moses put it, "the fair administration belongs to no architectural clique and worships at no artistic shrine." Photo © Bill Cotter.*

the opportunity to showcase their work at what was perhaps the ultimate commercial, bourgeois event. ("The real American architecture is McDonald's," Roy Lichtenstein once observed, "not Mies van der Rohe.")[20] Besides works by Lichtenstein, Robert Rauschenberg, James Rosenquist, and Claes Oldenburg on the exterior wall was John Chamberlain's crushed automobile fender mounted on a truck chassis and, rather startlingly, giant mug shots of the FBI's thirteen "most wanted" men as interpreted by Andy Warhol.[21] Right before opening day, however, Warhol's mural was mysteriously covered up by silver paint, the first reason being that he did not like the way it was hung and the second that the artist claimed to have received legal threats from one of the "most wanted." "One of the men labeled `wanted' had been pardoned, you see," explained Warhol, "so the mural wasn't valid anymore."[22]

The real truth, however, was that Warhol's mural was too much of a reminder of the problems outside the grounds, penetrating the Fair's safe, comfortable bubble. Governor Nelson Rockefeller was, not surprisingly, especially perturbed about the work as, one, many of the "thirteen" were apparently in the Mafia, and, two, he believed he might lose Italian American voters because of the men's mostly Italian names. Whatever the particulars, there was no doubt that the work, as Robert Rosenblum later observed, "prove[d] too disturbingly real to survive the Fair's glut

34. *"The Tent of Tomorrow," another part of Philip Johnson's elaborate New York State Pavilion, still stands, although the multicolored roof is long gone. Photo © Bill Cotter.*

of superannuated American dreams." The showman he was, Warhol was not giving up on exhibiting before millions at the world's fair, however. "I'm still waiting for another inspiration," he made clear, but his next effort—a silkscreen of Robert Moses—also did not pass muster, Johnson recognizing that Warhol had based the second work on the first. Another work on the exterior wall of the New York State Pavilion, Robert Indiana's neon "EAT" sign, was similarly out of commission early on. The sign was properly lit shortly after the Fair opened but soon went dark, with officials claiming the problem to be "electrical troubles." Indiana explained, however, that "the real story is that too many jokers came up and saw the `EAT' sign and asked for the restaurant which bothered the officials, so they turned it off." Indiana was understandably peeved that officials bent so easily to those fairgoers who did not fully appreciate his work. "In the case of art," he mused, "they should be willing to put up with some bother."[23]

The neighboring New York City Pavilion, which was cosponsored by the Mayor's Office, the Department of Parks (which Moses had reigned over for decades), and the TBTA (of which Moses was the current chairman), housed the only exhibit to celebrate the original idea for the Fair—the three hundredth anniversary of New York. Art, sculpture, photographs, and artifacts from the city's thirty-four museums traced the history of New York from 1664 to the present day, and a TBTA theater showed films of the city's bridges and tunnels. The real excitement in the

35. *Visitors roam Texaco's enormous terrazzo map of New York on the main floor of the state's pavilion. Photo © Bill Cotter.*

pavilion, however, was the Panorama of the City of New York, the world's largest (a half acre) three-dimensional model that featured every structure, bridge, highway, and park of the city.[24] One could (and still can in what is now the Queens Museum of Art) pick out one's home, school, or workplace, with binoculars for rent to make it a little easier. Besides the narration by announcer deluxe Lowell Thomas and the ability for the scale (one inch to one hundred feet) model to go from day to night and back again, one could take a seven-minute helicopter ride over the minicity, skimming over the panorama by just two feet. The model, which had taken Richard Lester of Lester Associates two years and the city six hundred thousand dollars to create, was not just an amazing piece of design but also without question a monument to Robert Moses's career. One could not look more than a few feet without bumping into something Moses had built, a fact that surely did not go unnoticed by the seventy-five-year-old man. The New York City Pavilion (which had served as the home of the young United Nations from 1946 to 1950) also briefly hosted Dick Button's Ice-Travaganza, which quickly folded, despite having, according to its pre-Fair publicity materials, the "most spectacular skating performances," the "most fascinating sets," the "most delightful musical score," and the "most beautiful girls on ice."[25]

With Moses at the helm, New York also was keen on promoting its transportation network. The Long Island Rail Road's exhibit in the Federal and State Area

36. *The New York City Pavilion was one of just three buildings remaining from the 1939–40 fair and is also one of the few structures to survive the 1964–65 Fair, now housing the Queens Museum of Art and the fantastic Panorama of the City of New York. Photo © Bill Cotter.*

gave visitors the chance to board a real locomotive or, for a quarter, take a ride in a miniature train that did a circle around the one-acre area. HO-gauge model trains ran continuously around a huge relief map of Long Island in one of the exhibit's tents, passing points of interest like Sagamore Hill and the Montauk lighthouse.[26]

Over in the Transportation Area on the west end of the grounds, New York had another self-congratulatory pavilion, the T-shaped Port Authority Heliport and Exhibit Building. Charged with running New York City's airports, docks, bus terminals, tunnels and bridges, and rail rapid-transit line (known as PATH), the Port Authority was (and is) a public agency Moses obviously had strong ties to, its building another symbol of his status as a power broker for almost a half century.[27] The pavilion's Top of the Fair restaurant served as Moses's favorite spot to entertain guests but could not make a consistent go at it because of its hefty prices. At the top of the building was a place for visitors to have a panoramic view of the entire fairgrounds and the Manhattan skyline, with the roof serving as a heliport for sightseeing flights and for the jet set to fly into or out of Flushing Meadows by chopper from or to area airports. Downstairs in the theater, audience members standing in front of a large screen took a trip around the port via a wraparound, 360-degree motion picture, which vividly displayed the city in all its glory as well as proved, as if there was any doubt, that Robert Moses was the master builder of

New York. Also in the building, interestingly, was a scale model of the planned World Trade Center that, when constructed a decade later, would remake the city's skyline once again.[28]

## Around the World in One Thousand Days

Backed up by the Fair's official theme of Peace Through Understanding, classic postwar rhetoric steeped in utopian international brotherhood, and an attempt to ease some of the tensions of the cold war, the State Department sent official invitations to take part in the Fair to no fewer than eighty-four countries around the world in January 1960.[29] The first delegation left for Europe in August 1960 for almost a month to personally extend invitations to heads of states, prime ministers, and other foreign officials, the start of what would be an amazing three-year mission combining Washington-style diplomacy, Loman-style salesmanship, and Barnum-style showmanship.[30] Political instability and governments overthrown in midnegotiations, not to mention high rental fees and the BIE ban, made the WFC's effort to make its Fair a world's fair an undertaking of truly epic proportions.

Led by Charles Poletti, vice president of international affairs, with support from his seven-member staff and the occasional outsider (such as former ambassadors), the WFC pitched separate pavilions to larger countries and joint pavilions to smaller countries who would have to pool resources if they wanted to exhibit at the Fair.[31] RSVPs quickly and steadily rolled in, with Italy, Bulgaria, Mexico, and the Republic of (or Nationalistic) China based in Taipei all accepting within weeks of receiving their invitations. Communist China, on the other hand, was banned from the Fair by President Kennedy, as the United States did not recognize the Peking-based government.[32]

Despite the Fair's official mission to blur or minimize geopolitical differences, organizers could not occasionally resist viewing and promoting the event from an American-centric perspective. In March 1960, for example, Deegan claimed that the Fair was an opportunity for the non-Communist world to put its "best foot forward," echoing Moses's view of it being a global competition of sorts.[33]

The Fair's grounding in international kinship also waffled from time to time, occasionally taking a backseat to a progressive theme celebrating Western values. In an August 1960 news conference, for example, the Fair's theme curiously and temporarily morphed from harmonic idealism to one centered around twentieth-century "inventions, arts, skills, and aspirations," the latter a more classic world's fair platform.[34]

Given that the Fair was not going to be officially sanctioned by the BIE, however, it was understandable that many nations were reluctant to sign up. The BIE's November 1960 barring of its thirty member nations from taking part in any fair in the United States except the Seattle Exposition until 1972 was a ruling that would certainly weaken the upstart New York event.[35] The WFC tried to strike a gentlemen's agreement with the BIE to allow its Fair to be an exception to the rules (as happened for the 1939–40 New York fair under the condition that officials would try to persuade the federal government to join the organization), but the French would not allow history to repeat itself.[36] Undeterred, Moses moved ahead, pronouncing that many if not most countries would not take the "three people living obscurely in a dumpy apartment" or "bunch of clowns" in Paris too seriously. The fact that there were about twice as many sovereign nations in 1963 than 1940 made it all the more likely that the WFC would at least match the previous New York fair's fifty-nine foreign entries.[37]

Austria became the first country to decline participation when officials there felt the WFC was treating them as a minor player. (Austrian officials changed their minds in July 1962 when they got over the snub.) In February 1961, however, three European heavyweights—Great Britain, France, and Italy—all declined their invitations to attend, saying that their membership in the BIE prohibited them from accepting. Naturally prepared for some countries to pass because his Fair was in clear violation of a number of the BIE's rules, Moses proceeded directly to Plan B, pitching unofficial participation sponsored not by governments but by private exhibitors and trade organizations. Over the next year and change, businesspeople from these three countries as well as West Germany, Belgium, and the Netherlands all signed up for commercial exhibits, eager to show off their products and services to millions of consumers at what promised to be the biggest trade show in history.[38]

Other nations, either not members of the BIE or simply seeing a New York world's fair as too big of an opportunity to miss in the increasingly global economy, quickly came on board. Reza Shah Pahlevi accepted Iran's invitation in January 1961, as did President Sukarno of Indonesia that same month. Soon after twenty-one representatives from various African nations visited Moses in New York, a total of twenty-four nations had officially signed up. Jordan confirmed its participation, adding that it would bring its collection of Dead Sea Scrolls along. Not to be outdone, Israel not only agreed to participate, reversing its previous stance, but also said it would exhibit the seven Dead Sea Scrolls in its possession, the beginning of the tiff that would climax with allies of each country slugging it out on the fairgrounds as season two got under way. Although Israel decided to withdraw in October 1962 because of the high cost, private Jewish organizations came forward to help pay for a building, resulting in the peculiarly named American-Israel Pavilion. Delighted to see that Israel, a member of the BIE, was back in, the WFC reciprocated by persuading U.S. government officials to exhibit at the former's upcoming, smallish 1964 Near East Trade Fair in Tel Aviv.[39]

Soon a flood of countries sent letters of intent to build or rent space in officially sponsored pavilions. Morocco, Tunisia, and the Sudan soon signed on, a result of a WFC whirlwind trip to the Middle East and Africa. The next six months were a bonanza for the WFC, with Turkey, Pakistan, Thailand, and Monaco throwing their hats in the ring in May; Ethiopia, Ceylon, Senegal, Mauritania, Sierra Leone, and Guinea in June; the Ivory Coast, Upper Volta, Niger, and Paraguay in July; and the United Arab Republic (Egypt, Iran, and Saudi Arabia), Venezuela, and Cambodia in September.[40] By October 1962, sixty-five countries had declared their intention to exhibit, with thirty-five having committed by contracting space.[41] Argentina had recently agreed to exhibit, only to drop out in May 1963, recommit the next month, show up at the Fair, and fold in just a month, a not-that-unusual example of the topsy-turvy, politically charged, financially rickety nature of global expositions.[42]

Matters got especially dicey when countries considered unofficial participation through industry groups. Knowing that having a presence at this Fair would be good for business but wanting to keep their membership in the BIE in good stead, governments not only allowed private groups to sponsor national pavilions but occasionally even offered to subsidize them. This situation was the case for Italy, whose government was working with businesspeople in early 1963 to put together a pavilion for the Fair. When Premier Amintore Fanfani resigned in May and the leadership shifted decidedly to the left, however, the plug was pulled on the previous government's pledge of three million dollars.[43] Some Italian Americans, however, were determined to do everything they could to persuade President Antonio Segni to back an unofficial Italian pavilion. Thirty-four prominent people of Italian ancestry, including eight members of Congress, sent a cablegram to the new leader in July 1963 asking him to reconsider, adding that a group of Italian Americans would help pay for the building.[44] The Americans worked out an arrangement with an Italian industry consortium after meeting with it in Rome, but Fair officials, thinking the situation too financially shaky and politically sensitive, killed the deal.[45]

The French situation was equally problematic and confirmed that the WFC made the right decision in passing on the Italians. Private French groups were eager to have representation at the Fair, thinking the Folies-Bergères, "slightly censored" for Americans' (or at least Moses's) tastes, would be a big hit at its pavilion, as would a knockoff of the famed Maxim's Restaurant. Another French organization was trying to get six ships from the United States's "Mothball Fleet" to take French visitors to the Fair, and still another took the plunge by contracting out space previously reserved for the Italians' pavilion. After a French and French American group decided to pay construction costs and exhibition fees so that the country could have an unofficial presence at the Fair, however, the BIE sued the WFC, charging unlawful conspiracy by bypassing its authority by building and operating a French pavilion. Still, by January 1964, Poletti remained "guardedly optimistic" on the French participating in some way and *voilà!*—the Pavillon de Paris et Industries de France was in business on opening day.[46]

The excitement of having the French participate was short-lived, however, as the Frenchest thing about the pavilion was its name. In less than three weeks after opening day, the Pavillon de Paris et Industries de France was shut down by the WFC because it was not, to put it simply, French enough.[47] After big companies like Renault, Air France, and Hachette passed, as well as Maxim's and the fashion and fragrance houses, a New York lawyer simply grabbed the space and rented it out to pretty much anyone who wanted to sell something at the Fair. Concessionaires there did not submit their proposals to the WFC as required, knowing that products like liquefying machines and services such as handwriting analysis would never have been approved. "The scene certainly detracted from the pavilion's French flavor," Poletti understatedly put it when he took a look for himself. The operator also owed the WFC more than one hundred thousand dollars in rent and connection charges, and the French Pavillon was history by the end of May.[48]

Although it would have been nice to have some French joie de vivre and Italian bon gusto at the Fair, West Germany presented a special case. Seeing the Fair as an opportunity to strengthen diplomatic ties and leverage his popularity with West Germany, President Kennedy made a rare personal appeal on behalf of the WFC (Moses once called JFK "a new salesman on the World's Fair team"). While visiting Bonn in June 1963, the president urged Chancellor Konrad Adenauer to allow manufacturers from the country to exhibit their goods, a clear sign of West Germany's support and endorsement of consumer capitalism. (West Berlin had already agreed to be at the Fair, its pavilion consisting of a plastic dome surrounded by a concrete wall to symbolize the barrier between it and communist East Berlin.) Although the chancellor granted JFK's wish and allowed West German firms to contract exhibition space at the Fair as they wished, only W. Goebel Company, the maker of Hummel figurines, made a commitment by the deadline. Politics, it turned out, was not a factor in West German firms' decision to pass on the New York Fair, as the cost of exhibition space was simply too rich for their blood.[49]

If the circumstances surrounding the participation of Italy, France, and West Germany were complex, the issues swirling around the USSR's possible participation were the stuff of a spy novel. (Moses once even referred to an agreement reached between the WFC and the Soviet Union as a "treaty.") The five-year saga began in September 1959 when Mayor Wagner invited the Soviet Union to take part in the Fair and Premier Khrushchev tentatively accepted.[50] The Soviet Pavilion was a big hit at the 1939–40 fair, and Wagner and the WFC were eager to have the Russians back in New York. A year later, the USSR's ambassador to the United States, Mikhail Menshikov, accepted the WFC's offer, but wanting further assurance, Deegan and others went to Moscow in December to formally extend an invitation (in parchment and leather) to Minister Andrey Gromyko, who was noncommittal about his country's participation.[51] Complicating matters was the fact that the USSR had announced in March 1960 that it would be hosting a world's fair in 1967 with the remarkably familiar slogan "Progress and

Peace," turning the cold war into somewhat of a fair war.[52] By 1962, the Russians had decided to cancel their fair, however, and, after intense negotiations, devoted their attention and resources to Flushing Meadows by leasing the largest space of any foreign nation (at seventy-eight thousand square feet, equivalent in size to what fifteen smaller countries had jointly contracted out for). Despite this calm in the cold war storm, soon the superpowers would be beating their chests, each country seeking to avoid not only an atomic-bomb gap but also a "fair gap." In exchange for the Soviets' participation and in lieu of their decision to cancel their own fair that the U.S. government very much wanted to attend, the State Department reportedly demanded that it be allowed to stage an exclusive two-year exhibition in Russia (one year each in Moscow and Leningrad).[53] This demand did little to promote peace through understanding between the two countries.

As wonks in Washington and Moscow played cat and mouse, the superpowers were also now duking it out to have the tallest exhibit at Flushing Meadows. Each country was, no surprise, keeping its building plans top secret, *déjà vu* for those fairgoers who remembered what had happened twenty-five years ago on the same site. All signs were that the two nations were about to play a my-pavilion-is-higher-than-yours game as they did at the 1939–40 fair when the United States put up a flagpole to make its pavilion taller, only to be trumped by the Soviets when they plopped a statue of a worker (rumored to be a young Stalin) on top of theirs.[54] Just when this "space race" was beginning to get really interesting, however, the USSR decided to withdraw from the New York Fair in October 1962 in light of the State Department's alleged insistence that America be allowed to stage its "reciprocal" exhibit in Russia. "Negotiations with the Soviet Union collapsed amid more confusion than the disarmament talks," as *Newsweek* described the situation. With the Russians' contract for exhibition space in hand, Moses furiously protested to Secretary of State Dean Rusk, calling the whole thing a "misunderstanding," and urged the USSR not to withdraw. In December, a few weeks later than originally planned because of some embarrassment lingering from the Cuban missile crisis, Poletti flew to Moscow in a last-ditch attempt to smooth over the incident and bring the Soviets back into the Fair fold, but the Russians would not come in from the cold, having by now lost interest in the whole affair.[55]

Even after opening day, however, the WFC was still courting the Russians, hoping they would change their minds and come to Flushing Meadows for the second season. In June 1964, Thomas Deegan, who had met with Premier Khrushchev in Moscow a couple of years earlier, was cautiously optimistic about a Russian pavilion for 1965. A group of Soviet scientists was about to visit the Fair, and the country's track team was considering holding its Olympic trials in the Singer Bowl that summer, each a positive sign that the Russians might show up en masse the following spring. "This is the big dream," Deegan said at the time, but the dream was not to be, a casualty of real-world cold war politics.[56]

## Mass Appeal

The conspicuous absence of a Russian pavilion at the Fair made it all the more important that the Vatican would be a major exhibitor. The WFC in fact considered the Vatican to be, with the exception of General Motors, the biggest fish to land if they were going to host anything close to the biggest event in history. It was a relief to all when soon after the Vatican was invited to participate, Pope John XXIII accepted, the pontiff knowing as well as any nation's minister of tourism or company's CEO that the Fair was a tremendous opportunity to show some seventy million potential customers one's wares.[57] In March 1962, it became clear that the Vatican would go all out for the New York Fair when, after the pope met with Francis Cardinal Spellman, the archbishop of New York and future president of the pavilion, it agreed to exhibit two of its most prized statues, Michelangelo's *Pietà* and the *Good Shepherd*.[58] The Carrara marble *Pietà*, which depicts the body of the dead Jesus in the arms of the Virgin Mary after the Crucifixion, had never left the Basilica of St. Peter in Vatican City in the 465 years since its completion, whereas the *Good Shepherd*, residing in the Lateran Museum, was believed to be the earliest representation of a beardless Christ.[59]

Although the coup made WFC staffers jump for joy (the corporation immediately predicted the *Pietà* would be the single largest draw at the Fair), the pope's rather bold decision did not go over well with the Italian artistic community, who feared the three thousand–pound statue might get damaged and resented their cultural icons even temporarily leaving the country. A few days after the announcement, a group of Florentine artists drove a truck carrying a plaster cast of the *Pietà* through their city, claiming it was the real thing that they had hijacked to keep it in the country. The clever hoax fooled more than a few Florentines and served as the start of a long global debate over whether the statue should be brought to New York. Many people, including the director of the Fogg Art Museum in Boston, were firmly against it leaving its native turf, agreeing with many Italians that the masterpiece should not be treated like an animatronic Abe Lincoln.[60]

Ignoring the party poopers, the WFC tried to parlay their winnings by beginning negotiations with the Louvre to bring over Da Vinci's *Mona Lisa*, while a Greek newspaper proposed that Praxiteles's *Hermes Carrying the Infant Dionysius*, a prized statue standing in south Greece's Olympia Museum, be sent to the Fair. (A reader of the newspaper agreed, thinking that the average American would be much more impressed by *Hermes* than "the chick-peas of Santorini or the prunes from Skopelos.")[61] Although Greek archaeologists made it clear that the risk of shipping the twenty-three hundred–year-old statue overseas was too great, Fair officials would not give up on the piece, urging the Greek ministry to bring it over and sweetening the deal by not only guaranteeing its safety but also offering four million dollars in shared revenues.[62] Neither the *Mona Lisa* or *Hermes* would make it to Flushing Meadows, however, turning the *Pietà* into that much more of the crown jewel of the Fair.

The WFC and the Vatican—the latter no slouch itself at public relations—made the most out of their exciting joint venture. On October 31, 1962, Pope John XXIII pressed a switch in his private study, and, a few thousand miles away, work began on the Vatican Pavilion on the future fairgrounds. The ceremony was broadcast on European television and American radio, with the sound of bells from St. Peter's Basilica mingling with the clamor of a pile driver in Flushing Meadows.[63] While Thomas Deegan presented a Fair medallion to His Holiness in Rome, Robert Moses stood formally among a group of reverends for the 3:00 A.M. groundbreaking in Queens.[64] In May 1963, Moses went to Rome to supervise the shipping of the *Pietà* and some other art objects from the Vatican's collection, while Francis Cardinal Spellman appealed for contributions to pay for the pavilion that would indeed be built in part by donated funds from American Catholics through their churches. The cardinal was pleased when he toured the completed pavilion in March 1964, even chatting up the workmen in Italian, but other men of the cloth were less so. The Reverend Gregory Smith thought the building and the exhibits were "out of touch" with the current Roman Catholic Church, a good example of the growing division between traditional, "Old World" Catholics and those faithful who believed the religion needed to change with the times if it was going to survive. ["I can] only question the wisdom that has made a Renaissance work of art the central attraction in a pavilion that should show a contemporary church looking toward the future," the Carmelite priest said, adding that the planned exhibition of Spellman's personal collection of Vatican stamps and coins "seems reprehensible."[65]

Despite its attractions, the pavilion was unapologetically religious, its official aim (clearly inspired by the Fair's theme of Peace Through Understanding) to "promote a deeper understanding of the Church as Christ living in the world, and, through this understanding, to bring men to that peace which He alone can give Who is called the Prince of Peace." The pavilion, which was divided into three areas—Church as Christ Loving, Christ Teaching, and Christ Sanctifying—also included a chapel that was frequently used by visitors wanting a break from the secular world of the fairgrounds.[66]

As could be expected, getting the *Pietà* to the fairgrounds was no easy feat, traveling by boat first to Naples and then across the Atlantic to New York Harbor. Pope Paul VI, who became the new pontiff in June 1963 upon Pope John XXIII's death, granted a special audience to American and Italian packers of the *Pietà* and the *Good Shepherd*, giving them medals when they arrived at the Vatican to take the statues. The packers lashed the *Pietà* to the deck of the *Colombo*, the pride of the Italian fleet, and equipped the statue's crate with steel guy wires and hydrostatic releases to raise it should the boat sink on its eight-day journey.[67] The six million–dollar insurance policy on the statue did not, as everyone was thankful, have to be cashed upon the work's safe arrival on the docks of New York, and church and

*37. A packed house attends mass in the 350-seat chapel in the Vatican's pavilion, one of no fewer than eight religious pavilions at the Fair. Photo © Bill Cotter.*

Fair officials decided not to accept the offer from a wealthy Catholic Manhattanite to keep the *Pietà* in his Fifth Avenue apartment.[68]

A new base was built for the masterpiece for better visibility, and Broadway stage designer Jo Mielziner was hired to build, in effect, a set for the star of the Fair. Mielziner, whose credits included *Annie Get Your Gun* and *A Streetcar Named Desire,* sprinkled hundreds of dark-blue flickering votive candles around the *Pietà* and had Gregorian chants played over the speakers, attempts perhaps to make the bulletproof glass in front of it and armed guards around it a little less obtrusive. Most visitors rode past the sculpture on a conveyer moving at two miles per hour, and then were invited to purchase *Pietà* souvenirs—medals, rosaries, charms, and miniatures—from the Vatican Pavilion's gift shop.[69] The *Pietà* may have very well been turned into a theme-park ride, as critics carped, but many fairgoers, especially Catholics, found the experience to be a powerful, deeply spiritual one.

As for the *Pietà*, there was much debate among the Spaniards whether El Greco's seminal painting *Burial of the Conde de Orgaz* should be shipped over and displayed at the Fair.[70] The work was removed from the Church of San Tome in Toledo for shipment—only the second time in four centuries that it left the building—but it was left to Generalissimo Francisco Franco himself to make the final decision of whether it would actually make it to the Fair. The difficulty of shipping masterpieces to and from Flushing Meadows and the slight possibility that they

*38. Until it made its trip to Queens, Michelangelo's* Pietà *had not left the Vatican since it was installed in 1499. Photo © Bill Cotter.*

could be stolen were not the only concerns among their owners; New York's high humidity could damage priceless works of art, which is exactly what happened to Sudan's thousand-year-old fresco of a Madonna and child that had been recently unearthed and exhibited at the Fair. *Burial of the Conde de Orgaz* not only had a "weak canvas," according to experts in such matters in Spain, but was also prone to deterioration because of the honey El Greco mixed into his primer paint. While Franco mulled it over, the Spanish government bought three Picassos to exhibit in case the president decided to keep the masterpiece in the country, which is what he did. Spain would ultimately exhibit a couple of dozen paintings in its pavilion, including the Picassos, two other works by El Greco, a Velázquez, a Dalí, and five Goyas. Spain's world-class art collection, much of it from the Prado Museum in Madrid, was immensely popular, all the more so because of the pavilion's sixty female guides, all wearing Balenciaga.[71]

Spain more than made up for the absence of *Burial of the Conde de Orgaz* by deciding to also send to the Fair a full-size replica of Columbus's *Santa María*, which would be moored in a fifteenth-century-style Spanish wharf in the Lake Amusement Area. Visitors walked over a drawbridge through a "castle's" doorway to enter the pier and then boarded the ship to see twelve dioramas that traced Columbus's life.[72] The voyage of the 110-ton ship, however, made the transportation of the *Pietà* seem like a piece of Italian wedding cake, rivaling the trip of the original ship in

39. *Spain's effort to send a full-size replica of the Santa María to Queens rivaled Columbus's journey across the Atlantic on the original. Photo © Bill Cotter.*

difficulty. Carried as deck cargo on a German steamship, the 90-foot vessel's trip across the Atlantic from Barcelona to Hoboken was the easy part. After floating the ship on a barge to a lumberyard a few miles from the fairgrounds, the latter-day *Santa María* had to be trucked overland on a flatbed trailer through the narrow streets of Queens, an effort that proved to be more complicated than any treacherous reefs, high winds, and mutinous sailors the Italian explorer may have faced. Low-hanging traffic lights, uncooperative tree limbs and telephone poles, and a suicidal small brown dog made the short journey especially complex for the crew of ninety-nine (eleven more than aboard the original) in charge of the operation. Fourteen special city permits and $7.5 million worth of insurance were required (Columbus's three-ship voyage cost the equivalent of $17,500) before the team of electricians, tree surgeons, truck drivers, and house movers led by a fleet of police cars could budge a single inch. When the trailer carrying the vessel finally arrived in one of the fairground's parking lots, it promptly bogged down in a sea of mud, requiring two cranes to take the ship the final couple of miles to the Lake Pond.[73]

## Common Ground

Even without the presence of some major players, the 1964–65 New York World's
Fair would indeed turn out to be, as a big chunk of the Coca-Cola Pavilion was
called, a "global holiday." Sixty-six nations ended up showing up for the Fair—
more countries than any other fair in history—making it seem that Robert Moses
had once again defied the critics by achieving what he said he would achieve even
if it meant bending or completely breaking every rule in the book.[74] Many of the
participating countries had not even existed during the last fair in New York and,
with no ties to the BIE, were excited to make what was in effect their international
debut or coming out before a global community. Moses and Poletti hoped that
even more countries would sign up for the second season after seeing what they
had missed out on in 1964. Moses's idea to launch what was in many respects a
private enterprise was undeniably brilliant, his knowing all along that foreign and
American businesspeople would chomp at the bit to package trade-oriented exhibits for countries that could not officially attend because of their BIE membership.
Peace Through Understanding may have been the Fair's official theme, but Dollars
and Cents was the actual motive for the entrepreneurs who were there strictly
for commercial purposes and using the name of a particular country purely as a
marketing tool.

Whether officially sanctioned or not, dozens of buildings sprang up in the
International Area throughout 1962 and 1963, more often than not kicked off by
a rather formal groundbreaking ceremony. Poletti (often joined by the Mrs.) was
almost always in charge of these affairs, with Moses a frequent speaker (especially
for bigger countries) and William Berns officiating when Poletti was on the road.
Ambassadors, consul generals, commercial attachés, tourism council executives,
ministers of commerce, and the occasional prince or princess would make a brief
speech, after which he or she would graciously accept a Fair medallion and perform the obligatory poke in the ground with a shovel. Architects and contractors
too were sometimes on hand, elated to be part of what was in their circles a highly
prestigious and quite competitive enterprise.[75]

Despite all the pomp and circumstance at these ceremonies, remarks by Poletti and other Fair officials were typically off the cuff, sometimes startlingly so.
At the foundation-laying ceremonies for the United Arab Republic on September
19, 1963, for example, Poletti made the following observations: "I made a great effort to persuade the United Arab Republic to come to this Fair. I think it is very
important for all of us to have a UAR Pavilion here. There aren't many countries
that have made great contributions to the civilization of the world—but certainly
the UAR is one. Greece is another, and Italy, the land of my ancestors, is another."
At the groundbreaking ceremonies for the Pavilion of Lebanon a month earlier,
Poletti had also felt the need to make a personal connection with the proceedings,
"Lebanon is a not a large country. I think it's about as large as the State of Vermont,

where I was born, which is about 150 miles long and about 40 miles wide—about the size of your country. But, of course, in Vermont we can't boast of all those wonderful things that you have in Lebanon." As the head of international affairs, Poletti typically received a gift from the many dignitaries who came to Flushing Meadows for their pavilion's groundbreaking ceremony. By opening day, Poletti's swag included some Philippine cigars, a Moroccan rug, a carved ivory cane from Sierra Leone, a Chinese dinner suit from Hong Kong, a Swiss music box, two bottles of aquavit in crystal flasks from Sweden, and almost as many dolls in colorful costumes as there were in the "It's a Small World" ride. The gift giving was not one-sided, of course. Poletti and his staff often bore gifts when visiting foreign officials as part of their effort to persuade them to come to the Fair. The shah of Iran's young son was the happy recipient of F. A. O. Schwartz's best electric train set, for example, part of the WFC's successful attempt to bring the country on board as part of the UAR Pavilion.[76]

By the time ground was broken for their pavilions, most exhibitors had at least a good idea about what they planned to present and offer visitors at the Fair. Trade fairs were exclusively about commerce, but a world's fair was much different, an opportunity for nations to tell other nations about their past, present, and future. Government officials had a number of options they could choose from in determining how they would like their country to be perceived by the rest of the world. At the groundbreaking ceremony for her country in April 1963, for example, Mrs. Gandhi made it clear that India's pavilion would focus on "progress" by contrasting life in the country before and after independence in terms of health, electric power, agricultural output, industrial output, and communications. A year later at the opening of the pavilion, Gandhi again spoke of what lay ahead for her nation, very conscious of the "excitement, the moments of uncertainty, and the conviction that there will be positive results when our plans are completed." Members of the Centralamerica [sic] Pavilion—Costa Rica, El Salvador, Guatemala, Honduras, and Nicaragua (all members of the Central American Common Market)—also adopted a progressive stance, planning its pavilion to be "a symbol of the vigor of the new Latin America on the march toward a brighter future of economic development and social justice."[77]

Whereas larger nations had a wide range of exhibition possibilities—history, natural resources and beauty, arts and culture, scientific and technological achievements—the simple fact was that smaller countries often did not have a heck of a lot up their sleeve to impress many visitors. Focusing on the limitless possibilities of the future was thus the safest bet, especially for countries that did indeed want to compete in the global marketplace. One of the main features of the African Pavilion (financially backed by an American banking syndicate), for example, was its "Hall of Aspirations" that examined the resources and economic development potential for an "Africa of the Future." Moses made the Africans' challenge (and the progressive ideology of the Fair as a whole) quite clear in his

40. *The thumbtacklike African Pavilion was, like most international exhibits, a mix of a proud cultural past and an economically prosperous future. Photo © Bill Cotter.*

address at a November 12, 1963, press conference. "Just what they will demonstrate, I don't know," Moses said, "but surely they will be able to show that their objectives are right, that their ambitions are correct, that they are willing to make tremendous sacrifices in the name of progress." Consistent with his habit of trading on the spirit of the Olympics, Moses saw the Fair as a friendly competition for nations (and companies) to show off their accomplishments and ambitions. In this particular case, however, he seemed most excited that the Africans might bring their Watusi dancers, whom he had seen and greatly enjoyed when he visited the continent on one of his recruiting missions.[78] Much to his delight, the dancers did indeed come, complementing the pavilion's film of scenic wonders, a tree-house bar and restaurant, cluster of *rondavels* (round huts), and a wildlife exhibit.

World leaders convened in Flushing Meadows the weeks before and after opening day to dedicate their pavilions. In addition to Mrs. Gandhi's appearance, Queen Frederika of Spain visited in February 1964 for her aerial view of the grounds, whereas King Hussein of Jordan arrived on the third day of the Fair, presenting an ancient stone column to Flushing Meadows Park (one of the few architectural remnants remaining on the site). Princess Christina (then a student at Radcliffe) dedicated the Swedish Pavilion a few days later, proud to show off the 676-year-old stock certificate for Stora Kopparberg, believed to be the oldest such document of any company still in existence. A parade of foreign dignitaries

*41. Many fairgoers (and Robert Moses) were delighted that the Africans decided to send their Watusi dancers to Flushing Meadows. Like much at the Fair, the Swiss Sky Ride in the background provided an odd juxtaposition of old and new, North and South, and East and West. Photo © Bill Cotter.*

came to the Fair the first season including West Berlin mayor Willy Brandt, Irish president Eamon de Valera, King Mwambutsa IV of Burundi, and the Shah and Empress of Iran (who, rather shockingly to some, held hands while on a Greyhound Glide-a-Ride).[79]

No single individual generated the level of excitement of Pope Paul VI's visit near the close of season two, however. Deegan extended an invitation to the pontiff between seasons one and two, exploring the possibility of his visiting the Vatican Pavilion in the summer of 1965. The Vatican's press office made it clear that the pope would not be able to make it ("the filial desire manifested by the [WFC] cannot be fulfilled," it proclaimed in Vaticanese), but many New Yorkers remained hopeful that he would perhaps change his mind.[80] Miracle of miracles, the pontiff arrived in Flushing Meadows on October 4, the final stop on a trip to New York. After leading a mass in a packed Shea Stadium, the pope, accompanied by Francis Cardinal Spellman, five other cardinals, and four American archbishops, arrived at the fairgrounds where he was greeted by a Catholic high school band, bursting fireworks, and ringing bells. The pontiff's motorcade swung by the Unisphere and then proceeded to the Vatican Pavilion where he was welcomed by Robert Moses and nineteen hostesses, the latter all wearing appropriate cardinal red. Some ten thousand people waited outside the pavilion as the pope inspected the *Pietà*, the Chapel of the Good Shepherd, and his own jewel-encrusted, gold and silver coronation tiara. Twelve minutes later, the pope was off to Kennedy Airport and back to Rome as cries of "Viva Il Papa" from the thrilled crowd filled the air.[81]

## People-to-People

With dozens of nationalities taking up residence in the International Area for a full year, a walk through this part of the Fair was no doubt a disorienting, surreal experience for many. The area consisted of pavilions from some 40 foreign countries or cities along with the International Plaza, a complex of buildings housing exhibits of smaller nations. The International Area was in many respects a "fair within the Fair," as its range of food alone proved. Of the 110 or so eating places at the Fair on opening day, 61 were in the International Area, creating an astounding multicultural buffet for the more adventurous fairgoer.[82] For example, "typical Korean cuisine, seasoned and flavored to please Westerner's [*sic*] palate," could be found at that nation's pavilion, which was, even better, "served by thirty young misses attired in traditional Korean costume." Likewise, besides the Japanese food, the restaurants in Japan's Pavilion featured more than 120 "charming young girls" as hostesses and waitresses, all of them kimono-clad and "carefully screened and selected from the highest type backgrounds." As for Korea and Japan, much attention was paid to the selection of the "girls" who worked in the Indonesian pavilion's restaurant, with President Sukarno personally choosing them and even advising them on their behavior ("I do not want you to wiggle around with tight skirts," the president made perfectly clear). The Indonesia Pavilion would exist just one season, however, as the country decided not to show up for 1965, reportedly in protest of the United States's economic support of its foe, Malaysia.[83]

For all the faux ethnic food at the Fair (the pineapple turnovers at Hawaii's pavilion were more Betty Crocker than King Kamehameha, and Luxembourg's restaurant was run by a Frenchman who formerly managed a joint called Lucky Pierre's in Laguna Beach, California), there was plenty of authentic cuisine to be found as well. The Swiss Pavilion's Alpine restaurant featured some very Swiss fondue, the American-Israel Pavilion served kosher foods and Israeli orange soda, and Sweden's *inlagd sill* (pickled herring), *stekt stromming* (fried Baltic herring), and *rokt renstek* (smoked reindeer) were as legit as anything one could find this side of Stockholm. Some critics bemoaned the fact that there was no culinary phenomenon at this Fair like there was in 1939, when chef extraordinaire Henri Soule made his U.S. debut at the French Pavilion and caused, at least in food circles, a sensation. The only thing that came close was the French cuisine being dished up at, oddly enough, the Spanish Pavilion, whose managers brought in Francisco Gonzalez, the head chef from Madrid's renowned Jockey Restaurant (along with no fewer than forty of his assistants). Having dinner at either of the pavilion's two main restaurants, the Toledo and the Granada (for about forty dollars for two, when forty bucks was forty bucks), became the talk of the town, even getting jaded New Yorkers off Manhattan Island for the wilds of Queens.[84]

Another case of a country successfully abandoning its native cuisine for another was at the Lebanon Pavilion. Of the thirty members of the BIE, Lebanon was the only nation to defy the organization's mandate by building an official pavilion.[85] The bold decision might have brought on some bad karma, however, as the Lebanese pavilion would first open late after some historic treasures were damaged in transit, and then, despite having what they thought would be a pretty good draw—the ancient sarcophagus of King Ahiram—attendance started off very slowly.[86] Exhibit managers rethought their mix of offerings, however, recognizing that they might have a better chance of winning fairgoers' hearts through their stomachs. After seeing the huge crowds at the Chun King Inn, the Lebanese decided to add an Oriental snack bar, and the BIE curse instantly disappeared.[87] Arguably the most popular food (and clearly the best remembered, based on anecdotal evidence) at the Fair was, however, the Bel-Gem (later Belgium) waffles that were invented at the Fair and served under the Swiss Sky Ride in the Belgian Village and at various other places on the grounds. To this day, visitors will talk dreamily about their encounter with Bel-Gem waffles in Flushing Meadows, salivating as they recall the ninety-nine-cent treat from forty years ago. That Bel-Gem waffles originated in Queens in 1964 and not, as one might imagine, in Brussels at its fair in 1958 is just one of the ironies to be found in the century and half of world's fair history.[88]

Like food, performing arts imbued the International Area and the entire Fair with the kind of multicultural joie de vivre the WFC knew would make visitors leave with a smile on their faces. Whether it was free, pay-as-you-see, or pay-as-you-eat, the incredible range of dance, music, and theater at the Fair vividly illustrated how people from the four corners of the earth could share a common experience but express it very differently—exactly what a world's fair should do. Spain offered a number of different dance ensembles from various regions of the country under the name Coros y Danzas de España, most impressively a troupe of Flamenco performers who wowed audiences every night. Besides the Watusis (who wore sneakers when they performed), the African Pavilion offered the Burundi Drummers, Zulu Singers and Dancers, Ivory Coast Dancers, and Sierra Leone Dancers, all authentic examples of the art form from different parts of the continent. Many of the African women dancers could be seen continually tugging at their halter tops, not used to wearing such an article of clothing back home. If not doing the twist at one of the Fair's discotheques the second

42. *Two women eating Bel-Gem waffles, a food conceived at the Fair and, as it turned out, one of the most memorable experiences. Photo © Bill Cotter.*

season, visitors might encounter some Hawaiian and Tahitian hula dancing, Moroccan belly dancing, Caribbean limbo dancing, Hopi Indian hoop dancing, and the birdlike "Dance of the Voladores" at the Mexican Pavilion. Although these dances were not watered-down examples of the art form, others were clearly designed for American tastes akin to any other "export" product. Indonesia turned its Javanese and Balinese temple and court dances into a floor show for its restaurant, for example, good entertainment perhaps but probably not something one would see in the South Pacific.[89]

Food, dance, and music in the International Area were thus not just a celebration of a particular country's heritage but conscious attempts to make visitors think more highly of, in today's terms, their "brand." Nations, just like corporations, were at the Fair primarily for commercial purposes, to promote their current and future cultural assets to consumers. A trade element had always been a part of world's fairs, of course, with countries proudly displaying their manufacturing capabilities and finished products for the import-export market. What made this Fair different from previous ones, however, was a new focus on tourism, as jet travel began to become widely popular in the mid-1960s. Many pavilions or exhibits in the International Area were thus, not surprisingly, sponsored by national airlines wanting consumers to "sample" their brand in hopes they would choose it when making vacation plans. "After visiting the Swiss Pavilion, you will want to spend your next vacation in Switzerland just a few hours away by twice daily Swissair DC-8 jet flights," promotional material told visitors, with representatives from the airline on-site to personally pitch the country as well. Similarly, the Spanish Pavilion's flamenco show, featuring Manuela Vargas, an Andalusian gypsy with, according to its promotional material, "dark eyes and a volatile temperament," was sponsored by Iberia, Spain's national airline. Exhibitors in the International Area were especially keen on positioning their countries as "exotic" or "escapist," part of or perhaps a backlash to postwar internationalism as many became increasingly sophisticated as worldwide travelers. "Adventure" thus emerged as a major theme within many foreign pavilions, an opportunity for visitors—especially Americans—to either go back in time or to a place steeped in sensory-based fantasy. For example, the Belgian Village, according to its brochure, was "now your adventure," specifically an "old world of charm and hospitality, craftsmen and shopkeepers so often forgotten in our age." Especially with its "1001 Nights" supper club, a Casbahesque experience of music and dance, Morocco played up its renowned exoticism. "Welcome to the Pavilion of Morocco," its interestingly worded promotional material began, "where the visitor breathes deeply and headily the aromatic mixture of space, mystery, craftsmanship. Here, one crosses the threshold of the gorgeous Pavilion, as though entering the opened gates of the

*43. Swiss Sky Ride cable cars, an ideal promotional device for Switzerland and a form of transportation that many believed would be commonplace in the ultramodern world of tomorrow, making their four-minute run to and from terminals near the Swiss and Korean pavilions. Photo © Bill Cotter.*

Casbah, to adventure into today, tomorrow, and yesteryear, melded glamorously and ingeniously for the instruction and entertainment that live memorably—an adventure second only to a visit to Morocco itself."[90]

No doubt also influenced by Disneyland, nations in the International Area were "theme parking" their pavilions, having learned by now that the mythology surrounding their nations' identities was, at least in economic terms, more important than the reality. International exhibitors seemed to be taking a cue from icons of global marketing such as Pepsi, whose Disney-produced boat ride took visitors through fairy-tale settings of many lands, and Coke, whose "Global Holiday," a fifteen-minute stroll through such exoticisms as a bustling Hong Kong street, serene Indian garden, and lush Cambodian forest designed to let one "smell, touch, and taste far-off places," infused its brand with the increasingly rare commodity of actual adventure.[91]

Besides using their pavilions as advertisements to get fairgoers to come and see the real thing, exhibitors in the International Area showed off their products

44. *With its interpretations of a Hong Kong street, Indian garden, Bavarian ski lodge, Cambodian forest, and Rio de Janeiro harbor, Coca-Cola's pavilion was all by itself a "global holiday." Photo © Bill Cotter.*

much as they would at any trade fair. The Swiss not only sold Swiss cheese but also showed visitors how it was made, reinforcing the nation's popular image as cheese makers deluxe. Two million dollars' worth of Swiss watches, including ones from Rolex and Patek Philippe, were also on display at the Swiss Pavilion, as was the "Master Clock of the World's Fair Time Center." The clock, which was reportedly "so accurate that it can measure imperfections in the Earth's rotation," was a clever way for the Swiss to leverage their heritage as the world's best watchmakers. The Nationalist Chinese Pavilion exhibited no fewer than 370 products to set itself off from its Communist cousins, but it was the Japanese (avid exhibitors at the 1876, 1904, and 1939–40 fairs) who stole the consumer-product show in Flushing Meadows. Visitors to Japan's pavilion got to see both a Toyota Corona (85 horsepower, maximum speed 85 miles per hour) and a racy Datsun 1600 (96 horsepower, maximum speed 106 miles per hour)—very different automobiles from the behemoths the American car companies had over in their buildings.[92] Anyone getting a look at the puny vehicles would never have predicted that a Toyota would in the future be the best-selling car in America and that the Japanese car company would one day outsell Ford on the latter's home turf.

Many Americans seeing so many Japanese electronic products for the first time became smitten by their technological innovation and small size, a harbinger of the sea change that would soon take place in the marketplace. Mrs. Dayton Roseberg of New York City was impressed with what she saw, especially a Riccar sewing machine. "I had no idea Japanese goods were so varied," she exclaimed. Cameras from Canon, Olympus, and Nikon too were well received, as was a Sony calculator ("Push the keys in arithmetical order and the answer is indicated in illuminated figures instantly," the machine's instruction manual had to tell readers). Small color TVs from Sharp and Toshiba were there too, moving bus driver John Bressort of Wayne, New Jersey, to declare that he "might buy one of the Sony midget television sets."[93] Sony also had on display a 145-pound "videocorder"—a very early (and certainly hefty) VCR. The PV-100, which even had an optional remote control, was intended for "industry, education, medical research, technology, airlines, sports, arts, etc.," with Sony completely missing its consumer possibilities.[94] Executives from GE or RCA, however, would never imagine in their wildest dreams that Sony and other companies over in the Japanese Pavilion were about to steal the shirts off their consumer-electronics backs.

## Lost in Translation

The cultural differences between the Japanese and the Americans at the Fair extended well beyond their contrasting approaches to manufacturing or consumer products. Even before opening day, it was apparent to the Japanese, who had no unions in their country, that East was East and West was West. In the fall of 1963, seven artisans from Shikoku brought to the Fair by the renowned

45. *One of Sony's "midget" TV sets sits atop a larger model in the Japanese Pavilion, with few fairgoers (or GE or RCA executives) able to conceive that such foreign-made, utilitarian-looking electronics would soon dominate the industry. Photo © Bill Cotter.*

sculptor Masayuki Nagare to build a replica of a Japanese castle were baffled by American unions' bureaucracy and rigid work schedules. The artisans—the only foreign group of construction workers at the Fair—could not understand why they had to stop working at 3:30 in the afternoon as well as collaborate with an American team, as labor rules mandated. To get ready for their visit, the artisans had spent six months learning English, eating American food, and getting familiar with New York City by reading the *New York Times* every day, but nothing could prepare them for the city's very un-Zen-like union regulations. The American workmen were equally thrown by the Japanese's more improvisational approach to construction. Stones for the pavilion were prenumbered for easy assembly on the site, and Nagare's sudden decision to interchange number 7 with number 43 did not go over well with union workers trained to think of architectural plans as the gospel. It took two hours and much persuasion for the Americans to agree to swap the two stones.[95]

Other Japanese workers at the Fair, along with workers from many more countries, were similarly puzzled by some of the peculiarities of American life. For instance, catcalls from construction workers ("Hiya, honey, how do you like New York?" yelled one carpenter to a kimono-clad dancer) were something Japanese women had yet to hear in their native land. Visitors from less developed countries, such as the dancers and drummers from Burundi, were curious, to say the least, of a number of sights, sounds, and tastes they encountered. Immediately upon their arrival at JFK Airport, for example, the Burundis promptly laid down on the escalator, having no familiarity with stairs at all much less moving ones (all the buildings in their country were single story). The Africans were particularly intrigued by Jack LaLanne's exercise show on television, all the more so because they could not speak any English. Also, unlike most New Yorkers and visitors to the city who created as much privacy as possible in tiny apartments and hotel rooms, all twenty-two of the Burundis slept in a single room just as they would have back at home. The Africans also insisted on maintaining their habit of drinking a quart of beer with every meal—including breakfast—although they found the American version very weak compared with their own banana-based brew.[96]

Much more concerning to foreign exhibitors than the cultural differences were the Fair's unexpectedly high maintenance costs. Officials who had helped the pavilion managers put together budgets had grossly underestimated the costs to run a building, putting many exhibitors in serious financial jeopardy. The Malaysians, for example, were spending more on just window washing in 1964 than their entire maintenance budget, making them wonder if they would be able to afford to be back in 1965. Huge pavilion lawns in the International Area were going unmowed, untrimmed, unwatered, and unweeded, the costs of landscaping upkeep simply too dear. Run-ins with unions were making it difficult for the Moroccans to keep their air conditioning running properly, and the Spaniards' garbage situation was even worse. The Japanese were paying two and a half times the amount in maintenance than they had planned, the Pakistanis three times, and the Jordanians a whopping ten times.[97]

Pavilions in all areas of the Fair were experiencing the same problem, making it clear that it was not just a matter of higher labor costs in the United States versus in other countries. Even flush exhibitors like GM and GE were angry over what Allied Maintenance, which had an exclusive contract with the WFC, was charging them. Stories of the Teamsters—Allied's union of choice—overcharging, doing shoddy work, and even sleeping on the job became almost legendary, causing talk about an all-for-one, one-for-all rent strike unless the situation improved.[98]

Although outrageous maintenance costs were certainly a major thorn in foreign exhibitors' sides, the issue seemed minor compared to cases in which international politics intersected with the Fair. One case involved a group of South Koreans, who were arrested by the United States Immigration Service in January 1965 for violating their visas by staying in New York and taking jobs over the winter. The nineteen South Koreans, who did not want to return to their country simply out of concern they would not be able to afford the trip back for the 1965 season, asked a federal court if they could stay in the States for the six-month break, but the Immigration Service would not budge. In a much more contentious case, twelve South African Zulu dancers decided not to return home after their six-month visa expired at the end of season one, claiming that they faced a "very real risk" of reprisals and persecution in their segregated country if they did so. Harry Belafonte became interested in the case, adding them to his gig at Carnegie Hall in December 1964, as did the Reverend Martin Luther King, who sought funds to fight the deportation of the remaining six in April 1965. After appealing to a number of civil rights activists ("from the front-line of Selma, Ala., or Greenwood, Miss., it is sometimes hard to think about the plight of others fighting for freedom," King wrote in a letter), the Workers' Defense League, a human rights organization, took up the South Africans' cause. The league urged the United Nations to intervene to award political asylum to the dancers and also asked the State Department to offer its opinion on the matter. Other civil rights leaders joined King in asking Secretary of State Rusk to show some international diplomacy toward and empathy for the South Africans, and, in May 1965, the federal government withdrew deportation proceedings of the five remaining dancers.[99]

It was the hundreds of foreign pavilion hosts and hostesses, however, who best displayed international diplomacy day in and day out at the Fair. "A large share of the burden of demonstrating the World Fair's theme of 'Peace and [sic] Understanding' falls on the graceful shoulders of about 300 pretty guides and hostesses at the 35 foreign pavilions," correctly observed the *New York Times*. The "junior diplomats," most of them college students, found Americans well meaning and eager to learn but often geographically, culturally, and politically challenged. A hostess at the Philippine Pavilion was amused to hear a couple ask if her country was part of Hawaii, for example, whereas another one at the Indonesia Pavilion was surprised to learn that many people thought the nation was part of India or Thailand.[100] Hosts and hostesses played an important and underappreciated role at the Fair by educating American and other visitors about their countries' whereabouts, culture, and political situation, creating an educational experience much like the one Robert Kopple had imagined.

International understanding was also achieved by the seemingly countless number of multilingual employees at the Fair. The WFC had multilingual operators answering phones to handle calls from the foreign press, and Hertz's multilingual attendants were ready to put visitors from near and far in the driver's seat. Eastman Kodak's "multilingual experts" answered questions about all things photography, whereas First National City Bank's multilingual staff specialized in foreign currency transactions. Billy Graham simultaneously translated his narration of his *Man in the Fifth Dimension* film into French, German, Spanish, Chinese, Japanese, and Russian to make certain that he, his pavilion, and his religion appeared like a world citizen. Some, however, thought that the Fair was not multilingual enough, especially when it came to helping fairgoers find their way to and around the grounds. "What discourtesy to our visitors—what negligence and inhospitality to find not even one sign either directing to the fair or at the fair in any language other than English," complained Ilsa Lebrecht to the *New York Times* editorial page.[101]

The fact was, however, that a number of efforts were made to turn the entire Fair into much more of a multilingual event in order to turn it into a true "global holiday." A year before the Fair opened, a New York–based group, the International Committee for Breaking the Language Barrier, called for some sort of system to assist non-English-speaking visitors "to facilitate and promote communication among people speaking different languages." Through signs and language, the group imagined, the upcoming world's fair would be the perfect opportunity to break down some of the barriers that unnecessarily separated citizens of the world.[102] Esperanto associations too urged speakers of the world language to visit the Fair in order to put a "non-native tongue" in greater circulation. "Vizitu la Novjorkan Mond Foiron!" exclaimed Esperantists in a pamphlet sent to fellow speakers of the artificial language, urging them, "Come to the Fair!" The state railways of Germany and Austria as well as the Netherlands' tourism information service were already promoting themselves in Esperanto, giving its proponents hope that the language was beginning to become a legitimate option for millions of travelers around the world.[103]

Perhaps the best example of international accord, however, was an essay contest sponsored by the Indian Consulate with the winners getting a free trip to India. Much like the contest sponsored by Consolidated Edison, this one was designed to, according to S. K. Roy, India's consul general, help people discover that "the barriers of geography and communication are not barriers at all" and that everyone "can instantly find a common ground with foreigners who share your interests." Ten people—six adults and four teenagers—from the United States and the Caribbean were off to Bombay, Madras, and New Delhi in January 1965, each of them interested in a particular aspect of Indian culture. An attorney from Long Island wanted to know more about municipal governments in the country, for example, whereas a recent graduate of Wells College was interested in the Oriental religions she had studied. A housewife from Santo Domingo yearned to see more Indian art, and a thirteen-year-old girl from West Hartford, Connecticut, impressed by a carpet she had seen at the Indian Pavilion, "wanted to know more about the people who could make such a thing." "We all tend to get lost in high policy matters, such as the United Nations, and forget what's ultimately important—the people," remarked the consul general, perfectly capturing what was most wrong and what was most right about the Fair.[104]

Such little stories, way off the larger radar screen, make it clear that the world's fair was just not the latest of Robert Moses's mammoth construction projects, an opportunity (or excuse) to turn the valley of ashes into a gleaming emerald isle. Because a world's fair had to, after all, be a world's fair, for twelve months Flushing Meadows was turned into what may very well have been the most culturally diverse place on earth. It was true that many bigger and older nations were not there, with much of the space in the International Area rented out by countries from Latin America, Africa, and the Far East using the Fair primarily to move up the global economic food chain. It was also true that many of the nations that did show up were in cahoots with or completely sponsored by private commercial interests, had strong ties with the United States (such as Japan and Mexico), or else were the recipients of U.S. aid (such as India and Pakistan). And it could not be denied that only some of the global holiday going on at the Fair was truly global, the rest of it as authentic as a pineapple turnover. "To visit any country's pavilion is to emerge laden with its most overworked tourist images," griped the hypercritic Robert Hughes.[105]

Take a look from a different perspective, however, and one can see that the Fair left a much more important legacy than another park in New York City. Millions of people's personal views of the world were changed after a day or two or three at the Fair, more the realization of Robert Kopple's dream than Robert Moses's. "The great fair succeeds in the end," wrote *Time,* because it "so abundantly contains the variety of the world." "You have only to walk through it to discover continents in the corners of your eyes," a reporter for the magazine concluded. Another reporter, Walter Carlson of the *New York Times,* felt similarly, first asking, "What is a World's Fair?" and then providing his own answer: "It's being able to sit in the Caribbean outdoor restaurant . . . sipping a tall mai tai while listening to a calypso singer on the stage, while outside a bagpipe band skirls by and across the street Mexican Indians swing upside down from a 114-foot pole in a prayer for rain."[106] It is no coincidence that the most enduring physical legacies were the Unisphere and the "It's a Small World" ride, each a persistent reminder of the global holiday that was the 1964–65 New York World's Fair.

# 6   Sermons from Science

*Here is a foretaste of tomorrow.*
*Here are triumphs of science and technology,*
*but here—most of all—*
*is man's abiding determination to make a better life for all.*
　　—GM Futurama brochure

HAD ONE VISITED THE FAIR on June 3, 1964, one might have seen hundreds of men eating lunch at the Louisiana Pavilion and, after their crab cakes and Rheingolds, taking a tour of certain buildings. The men were contractors, engineers, architects, and building-code officials from across the country, interested in, as a movie in a few years would make famous, just one word: plastics. It was "Plastics Day" at the Fair, when the construction material in all its chemical splendor was honored, as were the men who made it possible.[1] Although the WFC awarded many groups of people, industries, and companies their own special day, Plastics Day can be seen as a fitting tribute to the high profile of science and technology at the 1964–65 New York World's Fair, offering visitors and exhibitors an ideal blend of education, entertainment, and commerce.

Most world's fairs, in fact, treated science and technology as a central theme if not reason for being, a means to demonstrate past achievements and show off future possibilities. "Ever since the Great Exhibition at the Crystal Palace in London in 1851 set the style for international exhibitions," noted the journal *Science*, "no world's fair has been complete without science exhibits." *Newsweek* made a similar observation: "All the great fairs since 1876 primarily have been manifestations of the progress and potentials of the industrial arts." From electricity at the 1893 Columbian Exposition in Chicago to airships, phonographs, moving pictures, and the vacuum cleaner at the 1904 St. Louis fair to air conditioning, TV, and nylon stockings at the 1939 fair, world's fairs had served as showcases of scientific and technological breakthroughs and, of course, their consumer applications. The 1964–65 New York World's Fair was no exception, as exhibitors seized the chance to deliver, as one of them expressed it, "sermons of science" to millions of visitors (especially to Soviets thinking that the United States may have lost its postwar technological edge). "The 1964 fair both celebrates and illustrates the fact that in the last 25 years science has so far expanded the human imagination that anything seems possible," a reporter for *Time* wrote six weeks after opening day, a view that would ultimately serve less as prophecy and more as a last gasp for a utopian future.[2]

## Hall of Science

Although hardly the most impressive offering of science at the Fair, its official headquarters was the Hall of Science. Built by the Port Authority by diverting funds from an incinerator project, the Hall of Science was a highly politicized and contentious affair from the very start, with WFC officials, local politicians, and the scientific community all at odds as to whether it should exist after the Fair. The conspicuous absence of a museum of science and technology in New York City (a small one in Rockefeller Center closed in the late 1940s) caused many to look at the creation of a pavilion dedicated to science as too good of an opportunity to simply allow the building to be knocked down when the Fair was over. The elite New York Academy of Science was pushing for a twenty-one-story World Science Center near the paint-still-wet Lincoln Center, however, and board members and trustees for the Fair and the academy battled it out to be king of the city's scientific hill. The Academy of Science contingent argued that the Fair's Hall of Science was too small, too costly, and too hastily constructed, "hardly a promising beginning" for a world-class science museum. Another problem in turning the Hall of Science into the scientific equivalent of Lincoln Center, the Metropolitan Museum of Art, or the American Museum of Natural History, they pointed out, was its location. Making a pilgrimage to Queens for a world's fair was one thing, many would agree, but going to the borough to spend a couple of hours at a science museum was quite another. One more major issue was that the hall's exhibits, which would serve as the core of a permanent museum, were decidedly industry-centric, not too surprising given that exhibitors included the likes of Abbott Labs, Upjohn, and the American Chemical Society. A future museum, supporters of the academy suggested, would thus be nothing "more than a trade show for science-based exhibitors." Moses lobbied heavily to make the Hall of Science a permanent fixture on the grounds, however, as such an institution would no doubt help make his dream park a reality (one of Moses's aides called the hall one of his "pet projects").[3] And with no millions of dollars to go to education after the Fair, as many hoped future profits would be used, a science museum seemed like an ideal alternative legacy.

On June 16, 1964—almost two months after opening day—the basement of the Hall of Science was opened to the public.[4] Exhibits ranged from the workings

46. *The undulating and controversial Hall of Science, one of the few surviving structures on the grounds. Photo © Bill Cotter.*

of the human brain (Upjohn) to oceanographic research (American Chemical Society) and cancer detection (American Cancer Society). The clear highlight, however, was the exhibit sponsored by the U.S. Atomic Energy Commission (AEC), which had opted not to build a mobile atomic power plant at the Fair as it originally considered but did show up with something at least as interesting. For adults, the AEC (later split into the Nuclear Regulatory Commission and the U.S. Department of Energy) offered displays on nuclear energy in research, agriculture, and medicine, and Radiation and Man, an exhibit on nuclear fallout and how to guard against its hazards. For children aged seven to fourteen, the AEC had the Oak Ridge Institute of Nuclear Studies create "Atomsville, USA," which the *New York Times* described as "the atomic equivalent of a children's zoo."[5] The for-kids-only exhibit (parents could watch their little ones through one-way mirrors and on closed-circuit television) turned the normally frightening subject of atomic energy into a fun-filled educational romp, letting children twist knobs to create atom-shaped figures, weigh themselves on an atomic scale, and operate a remote control to handle make-believe radioactive materials. Kids were also invited to crawl over a map of the world and press buttons to reveal the location of large uranium deposits ("Plenty" for the Soviet Union, a sign announced, with a simple "Yes" for China). A chain-reaction simulator designed like a pin-ball machine was another feature of Atomsville, as was an equally hands-on (and talking) simulated nuclear reactor that gave off an eerie white-blue glow as charged particles passed through water.[6] Like the propagandist AEC-sponsored educational films and duck-and-cover drills at elementary schools, Atomsville, USA, attempted to seed positive feelings about atomic energy and all its possible applications among children by turning the worst-case scenario into a manageable and even fun exercise.

The Hall of Science was finally completed on September 9, at a cost of more than twice its original budget.[7] Referred to as both the "Permanent Hall of Science" and the "science center" in its dedication ceremony to make it perfectly clear that the final cost of $7.6 million would be worth every penny, government, corporate, and Fair officials basked in the glow at what they hoped was the birth of a world-class museum. "We are joining in more than a mere dedication of another building at the World's Fair," said Paul Screvane, president of New York's city council, in his opening address. "What we are doing today is taking the first major step in the creation of an enduring institution."[8] Mayor Wagner too was a strong supporter of the museum, adding that the building was "destined to be a permanent and major fixture and feature of the Borough of Queens and an important addition to the cultural and educational facilities of the City of New York."[9] James E. Webb, a top official of NASA, also praised the Hall as did George M. Bunker, president of the Martin Marietta Company. Martin Marietta chipped in $1 million for its exhibit, which featured the film *Rendezvous in Space*, produced by none other than Frank Capra. Bunker was hoping the center "would fire the ambition of young scientists and astronauts of the future," a reasonable wish, especially since his company was a leading manufacturer of space vehicles.[10]

Grounded in the child-friendly and progressive idea of "education," science could be found nearly everywhere at the Fair. The WFC undoubtedly encouraged scientific exhibits to help offset the overt commercialism of the Fair, but, because they were sponsored by companies, governments, or even nonprofit organizations with a vested interest, they only added to the feeling that everyone was selling something at every corner of the grounds. Even the U.S. Department of Commerce's Patent Office, not the most marketing-savvy organization around, sponsored the International Inventions Exhibit (in the neutral territory of the Belgian Village) in order to "give the people of the United States and the people of the world a clear picture of how a free government encourages and assists the creative efforts of its citizens."[11]

Interestingly, one of the most compelling presentations of the natural world came not from a scientific organization but from a religious one. Sermons from Science, located in the International Area, was a free exhibit sponsored by the Christian Life Convention of New York City that showed fascinating films of a variety of scientific subjects and nature using techniques such as time-lapse photography of cumulus clouds and growing roots.[12] (Sermons from Science had a similar exhibit at the 1961–62 fair in Seattle under the sponsorship of the Moody

Bible Institute.)[13] The 1964–65 films, which mentioned religion only at the end, were designed to illustrate the compatibility of faith and science, how both were miracles that could live happily side by side. Sermons from Science also held demonstrations on a stage, one in which a million volts of electricity safely coursed through a man's body while igniting a piece of wood in his hands, as fitting a display of the symbiotic relationship between science and faith as one can imagine.[14]

## The Wonderful World of Chemistry

It was the applied world, however, that drew the biggest crowds to hear sermons from science. Corporate America turned its lab experiments into entertainment fodder, building goodwill among a global audience by proudly showing how its technologies were making the world a better place. A battle was being waged on the fairgrounds, each exhibitor making its best case how its particular miracles of chemistry would not only lead to personal and society-wide happiness, comfort, and convenience but also solve problems many people did not even realize they had. The Interchem Color Center from Interchemical Corporation, a manufacturer of inks and other colorants, for example, "explored the phenomenon of color" in the Hall of Science, its exhibit featuring eleven demonstrations in color perception and no fewer than forty-three push-button operations. Such an understanding, the company explained, was "essential to successful solutions of the many color problems which arise in the home, fashion, the arts and in industry."[15] Interchem also had on hand the world's largest "Color Tree," a fourteen-foot thing with 240 colored "leaves" that certainly had never seen the inside of a forest.[16]

The loudest voice of the chemical paradise just around the corner, however, was clearly Du Pont, which, in classic postwar style, presented all things synthetic as superior in every way to what could be found in nature. Knowing that fairgoers had come to Flushing Meadows more to be entertained than for a science class, Du Pont presented *Wonderful World of Chemistry*, a forty-five-minute musical revue written and produced by Broadway composer Michael Brown that also featured some innovative product demonstrations. The company apparently looked to the chairman of the board, Frank Sinatra, for inspiration, describing its two-cast, two-theater show as a "free-and-easy, light and breezy swing through the fascinating world of chemistry." The theaters themselves were a tribute to the versatility of chemistry, made up of a bevy of Du Pont–branded materials including a Tedlar roof, Delrin doorknobs, Antron and Fabrilite seats, Dacron fire hoses, Zytel hinges, Mylar stage curtains, Hylene foam undercoating, and Nylon carpets. As well, Du Pont fibers were displayed in clothes created by top designers like Oleg Cassini, all the more interesting because the live actors wearing them interacted with filmed actors to tell the story of chemistry.[17] The experiments in the show were conceived by Dr. Jonathan Karas who, in a previous chemical life, had helped develop the atomic bomb during World War II.[18] The pièce de résistance was when the Du Pont chorus sang "The Happy Plastics Family," something that occurred, rather amazingly, forty cheery times a day.[19]

Joining the chorus in praise of "the happy plastics family" was, of course, the plastics industry itself, which relished the opportunity to show off the construction material at the Fair. Reservations about the material among many developers and restrictive building codes had limited its use in construction, but that situation could all change, plastics industry leaders believed, when people got a look around the grounds. The white siding on the House of Good Taste was made of plastic, for example, a monument to the, well, good taste of synthetic construction materials. Eager to seize the plastics day, the Society of the Plastics Industry scheduled its annual conference in New York to coincide with the Fair, the theme of the meeting being Plastics in Construction in Tomorrow's World, the climax of which was their June 3 plasticfest.[20]

The makers of another material, fiberglass, were also having a heyday at the Fair, with a million pounds of the stuff used in about two dozen pavilions. Fiberglass (originally fibrous glass) debuted at the World Columbian Exposition in 1893, with Owens-Corning introducing its version, Fiberglas, at the 1939 fair in New York (woven into, of all things, neckties and bedspreads). Owens-Corning was, twenty-five years later, by far the biggest producer of fiberglass in the world and went all out to show off the versatility of what it promised was "a material you're going to see a lot of in the future."[21] The biggest coup for Owens-Corning was its contribution to U.S. Rubber's giant tire-shaped Ferris wheel, which, oddly, was made not of rubber but of Fiberglas reinforced plastic. What appeared to be stained glass on the outer wall of the Federal Pavilion was also Fiberglas, as was the multicolored roof of New York State Pavilion, the bubble roofs of the Brass Rail kiosks, the (rust-proof) bodies of Greyhound's Glide-a-Rides, and much of the Monorail's red and white cars. Even the drapes in the Top of the Fair restaurant were made with Fiberglas yarn that not only could not catch on fire but also never needed ironing. Lighter, stronger, and cheaper than real glass, fiberglass did indeed appear to be in the right place at the right time at the world's fair.[22]

Not to be left out, more traditional construction-material manufacturers were promoting their products at the Fair, also eager to capture the attention of builders and consumers. The American Iron and Steel Institute made a movie about the use of structural steel in the skeletons of many pavilions that it showed to construction people and architects, and the lumber industry promoted the fact that all three houses at the House of Good Taste had wood frames, made by Weyerhaeuser. Perhaps the best advertisement for any pavilion could be found in the all-wood Austrian Pavilion, however, its sweet aroma appealing to the senses in a way that plastic or fiberglass could never match.[23]

With its innovative use of concrete, the Kodak Pavilion was an outstanding promotion for that building material, so much so that it was given a special award from the Concrete Industry Board of New York.[24] Kodak, expecting the Fair to be the most photographed event in history—quite an expectation, given the massive photojournalism campaign of World War II—invested heavily in its moonscapelike building and exhibits. In addition to its *Photography 63–64* show featuring some of the best current examples of the art form (the company had put on a similar show at the last New York fair), Kodak installed the world's largest outdoor color prints on the exterior walls of its pavilion. The company also commissioned Saul Bass of Hollywood fame to create *The Searching Eye*, a twenty-two-minute film offering a camera-eye view of the world's wonders through a child's eyes. Using a new multi-image, 70-millimeter projection process and shown in a circular theater, *The Searching Eye* undoubtedly helped Kodak sell a heck of a lot of Instamatics for many years by wonderfully illustrating the miracle of sight. The company was keen to tell consumers about its new automatic "no threading, no fumbling" feature on the Instamatic, even installing a robot in the front of its pavilion that not only greeted people but effortlessly loaded film into a camera, proving the ease of the product. Kodak also offered a special World's Fair camera with a built-in flash (and Unisphere logo) and, as part of its free expert advice to more serious photographers, recommended what f-stop or exposure setting to use when taking pictures of the more popular pavilions.[25] Removing much of the chemical goings-on that of course made photography possible, Kodak masterfully turned the complexities of science and technology into consumer-friendly products and services.

47. *Knowing that millions of fairgoers would be toting their cameras, Kodak turned its pavilion into a temple of photography. Photo © Bill Cotter.*

## Progressland

Also interested in infusing a less-than-show-stopping scientific subject with entertainment value and consumer appeal, the energy industry showed up at the Fair with impressive exhibits. Besides the Atomic Energy Commission's nuclear-a-go-go in the Hall of Science, the gas industry's Festival of Gas was a sexed-up showcase for that form of heating and cooking energy (featuring a rolling gas-powered cart that cooked food table-side). But as it had been at all world's fairs since the 1893 Columbian Exposition in Chicago, whose White City connoted not just its alabaster Carrara marble but also its literally electrifying power source (including the largest searchlights ever made, visible an amazing sixty miles away), the electric industry stole the energy show at Flushing Meadows.[26] Every night, the Tower of Light, the world's most powerful (twelve billion candlepower) searchlight was switched on with much fanfare, a tour de force of electrical power deserving of its superlative, carnivalesque nickname, the Brightest Show on Earth. Sponsored by 150 investor-owned electric utility companies, the Tower of Light also had visitors ride through a musical show about the benefits of the energy source, with an animatronic character, Reddy Kilowatt, chatting up the joys of electric living. In the show, Reddy introduced "Uncle Ben" (as in Franklin) and the latter's sidekick, an animated eagle named Sam, to the modern uses of electricity, with the circa 1964 appliances predictably amazing the venerable kite flyer. One scene compared a 1939 "vintage" home, which had only eight or nine electrical appliances, to a modern, "total-electric" home having forty different electrical appliances, "mak[ing] 1964 living more comfortable, convenient, and enjoyable."[27] Using 1939 as a historical benchmark was a clever conceit, as many adult visitors to the 1964 Fair had also attended the one in New York twenty-five years earlier, thereby making the "World of Tomorrow" perhaps seem less futuristic and progressive than they fondly remembered and raising the status of this new upstart fair.

The company most responsible for getting Americans, and everyone else for that matter, to plug in dozens of appliances in their homes was, of course, General Electric. GE's Progressland, which borrowed from its Electric Utilities exhibit from the 1939–40 fair, was a self-contained theme park of energy in which the company stuck its brand name on all things electric, including what many scientists believed would offer unlimited potential in the years to come. Via the pavilion's Medallion City, a modern community with all-electric school, hospital, steel mill, department store, and, of course, cluster of homes filled to the brim with all the latest appliances, GE showed consumers how to "live better electrically."[28] The company was not content to merely sell consumers on the benefits of electricity, however, equally interested in using the Fair to sell consumers on how to more efficiently create electricity through nuclear energy. It was hardly an easy sell, as nuclear energy was difficult to understand and, of course, instantly made people

*48. Looking more than a bit like Oz's Emerald City, the Tower of Light was a tribute to the wonders of electricity. Switched on every night, the searchlight rising from the center was as bright as 50 fully illuminated Yankee Stadiums or 340,000 car headlights. Photo © Bill Cotter.*

think of the atomic or hydrogen bomb (*Dr. Strangelove* and *Fail-Safe* were just a couple of popular bomb-themed movies that came out during the Fair's run). In order to get consumers to start thinking about how to, perhaps, "live better atomically," GE knew it had to do more show than tell. In its Sky-Dome Spectacular, "the epic struggle of man to harness the energy of the atom for peaceful purposes" was told on the world's biggest (two hundred–foot) projection screen. Using eighty-seven coordinated projectors, the show equated spinning atoms with natural sources of electricity—electrical storms, fire, the sun—to make nuclear energy as unthreatening as possible.[29]

It was Progressland's "Fusion on Earth" show, however, a real-life demonstration of controlled nuclear fusion performed every six minutes, that had visitors literally jumping out of their seats. In what sounds like the definitive "don't-try-this-at-home" exercise, a wee bit of deuterium gas was squeezed out of a magnetic field for a few millionths of a second at a temperature of 50 million degrees

Fahrenheit and, after a three-minute countdown, poof!—a bright flash of light was seen and a loud bang heard as atoms fused and free energy was created.[30] Some 7.4 million visitors saw what was reportedly the first real public display of thermonuclear fusion (which GE liked to refer to as a "man-made sun" rather than what caused a hydrogen bomb to explode) in the 1964 season alone, with nary a fairgoer turned into carbon.[31] GE had been performing the experiment internally when Walt Disney—knowing a good show when he saw one—suggested to the company they go public with it at the Fair.[32] With "Fusion on Earth," GE leveraged postwar Americans' awe of nuclear energy, positioning it as an opportunity to "win the peace" through a virtually unlimited power supply. Ultimately, nuclear energy was an unprecedented opportunity to make a lot of electricity on the cheap, meaning bigger profits if the company could figure out how to actually do it, something that GE conceded would take several decades.

## From Here to There

Like energy marketers, the transportation and travel industry used the 1964–65 Fair to remind consumers of its importance and value to everyday life as well as position itself for the future. Transportation and travel had in one form or another always been an integral part of world's fairs, most memorably perhaps when Sarah Bernhardt floated on a balloon over the City of Lights during the Paris fair of 1878. The last fair in New York would also be a tough act to follow when it came to transportation and travel, as automobile culture in all its glory was joyously celebrated in 1939 and 1940, a victory party of sorts of American know-how over the Depression. More than any other previous exposition, however, the 1964–65 Fair was itself an endorsement of travel, with cars, buses, trains, taxis, moving sidewalks, and the Monorail scurrying in all directions, both within exhibits and across the 646 acres of grounds. The Fair reflected and demonstrated postwar America's love affair with mobility and freedom and pointed the way to the new frontier of space travel.

Back on earth, however, Greyhound was still heavily promoting its mode of transportation against the increasing threat of air travel. In its exhibit, the company featured displays of attractions around the United States along its highway tours, trying to counter speed with experiences. Visitors to the pavilion also had the chance to see Lady Greyhound, the company's live spokesdog, model the latest in canine fashions four times a day. The bus company also ran the network of information booths at the Fair (its hostesses called Greyhound Golden Girl guides), a clever way to promote itself as an expert when it came to directions and how to get around.[33] Greyhound was fighting a losing battle, however, as the pace of American society escalated throughout the 1960s and the bus (and train) industry went into decline. Many nonbusiness travelers were in the mid-1960s trying airplanes for the first time, as prices gradually fell and as fears about safety eroded.

Also no doubt concerned that more travelers were taking to the air in place of the Great American Road Trip, Sinclair turned up the entertainment volume on its product, gasoline, by exploiting its corporate symbol, the dinosaur. Sinclair had featured dinosaurs in its exhibit at the 1933–34 Century of Progress Exposition in Chicago but, with the new animatronic technology, could almost resurrect the long-dead species to popular acclaim.[34] In its one-acre Dinoland exhibit, the company's nine different kinds of fiberglass, life-size dinosaurs, some of them animatronic, stood at prehistoric attention as erupting volcanoes, flashing lightning, and bubbling streams depicted what Earth was like at different points in time, starting 4.5 billion years back. Sinclair's geologic presentation of the time when dinosaurs roamed the planet was, as the company put it, "as life-like and authentic as modern science and painstaking research can make it."[35] Additionally, Sinclair's operations and future plans were laid out in color pictures and dioramas, and Sinclair service stations were located at both of the Fair's parking lots.

With the Fair sitting right on Flushing Meadows marina, the WFC was sure to include water travel in its entertainment mix. For those fairgoers who ventured out to the Lake Area, short cruises in Amphibicars—boats that were made from and looked a lot like sports convertibles but fortunately had waterproof bottoms and sides—were available (the twin-propeller boats could actually be purchased), with another watery experience the Log Flume Ride, a waterborne roller coaster.[36]

For the more nautically inclined, the U.S. Navy's exhibit in the Transportation and Travel Pavilion included the film, *Around the World with the Navy*, which showed off the department's greatest hits such as an atomic submarine cruising under the Arctic's ice, jets taking off from and landing on an aircraft carrier, and aerial acrobatics by the Blue Angels precision flying team. The navy also had skin divers perform an underwater drama narrated by Lloyd Bridges of *Sea Hunt* TV show fame and, perhaps inspired by the popular CBS show *My Favorite Martian*, offered a half-film, half–live show called "Flying Saucer" in which Martians visited the earth.[37]

All of the Fair's aquatic offerings, however, were underachievers, not only because the Lake Area was considered off the beaten track and expensive by fairgoers but also because travel by air was, by 1964, simply considered more exciting than travel by water. Just as the 1939 fair worshiped travel by automobile, the 1964 Fair was in many ways a salute to flight in all its incarnations. If the Jaycopter, a simulated helicopter ride, wasn't exciting enough, one could take a real one to or from the Port Authority Pavilion Heliport's 120-foot rooftop landing pad. A ride on AMF's Monorail was a lot slower than a helicopter (or even one of Greyhound's buses) but turned travel by rail into a futuristic, sci-fi experience. Trains hung upside down from an overhead rail 40 feet up in the air across the three-quarter-mile route in the Lake Area, something that previously could be imagined only in the comics. Airlines too, much more than ever before in world's fair history, pitched the wonder of jet travel to future passengers. United Airlines's *From Here to There,* a short film by the indefatigable Saul Bass, was for many visitors the first glimpse of what it was like to move through space at 600 miles per hour at 36,000 feet.[38]

Even more exciting in these heady days of the space age was the Cinerama film *To the Moon and Beyond,* sponsored by KLM. The film, which was projected onto an 80-foot domed ceiling in the Travel and Transportation Pavilion, borrowed many of the elements from a previous Cinerama film shown in the Spacearium at the 1962 Seattle Exposition. Over the course of the fifteen-minute show, one had the sensation of being hurled into outer space, swung by the moon, taken back to earth, plunged into a deep canyon, whisked into a pine forest, submerged into the ocean, squeezed down an ant hole, and, finally, sucked into the nucleus of a human cell. After the seventy-five-cent trip (twenty-five cents for children), astronauts in Bermuda shirts could complete their mission by eating lunch in the pavilion's Galaxy Cafeteria.[39]

Space exploration was in one form or another featured at thirteen different pavilions at the Fair, reflecting many people's desire to know more about what existed (or did not exist) beyond the earth's atmosphere. Rockets could be found at the 1939–40 fair, but most of them were made of plaster, looking like they were plucked right out of a B movie. This time they were the real thing or, at least, full-scale, precise models, part of NASA's intention to use the Fair to garner public support (and continued funding) for the U.S. space program and, specifically, JFK's commitment to land on the moon before the end of the 1960s. NASA had shown up at the 1961–62 fair in Seattle with an impressive two million–dollar display featuring models of satellites and tracking stations and, most exciting, the craft in which Alan Shepard had made the first U.S. suborbital flight in 1961, but this time the agency and its corporate partners went all out.[40] In the Hall of Science's Great Hall, the realistic "Rendezvous in Space" show took place, with three full-scale spaceship models (one "orbiting cylindrical space laboratory" and two supply "space taxis") hovering 50 feet in the air. After the Capra-produced animated film, one of the taxis docked with the orbital lab to exchange crews and supplies, not unlike what could be seen in a *Star Trek* movie some twenty years later.[41]

"Rendezvous in Space" was certainly a nice show, but to see and touch vehicles that had actually been in space—a thrilling experience to many in the mid-1960s—one had to visit the United States Space Park. Jointly sponsored by NASA and the Department of Defense, the two-and-a-half-acre park held what was the largest array of spacecraft outside Cape Kennedy. There visitors could run their fingers on the Aurora 7 (a Project Mercury spaceship in which Scott Carpenter had orbited Earth in 1962), as well as get a look at a full-scale model of a Gemini two-man spacecraft and a model of the Apollo rocket planned to carry men to the moon. Youngsters could take a simulated space ride in a Mercury capsule, no doubt making many kids instantly change their future career plans from fireman, nurse, or baseball player to astronaut.[42] Major L. Gordon Cooper himself showed up at the Space Park early the first season, the first of a number of astronauts to

*49. A couple of the assortment of rockets in the U.S. Space Park that, for many fairgoers in the heady days of the midsixties' space race, was nothing short of thrilling to see and touch. Photo © Bill Cotter.*

visit the Fair to promote the nation's space program. Also scattered around the park were an X-15 rocket plane, a recovered Discovery XIV spy satellite, the Mariner II that had probed Venus, the propulsion section of a Saturn V, and a disparate collection of Thor-Delta, Atlas, and Titan II rockets. Twenty-one science and engineering college majors in blue jackets acted as guides, roaming the park and answering questions from all comers (for a cool one hundred dollars a week). For many visitors, this visit was the first time they gained any real understanding of what NASA and the Department of Defense referred to as the nation's "peaceful exploitation" of space. "I had read a good deal in newspaper and magazines about the U.S. plans to land on the moon," observed one visitor from New Jersey, "but it wasn't until I saw the actual models of two lunar spacecraft here and had a host explain step-by-step how ... two men would set foot on the moon that I could understand it clearly." The biggest coup for the Space Park took place in August 1965 when the tin can–size Gemini IV capsule arrived, almost still warm after its four-day orbit around Earth just two months earlier, during which astronaut Ed White took the first "space walk."[43]

## Computer Day at Midvale

Like cast iron and steam power at London's 1851 Crystal Palace, steel in Paris's 1889 Eiffel Tower, and the internal combustion engine at the 1939 fair, the computer was featured as one of the leading technological "stars" of the 1964–65 Fair. Unlike these previous technologies, however, the computer is not what we think of when it comes the Fair, or at least not what we think of first. Technology-based businesses, most notably IBM, tried to get across the major advantages of information technology—speed, miniaturization, logic, and problem solving—with gusto and flair, but audiences largely or entirely unfamiliar with computers often found the exhibits abstract and difficult to understand. One sign that visitors were less than ready to embrace computer technology was their overwhelming choice to go to information booths staffed by real people versus use the automated guides on the grounds that answered questions and provided directions.[44] It would, of course, take decades for consumers to start getting comfortable with computers and, eventually, to use them in an entirely different way than even the brainiacs at IBM envisioned in the 1960s.

For the most part, computer technology, which was spread liberally throughout the grounds (even present at the Protestant Center), was explained using the popular "question-and-answer" model of the times, with binary logic capable of figuring out the most difficult problems quicker than you could say "UNIVAC." At United Delco's exhibit in the GM Building, for example, a mechanic placed a punch card with the performance levels of a vehicle's shocks, brakes, engines, and ignition into a computer and, in minutes, "he knows *exactly* how everything is functioning, and what needs to be done." "This peek into the future is awaiting you," Delco's "Auto Service Center of Tomorrow" promised, correctly anticipating the age of advanced computer diagnostics for cars. Over at National Cash Register's pavilion, visitors typed out questions about food recipes and historic events on keyboards, and a computer magically printed out the answers (on forms they could take home as free souvenirs). And at the pavilion's "Microworld," visitors gaped at feats of miniaturization like a small stack of cards that held as much information as a multivolume encyclopedia, never in their wildest dreams thinking that one day this same amount of data could be put on a pinhead. Bell had a "Tic-Tac-Toe Machine," described as an "electro-mechanical brain" that could be tied but not beaten by a mere human. The "Electronic Travel Brain" (a Fujitsu FACOM computer) over at the Japanese Pavilion let visitors use a simple push-button switch to light up places on a world map and learn the best route from here to there. In the future, however, the Japanese told visitors, "a miraculous electronic computer will give you the sensation of riding in a rocket to prepare you for the day when you can book a passage to the moon."[45] Though one certainly can't argue with the value of having a travel agent for all one's lunar needs, this sort of mumbo jumbo only added to visitors' confusion about what computers could currently and one day might do.

The clearest and most compelling explanation of computer technology was made by the undisputed king of information machines, IBM, whose pavilion was so popular that the company offered entertainment to those fairgoers standing in line for an hour or more. Although most of its pavilion was dedicated to making visitors warm up to the strange, new frontier of computers, the company was also sure to have on display ten of its new Selectric typewriters. (IBM also designed its auditorium's exterior as a giant Selectric ball, the company's abbreviated name repeatedly substituted for the whole keyboard.) Fairgoers could type free postcards at the "Typewriter Bar," a fun way for IBM to get folks to try this "uniquely different machine that has no moving carriage." The company was influential enough for the WFC to declare July 8, 1964, "IBM Day," when twelve thousand employees from all fifty states and thirty-two countries gathered at the Fair. Mayor Wagner, Moses, and former president Eisenhower also took part in the day's festivities, the latter the keynote speaker at ceremonies held in the Singer Bowl. In his speech,

50. *Eero Saarinen's egg-shaped IBM Pavilion, one of the legendary architect's last commissions. Photo © Bill Cotter.*

the septuagenarian confessed he did not have "the slightest idea how a computer works" and was "confused" by the entire concept, something most Americans would likely admit if asked.[46] With the Fair, IBM was determined to try to change that confusion.

The 1964–65 Fair was not the first time IBM used a world's fair to show off its products to primarily a business audience, proudly displaying technologically advanced business machines that could automatically sort checks and grade papers at the 1939–40 fair. Twenty-five years later, however, the company had much more work cut out for itself, its challenge to explain in simple terms an incredibly complex concept—how a machine "thinks." With the help of an all-star team—the late Eero Saarinen as architect, display area and film by Charles Eames and Ray Eames, and music by Elmer Bernstein—IBM attempted to bring the cold and alien world of computers to life. The main event was the "People Wall," in which an audience of five hundred filed into neat rows on steeply (forty-five-degree) tiered bleachers and was greeted by a master of ceremonies dressed in white tie and tails who was suspended in midair. The audience was then raised fifty-three feet, plopped into a ninety-foot-tall egg-shaped theater, and shown the Eameses' twelve-minute film. Projected onto a whopping fifteen screens, the film featured a series of vignettes showing how computers and the human mind solved problems in much the same manner.[47] One sequence involved the logistics of planning a dinner party (the hostess using a mathematical model to properly seat people), while another broke down the steps of a football coach planning a pass play. With the People Wall, IBM was trying to deflect Orwellian concerns about the emerging information society by demonstrating how people and computers "thought" in a remarkably similar way and that man and machine were not that different after all.[48]

"Puppets in the Park" was another way IBM illustrated man's and machine's shared reliance on binary (or, at the time, "two-valued") logic. In miniature Punch and Judy theaters, mechanical figures acted out skits involving speed, logic, and information handling, one in which Sherlock Holmes solved "the case of the elusive train, or the plurality of the single green moustache." In the skit, Holmes showed Dr. Watson how to catch robbers using problem-solving skills similar to the abilities of a computer, making visitors realize "computers are not so mysterious after all." Another skit was *Computer Day at Midvale* in which a mayor of Anywhere, USA, sang the praises of computer technology, further positioning the machines as just another part of normal, everyday life.[49] By reducing the complexities of computer technology to the lowest common denominator possible, locating them in ordinary settings, and challenging the idea that they were perhaps smarter than us, IBM attempted to lessen the perceived threat they posed for many people (including no doubt businessmen fearing they may one day lose their jobs to such a machine). To some, especially in the science community, IBM's exhibit was as persuasive a case for computer technology as could be imagined. "If the 3-ton people wall returns you to Earth *still* wondering why data producing machines are useful, it's no fault of IBM's," commented Henry B. Comstock of *Popular Science.* Arthur Knight of the *Saturday Review,* on the other hand, had a much different opinion. "The spectator leaves . . . with only the vaguest idea of how the computer operates but with a vast respect for the human brain," Knight thought.[50]

Although the computer was universally praised at the Fair, there was little tolerance for one that smacked of the dreaded carnival and midway. On six separate occasions, an undercover investigator for the local Better Business Bureau paid one dollar to have his handwriting analyzed by a card-sorting machine in the Better Living Center, but the alleged "hidden secrets" of his personality traits turned out different each time. Concluding that the handwriting-analysis machines, which could also be found in the Bourbon Street, Hall of Education, and Transportation and Travel Pavilions, were "phony," the investigator forwarded his findings to Attorney General Louis J. Lefkowitz. In his 26-page (!) report to the state's supreme court, Lefkowitz asked that the machines be barred from the Fair despite their impressive blinking lights and "meaningful hum," adding that their operators were suggesting that the devices were made by IBM or UNIVAC.[51]

A real UNIVAC was blinking and humming in the Federal Pavilion, whose "Library USA" exhibit featured a computerized reference system. Visitors could choose from any of seventy-five subjects, and, after a librarian pushed a button, a seven hundred–word essay along with a bibliography would print out. George Lewicky, assistant director for Library USA, wisely believed that in "a matter of years" computers would be widely used in reference libraries, although no one could imagine the Googling and Yahoo!ing that lay ahead in the future as search engines emerged as one of the computer's principal applications.[52]

## See-as-You-Talk

New technologies were also on display in the many exhibits at the Fair focusing on communications. Even older methods of communication were presented with some new twists to make them seem modern and sophisticated. The U.S. Post Office set up not just a real mail-sorting exhibit but also a "working laboratory . . . of the most advanced technologies on mail processing [using] the latest high speed electro-mechanical devices and machines yet developed." Uncle Sam's postal exhibit was, its promotional material boasted, "a visual demonstration of the mechanization necessary to move the mails in the immediate future." The post office also sold the official world's fair five-cent stamp (a scene of the Unisphere and main mall) and envelope, which served, of course, as free advertising for the WFC as they winged their way across the country and around the world to potential fairgoers.[53]

Another tried-and-true form of communication, ham radio, could be found at the Fair, appealing to the hobby's millions of enthusiasts during the postwar years. Coca-Cola invited visitors to its pavilion to dial up fellow operators near and far, a subtle way the company emphasized its international presence and re-inforced its ownership of the most recognized brand on the planet.[54]

An icon of America's communications past, Western Union, let fairgoers send a telegram for the special rate of one dollar, even making available prepared messages such as, "Greetings from the New York World's Fair. It is simply tremendous. You must see it." Another one went, "New York World's Fair exceeds my expectations. Am staying over an extra day." Visitors to Western Union, located in the American Express Pavilion, could also contact their hometown bank to wire funds if one ran out of cash, a not-uncommon experience at the Fair.[55]

Much more exciting, however, were the truly new communications technologies or innovations at the Fair, some of them seen by the public for the first time. In what was the most (perhaps only) truly useful example of the Fair's push-button mania, the Bell System scattered fourteen hundred "touch-tone" telephones across the grounds (with the price of a local call still just a dime). The phones, which had been test-marketed in several cities for a few years, promised to shave off a full five to eight seconds in dialing time from the conventional rotary dial's average of ten seconds. One such "time-saving" phone was ceremoniously installed on Moses's desk in October 1963, the first push-button in fact to be put into use in New York State. Its monopoly of the telecommunications industry still very much in place, Bell had a total of seven thousand public telephones in Flushing Meadows, many of them bringing curvy space-age design to the boxy phone booth. Also on the grounds were a number of "family telephone booths"—jumbo, "ultra-modern, semi-private" stalls that allowed as many as six people to crowd around and speak into a phone. In its main exhibit, Bell's moving ride traced the history of communications (from "primitive signaling by drums to . . . communications satellite orbiting in space"), its 140-foot microwave tower transmitting RCA's television programming that originated from the Fair.[56]

The star of Bell's exhibit was, however, its Picturephone that allowed caller and callee to see each other while chatting. Such a device was long the stuff of science fiction (Tom Swift had used one about fifty years earlier), and most visitors who saw or tried the phone were amazed that such a device might soon be in their homes (especially when learning that it could be switched to one-way viewing if one was, say, coming out of the shower). The day before the Fair opened, Bell demonstrated its Picturephone for reporters with a coast-to-coast "see-as-you-talk" call between William D. Laurence, the WFC's top science consultant, and Donald Shaffer, managing editor of the *Anaheim Bulletin* (who was conveniently located at Bell's exhibit at Disneyland).[57] At the Bell exhibit, visitors could see each other on the $4^3/_8$" by $5^3/_4$" screens while holding conversations in separate booths, the push-button console adding to the Jetsonesque effect. Although the Picturephone was without a doubt one of the most impressive things at the Fair, Bell was clear that it was experimental and not headed to the home market anytime soon. The company did, however, interview visitors about their level of interest in it and

*51. Push-button phones in such swanky booths suggested that Bell would continue its dominance of the telecommunications industry for decades longer. Photo © Bill Cotter.*

how they would use the rather amazing device, a sign that Bell hoped that one day people would reach out and see someone from their homes.[58] Bell also set up "Picturephone Centers" in New York, Chicago, and Washington, D.C., where, on an appointment basis, the public could use the phones (for a pricey sixteen to twenty-seven dollars for the first three minutes). To kick off the service in June 1964, Bell had been able to get Lady Bird Johnson in Washington to call one of the company's scientists in New York, quite the promotional coup.[59]

As in the telephone business, leaders in the television industry used the Fair to, in effect, reintroduce television to consumers with recently developed technologies. Having introduced television to the public at the 1939 fair, RCA was well aware that the new one would be an ideal opportunity to show off color technology to millions of existing and new viewers. In the early 1960s, in fact, when color television was still largely experimental, RCA already had plans to use the Fair to kick off what was the most sensational thing to happen in the industry since the quiz-show scandals. In January 1961, before a group of RCA TV-set dealers at a swanky dinner at the Waldorf-Astoria hotel, David Sarnoff, chairman and

CEO of the company, delivered the exciting news that Robert Moses himself was hoping that their company would "take the lead" in broadcasting the opening of the Fair around the world in color. The "General" explained that the broadcast "in natural color over remote parts of the world" would be achieved by satellite communications, although no such system yet existed. AT&T planned to have an experimental satellite in orbit a year after it got the okay from the Federal Communications Commission, which was still figuring out what frequencies to assign to the system. In another example of his conscious attempt to bridge the 1939 and upcoming fairs, Moses acknowledged RCA's landmark role twenty-two years earlier when it aired the opening of *World of Tomorrow,* the first mass telecast in history (in less-than-natural black and white).[60] Like the Fair itself, this repeating of history, but new and improved, would serve as a win-win way for Moses to promote his event around the world and for Sarnoff to sell a lot of brand-new color TV sets and more advertising on subsidiary company NBC, which was leading the color-broadcasting way.

Throughout the Fair's run, RCA spread its televisual presence everywhere it could as a way to incite fairgoers to lug their old black-and-whites out of their living rooms and trade up to color. At its pavilion's Color Television Communications Center, visitors could watch a real television station at work and see themselves on color TV (actually twice, once "live" and, amazingly, a few seconds later on tape).

*52. NBC cameras were a visible presence at the Fair, airing live broadcasts on closed-circuit TVs to get consumers excited about buying new sets "in living color." Photo © Bill Cotter.*

The studio was linked by closed circuit to more than two hundred RCA color sets around the grounds (the Japanese and General Electric opted to use their own brands), airing concerts, taped interviews, exhibitors' institutional films, live coverage of pavilion dedications, and news, both Fair related and national, for a full twelve hours a day. Images of lost children too were broadcast on the sets, helping parents locate their gone-missing kids.[61] Soon after their trip to Flushing Meadows, millions of fairgoers would indeed be heading to appliance stores, excited at the prospect of watching *Bonanza* and some of their other favorite shows now being broadcast in living, peacocklike color.

## Futurama

How can a world's fair out-tomorrow one held on the very same spot called "World of Tomorrow"? That was a question WFC officials might have asked themselves as they planned for 1964, knowing full well that the 1939–40 fair remained a powerful memory for many. Not only did the previous New York fair carry a futuristic theme, but many of the predictions made by exhibitors—rockets, air-conditioned homes, a national network of superhighways, and others—had come true as well. When it came to tomorrow, the World of Tomorrow would be a tough act to follow, permanently ingrained in the public's consciousness as one of the seminal symbols of the future in the twentieth century. With postwar America's worship of science and technology as a cultural backdrop, however, the WFC and many exhibitors eagerly embraced the idea of the future, sprinkling visions of tomorrow all over the grounds. Most of these visions were, like the Fair as a whole, heavily commercial attempts by exhibitors to, in effect, brand the future. From General Cigar's Hall of Magic, where one could take in "the magic of the future," to the "Futorian" upholstered furniture in the Pavilion of American Interiors and the Fair's aluminum, prefab Atomedic (for Atomic Age Medicine) hospital, which the *New York Times* considered "as futuristic as a flying saucer," the world of tomorrow could be found in Flushing Meadows almost everywhere one looked. "The common man is being given a splendid opportunity to stand in awe at what he can do and comprehend, now and in the future," Barbara Tufty of the *Science News Letter* wrote shortly before the Fair opened. "The New York World's Fair offers many brief vistas into secrets of the earth and universe which science is probing and technology is using," a sentiment many visitors shared after their journey to Queens.[62]

The biggest, most popular, and most commercial presentation of the world of tomorrow at the Fair was, of course, GM's Futurama, its optimistic, even utopian perspective a ringing endorsement for what could be called corporate colonialism. Under its umbrella theme of General Motors—Many Minds and Many Hands Serving the Needs of Mankind, the company made the case that "mobility" in all its forms was the solution to the world's problems. Although

Futurama's fifteen-minute ride and "Avenue of Progress" included plenty of futuristic eye and ear candy like demonstrations of laser light and the sound of stars as "heard" by radio telescope to warrant their names, GM chairman Frederic G. Doner had told the exhibit's designers he wanted "no fantasies, nothing that can't be backed up with hard facts as a definite, practical possibility."[63] What Doner did want was for his company to be perceived as the future solver of many of the world's present problems, a messianic messenger that would deliver a better tomorrow through incredible leaps in transportation-based technology. If man could only devote all his energy and know-how to peaceful purposes rather than to war, Futurama told visitors, a more prosperous and more leisurely society lay ahead for all. Family farms, for example, would not only survive but thrive in the years ahead, a result of (GM-produced) push-button controls allowing farmers to plow, seed, cultivate, and harvest the land without taking a step outside. Traffic congestion, a problem GM had, of course, helped create through its aggressive dismantling of many cities' very efficient cable-car systems, would be solved by adding another level of highways in the air. By means of its extremely entertaining, easily understood, and overtly optimistic of the future, Futurama, with seventy thousand people a day moving through it in 463 three-passenger Fiberglas cars, became the most popular exhibit at the Fair and, probably, in world's fair history.[64]

Although the company can't be blamed for presenting a self-serving, auto-centric vision of tomorrow, how GM planned to achieve its utopia was, even for the times, myopic and ignorant. The 1964–65 version of Futurama was rooted in the missionary-style "conquest" and exploitation of various natural environments—jungle, desert, ocean, Antarctica, and outer space—for the expansion of man, an idea whose popularity had peaked in the nineteenth century or even earlier. "Everywhere you go," a brochure for Futurama stated, "you will see man conquering new worlds, to a large degree because he will have available to him new and better methods for transporting machines, materials and people." The ocean floor would be drilled for oil and mined for diamonds, GM proudly announced, while the ocean floor in the ride was "composed largely of coral removed by divers from deep beneath the Caribbean Sea." Even Antarctica would be "probed," its "frozen wastes" turned into "resources needed by a growing world population." In one segment, giant machines of the future invaded a primordial jungle, taking down ancient trees with red laser beams right out of *War of the Worlds*. The machine proceeded to gobble up the trees and undergrowth and then, miraculously, extract a four-lane highway from its rear. Cities would then rise out of this "wasteland," and resorts (Hotel Atlantis, naturally) would be built under the sea, each a solution to the growing population explosion as man established outposts in the most remote regions of the world.[65]

Futurama, like most exhibits at the Fair, was designed first and foremost not for education or even entertainment purposes but for commercial ones, intended

*53. As seen in GM's Futurama exhibit, "home, sweet home" in the new frontier might very well be underwater. Photo © Bill Cotter.*

to pave the way, so to speak, to make a favorable future a self-fulfilling prophecy. With nature now conveniently out of the way, GM explained, "an extensive freeway network [would] speed traffic to a park-like industrial sector or to festive recreational and cultural areas" (despite the less-than-speedy scenario actually taking place on the expressways right outside the fairgrounds).[66] Rather than offer solutions to the growing problems of pollution or the destruction of thriving urban neighborhoods owing to continued encroachment of highways, GM proposed that the introduction of the automobile into virgin land was the path to a better tomorrow. As well, despite the blossoming of the 1960s ecology movement (Rachel Carson's *Silent Spring* had been published in 1962), Futurama was completely blind to the role of jungles in creating oxygen or to the "ozone effect." Ironically, Futurama was not progressive but regressive, an all smoke-and-mirrors spectacle that looked backward versus forward in order to promote a way of life centered around and dependent on the combustion engine. The exhibit was in fact as dated as its name, an anachronism grossly out of touch with not only the future but the present as well. Still, visitors loved Futurama, more so than any other exhibit at the Fair, precisely because it solved major problems with a quick flick of its magic technological wand. The future of Futurama was, although fantastic, somehow comfortable and reassuring, just the thing visitors wanted to experience and feel before returning to the much more complex and challenging real world.

Ford's centerpiece exhibit, the Magic Skyway, on the other hand, was a harmless piece of Disney fluff, geared toward promoting its new models and moving product after or even during the Fair. Hoping to hear a resounding yes from visitors after posing its advertising question, "Is there a Ford in your future?" the company featured advanced research projects in progress at its labs as well as at its subsidiary, Philco. Like GM, which displayed experimental cars such as the Firebird IV, the GM-X (which looked like a cross between a Jaguar XKE and a rocket), and the Runabout (a three-wheeled vehicle designed specially for the woman of the house by incorporating a removable shopping cart), Ford offered dream cars up for inspection to position itself as a company with big plans for the future. Ford's star dream car was the Aurora, which Gene Bordinat, vice president and director of styling for the company, pointed out meant "beginning or rising light in morning." A "luxury lounge" station wagon (and forerunner of today's tricked-out minivans), the Aurora included a children's compartment, which could be "sound-isolated" from the rest of the car with a flick of the power-operated glass switch. The rocketlike car also had a communications console with a TV set, "sound recorder," and bar, the latter presumably for passengers versus drivers. Also built into the auto of the future was a swivel armchair and a curved sofa that could accommodate no fewer than four adults, turning the vehicle into a living or rec room on wheels.[67]

*54. One of a handful of experimental "dream" cars shown by GM and Ford that pointed the way to an exciting automotive future. Photo © Bill Cotter.*

Still trying to figure out the answer posed in *Why Johnny Can't Read,* the landmark 1955 book that exposed the fault lines in America's educational foundation, teachers and assorted experts also made the future an integral part of the Fair's Hall of Education. Located in the Industrial Area—a tip-off that the pavilion was corporately sponsored—the Hall of Education included a "School of Tomorrow" consisting of a scale model of what schools in a few decades might be like. The most forward-thinking views regarding the School of Tomorrow, however, could be found in a 128-page booklet the Hall of Education published, *Education in the Year 2000 A.D.*" The booklet, which could be purchased for one dollar, included predictions from various experts in the education field, some of them remarkably prescient and others less so. One prediction was that classroom desks would by the year 2000 be replaced by a "studysphere," an egg-shaped plastic pod in which each student would sit. In their own studysphere, students would have at their fingertips temperature and ion air controls "to make [a] chemical atmosphere favorable to study." Also in the unit was a set of state-of-the-art electronic equipment that included a television, film screen, microphone, tape recorder, and built-in stereo speakers (manufacturers of which all happened to be among the sponsors of the exhibit). Interestingly, also in the studysphere were computer controls and a keyboard that would serve as "a complete retrieval system for information from any part of the world," an eerily accurate forecast of what was to come. Prognosticators imagined that in three and a half decades, "great teachers" would lecture to students who were "plugged in," now able to learn "without leaving their homes." Although it was unclear exactly how all of it would happen, the designers of the studysphere had captured the essence of what would be the Internet and online learning programs, prompting at least one journalist to consider the cultural implications of such a device. "In the absence of a live teacher," wrote Fred M. Hechinger of the *New York Times* in July 1964, "children of tomorrow may have to throw spitballs at Central Control."[68]

Another section of *Education in the Year 2000 A.D.* included forecasts about what the schoolhouse of the future might look like. One scenario, which appeared as an illustration on the front cover of the booklet, was that kids would be learning their ABCs in a multistory cluster of flying saucers. Dr. Charles Raebeck, director of teacher education at Adelphi Suffolk College, foresaw it differently, predicting that schools would be located "on huge building sites so that as many of the dimensions of nature as possible (water, forests, flora, fauna, fish, wild life) will become an integral part of the life experiences of the child." Another expert, Dr. Leonard Price Stavisky, chairman of International Fair Consultants (the firm that planned the Hall of Education), was thinking big when it came to the School of Tomorrow, his version taking up fifty city blocks with an enrollment of 60,000 students. An architectural firm, Frederic P. Wiedersum Associates, believed that because school-building windows were apparently an obstacle to learning, they would be thrown out the proverbial window in the future in order "to provide a

completely controlled environment for concentration on tasks." Thankfully, however, Wiedersum Associates' plan allowed for open-air balconies so that students
could "step outside and relax as they enjoy the panoramic vista without having to travel down and leave the center." Dr. Raebeck also believed that many
of the "unnecessities" of life, notably advertising, would go away as the School
of Tomorrow produced smarter citizens. No mention was made of the fact that
*Education in the Year 2000 A.D.* included a three-page advertising section listing the
companies that sponsored the exhibit.[69]

One more thinly disguised commercial enterprise at the Hall of Education
was its on-site, twenty-five-by-seventy-foot "Playground of Tomorrow," or Playscape (a riff on "moonscape"), which let as many as 150 kids at a time crawl, jump,
climb, wiggle, or cling onto or through an array of domes, towers, and other "futuristic" forms. Playscape was a new product from the Playground Corporation
of America, which no doubt envisioned its own future as installing these play-
grounds of tomorrow all across the elementary school landscape. Although many
kids loved this new kind of playground (and welcomed the chance to take a break
from mom's and dad's exhibit choices), others were less impressed. Neil Millstein,
a ten year old from Yonkers, for example, conceded that the Playscape was "fun"
but that, if given a choice, he would "rather play baseball."[70]

With much of the Fair (and world's fairs in general) dedicated to the world of
tomorrow, social scientists, cultural critics, and other people in positions of leadership could not help but use the exposition as a timely opportunity to peer into the
more distant future. Three days before the Fair opened, for example, the *New York
Times* asked an all-star panel of such notables as anthropologist Margaret Mead
and English historian and author Arnold J. Toynbee to speculate on the state of
the world in the year 2000 (the latter predicting the demise of all forms of public
transportation as well as waitresses and nurses). Isaac Asimov, the famous writer
of science fiction (and "science fact," he liked to make clear), too mused about what
both life and a world's fair in the year 2014 might be like. In fifty years, Asimov
predicted, underground homes like the one at the 1964–65 Fair would be common,
"free from the vicissitudes of weather." And with most of us living beneath the
surface of the earth, the scientist happily concluded, "less space [would be] wasted
on actual human occupancy." Asimov went even further by proposing that people
would be living not only underground in 2014 but underwater as well. "The 2014
World's Fair will have exhibits in the deep sea with bathyscaphe liners carrying
men and supplies across and into the abyss," he prophesied. And just as living
underground would make weather irrelevant, living under the sea would have its
side benefits as well. "Underwater housing will have its attractions to those who
like water sports," the esteemed scientist wrote in all seriousness.[71]

In addition to some less-than-inspired futurism including a "large, clumsy,
slow-moving" robot housemaid uncannily like "Rosie" on *The Jetsons,* a show that
had already been on the air for a couple of years, Asimov also did anticipate a

"sight-sound" communications screen allowing for "studying documents and photographs and reading passages from books" at the 2014 fair, another Internet-like reference. He likewise expected that "wall screens will have replaced the ordinary [television] set" in a half century, a dead-on description of today's plasma TVs, and believed that 3-D television too would be a hit at the 2014 fair, much like black and white was at the 1939 fair and color in 1964 (an idea that engineers at RCA, GE, and Sony may want to start thinking about). A much different interpretation of the future was depicted in "Time Machine," an episode of *The Flintstones* that aired on ABC in 1965. In the show, Fred, Wilma, Barney, Betty, and the kids took a trip to the "Bedrock World's Fair" where, while visiting the Hall of Science, they met a scientist who sent them on a trip into the future using a time machine he had invented. The modern Stone Age family and company visited no fewer than four time periods, ultimately ending up in Flushing Meadows circa 1965.[72]

On October 16, 1965, the day before the exposition closed, VIPs gathered in Flushing Meadows to put the 1964–65 New York World's Fair into their own time machine. Just ten feet south of where a similar ceremony occurred a quarter century earlier, guests signed their names in a special book that was then put into a time capsule to be opened in five thousand years. The capsule was a replica of the one buried in 1940, when officials of that fair along with executives from the Westinghouse Electric Corporation buried circa 1930s artifacts and microfilmed records to document their time and place for the benefit of those individuals finding themselves in Queens in the seventieth century. Such things as a woman's hat, a slide rule, and an assortment of newspaper and magazine articles describing the (mostly sorry) state of world affairs at the turn of the decade were sunk into a fifty-foot steel shaft, not to be opened until the year 6939. Dozens of experts also deemed that the Lord's Prayer (in three hundred languages), a newsreel of a Miami fashion show, and a copy of the book *Gone with the Wind* were worth preserving for five thousand years. The location (in longitude and latitude) and a description of the time capsule's contents were recorded in a *Book of Records,* hundreds of copies of which were scattered around the world to help humans (or others) in five millennia find the thing and decipher what was inside.

Time Capsule II, also sponsored by Westinghouse, included twice as much material as the first, reflecting how much had occurred over the past twenty-five years. "In a quarter of a century," stated Westinghouse in its brochure for Time Capsule II, "man split the atom, danced the twist, ran the four-minute mile, scaled Mt. Everest, fought another World War and began to probe space and the seas."[73] The eighty-plus items were selected by a fourteen-person committee led by Dr. Leonard Carmichael, vice president of research and exploration for the National Geographic Society, with input solicited from fairgoers. Included in the seven-and-a-half-foot-long, torpedo-shaped, three hundred–pound metal (a new "super" alloy called Kromarc) capsule were such recent innovations as a few credit cards, a bikini, contact lenses, birth control pills, tranquilizers, a plastic heart valve, a pack

55. *Twenty-five years after it buried its first time capsule at a New York world's fair, Westinghouse buried a second, also to be opened in five thousand years. Westinghouse and fairgoers wondered what people in the seventieth century will make of a Beatles record and a bikini. Photo © Bill Cotter*

of filter cigarettes, an electric toothbrush, and a heat shield from Apollo 7. The arts too were represented, with such items as photographs of an Andrew Wyeth painting (Wyeth was a member of the selection committee) and Henry Moore sculpture, a microfilmed book by Ernest Hemingway and poetry by Dylan Thomas and Robert Frost, and a tape of a Danny Kaye television show. Records by the Beatles, Joan Baez, and Thelonious Monk were also part of the capsule—progressive music by artists that the WFC never considered inviting to the Fair because they were, ironically, a bit too ahead of their time. Photographs of important cultural figures of the 1940s and 1950s, including the rather odd triumvirate of Joe DiMaggio, Errol Flynn, and Adolf Hitler, were also tossed in the airtight glass envelope within the capsule. A photo of Robert Moses, who would definitely qualify as an important cultural figure of the last generation (or two), was, interestingly, not slipped into the capsule, an indication perhaps of his sullied reputation or, conversely, a sign that he and others knew that his legacy was already ensured.[74]

## Back to the Future

The long-range plans of the site of the Fair too were being given careful thought as the Fair wound down. Further encouraged by the attendance windfall of October, the WFC and the city's top politicians were making grandiose plans for a future permanent multibuilding science museum on the site. The WFC put a handsome booklet it had published, *Post Fair Expansion of the Hall of Science,* into the hands of influential New Yorkers to make their best case for a permanent museum in Flushing Meadows. "In this Age of Space," Paul Screvane argued in the preface, "our nation's ability to lead the Free World depends substantially upon our ability to maintain scientific leadership." The president of the city council also argued that "for New York City to continue to go without a Museum of Science would be unthinkable, the need for this Museum ma[king] prolonged debate—even the best-intentioned—indefensible." In his consultant's report, William D. Laurence served up his ambitious plans for the museum that called for a Hall of Discovery featuring exhibits relating to the pure sciences (astronomy, mathematics, physics, chemistry, biology) and a Hall of Inventions dedicated to the applied sciences (engineering, transportation, communication, space, medicine, nutrition, and public health). For a scientist, Laurence had an especially creative approach to how some of the exhibits should be presented: "Actors playing the parts of great scientists and inventors—such as Newton and Einstein, Edison, and Tesla—demonstrating each major discovery or invention made by them, would make such presentations not only highly instructive, but highly dramatic and entertaining as well."[75]

Its plans for the science museum in hand, which appeared to be inspired more by Disney than Darwin, the WFC started to eye different pavilions on the grounds like kids in a candy shop. Annexing the Space Park would be a great addition to the museum complex, Moses, Screvane, and the hall's board of trustees all agreed, as would the Ford Rotunda and the Federal Pavilion, even though the latter two were currently planned to be demolished after the Fair. Millions of dollars would have to be found for their rescue and conversion before the bulldozers started arriving, a challenging proposition to say the least given the Fair's troubled financial history. Moses was hoping to find a wealthy angel along the lines of Julius Rosenwald, whose huge donation to the Chicago Museum of Science and Industry got that great institution off the ground and continued to provide momentum. Even though it would be just a couple of blocks from a subway stop, as Screvane (a Queens resident) liked to point out, the future museum's provincial location was proving to be scaring off such an angel. With the necessary $5 million not forthcoming or even in sight, the Hall of Science closed its doors along with the rest of the pavilions when the Fair closed.[76]

Undaunted, in the spring of 1966 the hall's board of trustees put a new plan together to bring a great science museum to New York City. As important, they had a new champion, Mayor John Lindsay, who pledged that the city would pick up half of the initial $7.6 million needed to build it. A Nuclear Science Center with a real, operating reactor was now a major part of the vision for the Flushing Meadows complex, with the Atomic Energy Commission offering to fill the building with $3 or $4 million worth of exhibits. (It was no coincidence that the chairman of the Hall of Science's board, Dr. John R. Dunning, had been both a member of the team at Columbia University that first split the atom and a leader of the Manhattan Project.)[77] Another few million dollars was needed from individuals, private foundations, or government agencies to construct an education building for the complex, however, a giant chunk of change that remained elusive.[78]

Hoping to make a truly great scientific institution a self-fulfilling prophecy, the city reopened the Hall of Science on September 21, 1966, albeit a rather tired version of the one from the Fair.[79] Much more exciting was that, by the spring of 1967, baseball and soccer fields, an eighteen-hole pitch-and-putt golf course, a playground, and scenic paths had appeared in Flushing Meadows as the downsized but still alive WFC delivered on its promise to convert the grounds into a park. Just as he said he would, Moses (with cooperation from new parks commissioner August Hechscher) was building his park not from Fair revenues but with $6 million of TBTA money, taking full advantage of the law allowing the authority to develop land adjacent to highways and bridges. Another sign of new life springing up in the valley of ashes was the return of pheasants and rabbits to Flushing Meadows, the critters having scurried off when bulldozers arrived five years earlier to build the Fair.[80] On June 3, 1967, the fledgling 1,258-acre park was officially dedicated, making Flushing Meadows–Corona Park, as it became known, the largest in the city. WFC and city officials still dreamed of the area one day being "the Central Park of the twentieth century," however, with none other than Robert Moses offering an inspirational challenge at its dedication. "Guard it well, Mr. Mayor and Mr. Parks Commissioner," the now seventy-eight-year-old Moses advised. "The park has echoed to the sounds of many footsteps and voices, the world has beaten a path to its doors [and] now," the warrior closed, "we return it to the natives."[81]

Within just a year of its reopening, about a million people, many of them students, visited the Hall of Science, a clear indication that a science museum could thrive in the Netherlands of Queens. Also clear was the need for a new building designed specifically as a museum versus the existing one that was constructed for a world's fair, a much different kind of enterprise. Lindsay pushed hard for the new building in 1967, trying to squeeze a $10 million appropriation for it into the city's $1 billion budget. A new Hall of Science would, the mayor argued in June of that year, "attract to the city some of the foremost talents in the world of science [and] the best young students [as well as] act as a magnet for commercial and industrial developers." Helping Lindsay's cause was a report from the City Planning Commission that deemed the existing Hall of Science "unworkable," hardly worth salvaging for scrap. The hodgepodge of industrial—and government-sponsored—exhibits, the commission said in November 1967, was only made worse by the hall's poorly designed space that was, to boot, "an acoustical nightmare." The commission approved $10.8 million for a new building, with just approval from the Board of Estimate and the City Council to make the funds available.[82] It appeared that the original Hall of Science would soon be history, leaving just the Unisphere, the New York State building, the Singer Bowl, and, for the moment at least, the Federal Pavilion and post office (as well as the New York City building from 1939) as the only structures from the Fair standing.

In the quagmire that was and is New York City politics, however, the new Hall of Science project got stuck in the Flushing Meadows mud much like the scale reproduction of the *Santa María* back in 1964. It took a full two years for contracts to be awarded to build the infrastructure for the new building and another two years for the foundation to be completed, with the scale of the project continually decreasing as estimated costs to finish the job skyrocketed. By August 1971, the museum's board was hoping to put up just a large addition to the existing Hall of Science in late 1974 or early 1975 at a whopping cost of almost $25 million. As construction on the addition continued that summer, the hall was closed, its exhibits sent on the road throughout the state.[83] A year later, however, hopes for even the addition were all but dead as the now nearly broke city cut funding for all museums, parks, and schools, promising just $1 million to refurbish the hall and to keep the foundation for the addition from collapsing.[84] And despite the still lofty ambitions for the park, it appeared by the fall of 1972 that the ghost of Frederick Law Olmsted had little to worry about. The Federal Pavilion lay abandoned except for some squatters and, while the New York State Pavilion had a recently installed roller-skating rink, its two towers were empty with no high-end restaurant in sight. The Hall of Science remained closed, as did the Singer Bowl, and the park's zoo was losing money as fast as its seals went through fish. Still, some thirty-five thousand people visited the park on the average weekend day, making some, especially local residents, wonder how many people would come if the thing wasn't such an eyesore.[85]

When all hope looked lost, there was some good news in Flushing Meadows–Corona Park, at least for its once biggest draw, the Hall of Science. The hall had finally found a sugar daddy, with several grants from the Ford and Rockefeller Foundations making possible a gut renovation and all new exhibits. The new and improved (and free to the public) museum opened in November 1972, with a new planetarium made possible by a Charles Hayden Foundation grant added in the spring of 1973.[86] As before, however, the good news turned out to be just a short-term blip. Funds for the museum, even the $1 million that the city promised to keep the reinforced concrete building standing, disappeared as Mayor Lindsay found a new, more important pet cause—the overhaul of Yankee Stadium. "Everybody had big plans for us a few years ago and then the money we were supposed to get for refurbishing and expansion was diverted elsewhere," said a disappointed and angry Robert C. Reiley, the hall's executive director, in October 1975. Like the city, wealthy trustees of the museum were rapidly abandoning ship as the eleven-year-old buildings and grounds began to appear, as the *New York Times* put it, "as if they belong in the `before' picture photograph [*sic*] of an urban renewal project."[87]

Ironically, however, the Hall of Science was still bringing in almost a million visitors a year, making it the third-most-popular museum in the city and the third-most-popular science museum in the country. An ever evolving array of quasi-scientific exhibits, such as trucks from the 1920s and 1930s that were featured in the movies *The Godfather* and *The Valachi Papers,* was making the museum as fresh on the inside as its exterior was decrepit. Although Reiley and his fifty employees remained committed to giving "the public a better understanding of what science and technology really is" (an interesting echo of the Fair's theme), even staffers had begun to refer to their workplace as the "Hole of Science."[88]

The Federal Pavilion, which had yet to be used for anything after the Fair, was about to become a literal hole as demolition plans drew near in 1976. Local civic groups and the occasional entrepreneur tried to save the $14 million Charles Luckman building, coming forward with an assortment of proposals for potential new uses (all of them called by Moses "an extremely dubious business"). The city agreed with Moses, and the mammoth building was soon razed, making room for what would be the National Tennis Center's Arthur Ashe Stadium twenty-five years later (located right next door to Louis Armstrong Stadium, which was in a previous life the Singer Bowl).[89]

The saga of the Hall of Science continued through the next decade. In 1980, the building was closed again, not for lack of funding but for yet another major renovation as the city's finances improved. Although it was ready to go in November 1983 under the Koch administration, cultural commissioner (and former Miss America) Bess Myerson blocked the reopening, claiming that the museum's board was not fit to run it. An independent report commissioned by the city also determined, surprise, surprise, that the museum's location in Queens was "an incontrovertible minus," fueling a contentious feud between Myerson and Queens borough president Donald R. Manes (who correctly pointed out that next-door-neighbor Shea Stadium was doing just fine, thank you).[90] Myerson won the battle, however, keeping the Hall of Science closed as millions more dollars were spent on further renovations and additions. Rather than rely exclusively on "experts," the norm for museum design, the new director of the hall, Dr. Alan J. Friedman, actively solicited input from kids to make sure the toughest critics of all liked what they saw, especially the many hands-on, interactive exhibits.[91]

Finally, on July 30, 1986, the Hall of Science once again opened its doors, with Myerson referring to the museum as "an almost brand-new test-tube." "For the first time," she proudly announced, "the much-stated goal of making this institution a world-class center for science and technology is more than pleasant but empty rhetoric." Critics were almost as gung-ho as Myerson over what had sprung up in Flushing Meadows. "Although it takes 40 minutes to reach the new New

York Hall of Science from midtown Manhattan," wrote Malcolm W. Browne of the *New York Times*, "a traveler is amply rewarded for the inconvenience." Buoyed by his shiny new toy in Queens, Mayor Koch announced an $80 million, ten-year restoration effort for Flushing Meadows–Corona Park. Almost a half century after Robert Moses had first proposed it, the city had decided to put in place, in the words of a spokesman for the mayor, "a master plan for the conversion of a fairground into a park."[92] Major changes had occurred in and around the park since the last fair, allowing others to finally grasp the master builder's vision for the huge piece of land. The U.S. Open at the tennis center was a roaring success (the most highly attended and profitable sports event in the world, in fact), and, when a true miracle in Queens took place—the once Keystone Kops–like New York Mets winning the 1986 World's Series—the much-maligned borough had another reason to pronounce itself as a home of champions.

After the New York City Building was converted into the Queens Museum, further raising the park's profile, Koch and parks commissioner Henry Stern knew that the time was ripe to take the park to the next level. The city, it seemed, was finally ready to bury the ghosts of two fairs past in order to move into the future. "Now we're trying to give it some identity and unity, and make a park out of what has been a collection of structures and plains," said Stern in November 1987. Grass had already been planted over the paths and roadways of the two fairs, new and better signs inside and outside the park were going up, and a promenade for strollers along the waterfront had been installed. Footbridges into the park from nearby neighborhoods (not just Flushing and Corona but also Forest Hills, Elmhurst, Kew Gardens, and Jamaica) were planned to allow residents to walk over Moses's beloved spider web of highways.[93] By 1990, eight million people a year were barbecuing, Rollerblading, and otherwise frolicking in, as Fitzgerald described it sixty-five years earlier, the "fantastic farm where ashes [grew] like wheat into ridges and hills and grotesque gardens." Flushing Meadows was rising like a phoenix out of the literal ashes, second only to Central Park in number of visitors, as immigrants infused the area with new energy and life. Asian Americans in particular were making the neighborhood resemble, at least in spirit, the Fair's International Area. Japanese groceries, Chinese supermarkets, Korean bakeries, and Indian sari shops were visible signs that this part of Queens had become one of the most culturally diverse places on the planet. "Flushing nowadays is a virtual world's fair of its own, a kaleidoscope of scenes," observed Richard F. Shepard of the *New York Times* in April 1989, as real an example of peace through understanding as could be imagined.[94]

Today, Flushing Meadows–Corona Park is more alive than ever. Every spring, thousands of local Latinos flood the park's soccer fields, their grass turned into dirt by fall because of such heavy use (an interesting twist of what Moses envisioned). With its plays, concerts, puppet shows, and annual Latino festival, Queens Theater in the Park holds court in the restored Theaterama, now one of the borough's leading performing-arts centers. Expansion plans that would do tribute to Johnson's architectural style are now under way for the theater because of its popularity among the borough's immigrant communities.[95] The zoo, restored in 1992, sits happily in what was the Transportation Area (using Buckminster Fuller's geodesic Winston Churchill Center as the aviary), complemented by a very respectable Wildlife Center (and vintage carousel from Coney Island). The Unisphere was restored in 1994 and designated a city landmark the following year, its cleaned-up fountain no longer a giant trash bin and perfect breeding ground for mosquitoes. Another overhaul of the globe is in the works to keep the fountain gushing all summer rather than just on special occasions (and to fix the leaks in the forty-year-old pipes that have a habit of spilling water into the basement of the Queens Museum of Art).[96] The Top of the Fair is now Terrace on the Park, a highly profitable banquet and catering hall owned by the city, while Philip Johnson's tentless "Tent of Tomorrow" and towers lay in ghostly ruins, fodder for the occasional sci-fi movie.

The Hall of Science, meanwhile, is bigger and better than ever, having gone through yet another round of major renovations in 1992, reopening in 1996 with a "Science Playground" added the following year.[97] Consistent with its once-every-decade reinvention, an ambitious $89 million expansion was recently completed at the hall, adding a fifty-five thousand–square-foot "Science City" that will help the museum continue to compete for the public's attention. New high-tech exhibits complement old standbys like "Mathematica" (originally created in 1961 by the Eames brothers for IBM's pavilion at the Seattle fair), and the refurbished outdoor rocket park looks as good as new. The nonprofit (but no longer free) institution may still be outclassed by science museums in Philadelphia and Chicago, but its hands-on interactivity is highly regarded if not legendary in the field. And despite the trend toward "edutainment," the Hall of Science really is about science, not willing to compromise its mission in order to attract a broader audience. With its 250,000 visitors a year, the Hall of Science is teaching kids things they are typically not learning in school, keeping the original vision of the 1964–65 New York World's Fair alive for future generations.[98]

# Conclusion

ALTHOUGH HIS WORLD'S FAIR may very well have put an end to his already damaged career, Robert Moses, as usual, is no doubt having the last laugh in the big construction site in the sky. Largely obscured in the critical maelstrom that has swirled around Moses and the Fair as a whole is that he achieved much of his original vision for that particular piece of New York City and fulfilled his primary purpose for taking the job. A full century after seeing the valley of ashes and its potential as a teenager, Moses's dream park is now no longer a dream. It may not rival Central Park in beauty and grandeur or bear his name, but, who knows, maybe in another hundred years it will do both. Stranger things have certainly happened in Flushing Meadows.

Besides deftly using the 1939–40 and 1964–65 New York world's fairs as a massive, long-term public works program to beautify a big, ugly chunk of Queens, Moses can also be credited with his constant claim that critics don't know anything, or maybe it's that they simply know too much. Critics of the Fair, both at the time and to this day, have focused on its political and business mess; profoundly conservative tone; overabundance of kitschy, over-the-top commercialism; and absence of many European nations. What has been largely left out of the Fair's story, however, are individuals' experiences, which were not only joyous at the time but often left a deep, lasting impact for the rest of their lives. Even more significant than the effect that the Fair had on adults was its effect on children and teenagers, something that Ilene Sheppard observes. The 1964–65 New York Fair, Sheppard believes, "permeated the memory of an entire generation," showing young baby boomers that the world was a big, wonderful place where anything was possible.[1] The Fair may have marked the end of postwar America's innocence, but, for the tens of millions of kids who went, it also planted a seed of the possibility to achieve great things. It may be safe to say that some of baby boomers' überachievement ethos that hit full stride in the 1980s is a result of their visit or visits to the Fair.

There were, then, really two Fairs in Queens in 1964 and 1965, or at least two constructions of its past. The first is steeped in its official memory—the business enterprise that lost money, overcharged exhibitors, and offended the intellectual and aesthetic elite. The other can be found in its popular memory—the experience that most visitors found thoroughly enjoyable if not enthralling, that sparked imaginations and reshaped people's vision of the world. It is more this second Fair that we should better remember, as it is this one that has endured and is still relevant today. It is also long overdue that the Fair be recognized for how successful it was based on sheer numbers. The event was the most highly attended, and thus the most popular, American world's fair of all time, a fact that has somehow been obscured by its many sideshow shenanigans. With so much attention paid to the eighteen million people who did not show up, not nearly enough attention has been paid to the fifty-two million people who did. From this perspective, then, the 1964–65 New York World's Fair was not only a huge success but arguably one of the most popular events of all time (World War II may have indeed been the "good war," but I would hesitate to call it "popular").

Although credit for the 1964–65 New York World's Fair has been sorely lacking these past forty years, criticism of it has also been, I believe, largely misdirected. What was most regrettable about the Fair is not things like the Broadwayized *Pietà*, the underground home with the painted nature scenes, or the "atomic Coney Island" that was Atomsville, USA, but that more progressive ideas and activities were not allowed to penetrate Moses's safe bubble in Queens. Filtering out much of the real world in order to create the happiest place this side of Disneyland came at a cost, of course, the cost being the exclusion of people and things that Moses believed threatened the Fair's orderly universe. Very popular musicians of the day, for example, were right in the neighborhood throughout the Fair's run but were never invited to Flushing Meadows, something that not only compromised the event's mission to showcase "man's achievement in an expanding universe" but also was a bad business decision because such artists would have undoubtedly boosted attendance. Why did Moses allow wax Beatles to appear at the Fair, one might ask, but not the real ones (who played nearby Forest Hills tennis stadium during season one and were reportedly thrilled to fly over the fairgrounds by helicopter)? Why wasn't there more jazz, rhythm and blues, or folk music at the Fair? (Ray Charles played Carnegie Hall at the beginning of the Fair's run in May 1964, whereas Bob Dylan and Judy Collins had gigs there at the end of the run in October 1965; other folkies including Pete Seeger and Peter, Paul, and Mary played at the Forest Hills Music Festival in the summer of 1964.)[2] More to the point, how could a world's fair predicated on the idea of progress be so nonprogressive? As itself a giant time capsule, the Fair could have done a better job in capturing the popular culture of the times. Rather than its ticky-tacky architecture, its epic artificiality, or its finishing in the red, the Fair's real failure was that it fell short of its full potential to educate people about the world around them by not embracing a wider range of human expression, especially that of youth culture and African Americans.

Still, even with this major fault, the Fair lives on as a seminal moment in millions of people's lives and in the nation's history. The Fair did not turn out to be a three hundredth birthday party for New York City, as originally conceived, but it was a party nonetheless, a party celebrating what had turned out to be, in Henry Luce's words, "the American century." It was the last hurrah for a nation that had triumphed over adversity and, by doing so, had fulfilled its destiny of becoming the "city on the hill." As America emerged from its postwar cocoon, it was the end of its innocence, with a much different chapter in its history soon to be written.

Notes

Bibliography

Index

# Notes

## Introduction

1. "The greatest event in history" claim may not be as far-fetched as it seems. In his eminently readable *The Devil in the White City: Murder, Magic, and Madness at the Fair That Changed America,* Erik Larson claims that the Paris fair of 1867 (Pavillon de Paris et Industries de France) "had drawn more people than any peaceful event in history" (60). The 1964–65 Fair drew many millions more.

2. Ilene Sheppard, "Icons and Images: The Cultural Legacy of the Fair," 167.

3. Robert W. Rydell, John E. Findling, and Kimberly D. Pelle, *Fair America: World's Fairs in the United States,* 105–6; Arthur Gelb, *City Room,* 386; Sam Roberts, "Sports and the Wide World of Tomorrow," *New York Times,* Apr. 27, 2005, B1.

4. Robert Stone, "The Prince of Possibility," *New Yorker,* June 14 and 21, 2004, 88. A key leg of Ken Kesey and his Merry Pranksters' journey in their magical bus tour was to the Fair in 1964, documented, of course, in Tom Wolfe, *The Electric Kool-Aid Acid Test.*

5. Jon Margolis, *The Last Innocent Year: America in 1964—the Beginning of the Sixties,* xi.

6. Like Moses, the head of the 1893 World Columbian Exposition in Chicago, Daniel Burnham, hired a large private police force, the Columbian Guard, to quickly nip any crime and vice at the fair in the bud (Larson, *Devil in the White City,* 137–38).

7. Morris Dickstein, "From the Thirties to the Sixties: The World's Fair in Its Own Time," 34.

8. Margolis, *Last Innocent Year,* vii.

9. Marc H. Miller, "Something for Everyone: Robert Moses and the Fair," 56. At 1,255 acres, Flushing Meadows–Corona Park is the city's second biggest, the largest being the more than 2,700-acre Pelham Bay Park in the Bronx. (Flushing Meadows–Corona Park is home to what is now the city's largest lake, the 84-acre Meadow Lake.) Although Central Park comes in at only 843 acres, its land value of course makes the value of its larger Bronx and Queens siblings seem puny.

10. See Susan Strasser, *Satisfaction Guaranteed: The Making of the American Mass Market.*

11. See David Gelernter's *1939: The Lost World of the Fair* for an interesting take on that fair and E. L. Doctorow's *World's Fair* for a compelling novel with the "World of Tomorrow" as backdrop.

12. The 1939–40 New York Fair would prove to be the last for almost a decade, as the war put all international expositions, BIE sanctioned or otherwise, on hold. There were no fewer than twelve official BIE expositions between 1947 and 1957 (1947 Paris, 1949 Port-au-Prince, 1949 Stockholm, 1949 Lyon, 1951 Lille, 1953 Jerusalem, 1953 Rome, 1954 Naples, 1955 Turin, 1955 Helsingborg, 1956 Belt Dagon [Israel], and 1957 Berlin), none of them especially memorable.

13. See Robert H. Haddow, *Pavilions of Plenty: Exhibiting American Culture Abroad in the 1950s.*

14. Ibid., 74.

15. Rydell, Findling, and Pelle, *Fair America,* 103–5.

## 1. The Greatest Event in History

1. Philip Benjamin, "Blending of Ideas in 2 Opposing Minds Went into Creation of the Exposition," *New York Times,* Apr. 22, 1964, 22. Interestingly, the 1939–40 New York was reportedly born after another father, Joseph Shadgren of Queens, asked his child what she had learned in school that day.

2. World's fairs, especially American ones, were typically tied to an important historical anniversary. The 1904 Louisiana Purchase Exposition in St. Louis commemorated the centennial of the signing of the fifteen million–dollar real estate deal between Thomas Jefferson and France that doubled the size of the nation, Chicago's 1893 World's Columbian Exposition celebrated the 400th anniversary of Columbus's arrival in the New World, and the 1939 fair recognized the 150th anniversary of the inauguration of George Washington. Interestingly, however, the 300th anniversary of New York celebration all but evaporated as the 1964–65 Fair took shape. Two months before the Fair's opening, in fact, Mayor Wagner stated that he did not want the city's anniversary to "interfere" with the event.

3. Martin Mayer, "Ho Hum, Come to the Fair," *Esquire,* Oct. 1963, 117. A committee of prominent businessmen in a particular community has always been the primary engine to get a world's fair off the ground. Larson notes that this situation was indeed the case for the 1893 World's Columbian Exposition in Chicago (*Devil in the White City,* 16).

4. "How New York Won World's Fair," *Business Week,* Nov. 7, 1959, 70–71.

5. Run by "Fishhooks" McCarthy, the Corona Dump received about a hundred railroad carloads of ash (produced by Brooklyn's coal-burning furnaces) every day. In cahoots with the Democrats of Tammany Hall, McCarthy and his Brooklyn Ash Removal Company had a great run until 1934 when the city cleaned up its act and the site (Roberts, "Sports and the Wide World of Tomorrow" [see chap. 1, n. 3]).

6. Rydell, Findling, and Pelle, *Fair America,* 13.

7. "Beckoning the Billions," *Newsweek,* Nov. 9, 1959, 37. See Larson, *Devil in the White City,* for a fascinating account of the battle over which city would host the 1893 fair (16–18, 31–33).

8. "Beckoning the Billions."

9. "U.S. Aid to '64 Fair Opposed in Senate," *New York Times,* Sept. 12, 1961, 1.

10. "Anyone for $100,000?" *Newsweek,* Dec. 28, 1959, 54.

11. New York City required its employees to retire at age seventy, but Moses was able to hold his eight city jobs through a "special extension."

12. Robert A. Caro, *The Power Broker: Robert Moses and the Fall of New York;* "1964: Who'll Be Away at the Fair?" *Newsweek,* Feb. 27, 1961, 73; "1964 Fair Slogs Ahead," *Business Week,* Jan. 12, 1963, 103–4; "The World of Already," *Time,* June 5, 1964, 40–52.

13. Caro, *Power Broker,* 1059–60.

14. Ira Henry Freeman, "Originator of Fair Dropped by Moses," *New York Times,* Apr. 9, 1960, 6. Moses, who later referred to Kopple as "that fellow who had something to do with the idea of a fair," explained, "These fellows that started it had to get out, so I could have a free hand. They were not the kind of people I would hire. They had to go, and they were paid" (Benjamin, "Blending of Ideas").

15. Richard J. H. Johnston, "Moses Is Elected President of Fair," *New York Times,* May 25, 1960, 2.

16. Caro, *Power Broker,* 1060, 1091. Moses's secretary, Hazel Tappen, had been with him since the 1920s (George W. S. Trow, *Within the Context of No Context,* 107).

17. "Fun in New York," *Time,* May 1, 1964, 40–41.

18. Alfred E. Clark, "Thomas J. Deegan Jr., Organizer of '64–65 World's Fair, Dies at 67," *New York Times,* Nov. 17, 1977, 90.

19. Richard Goldstein, "Charles Poletti Dies at 99; Aided War-Ravaged Italy," *New York Times,* Aug. 10, 2002, A11.

20. Susan Heller Anderson, "W. E. Potter, 83, Army Engineer," *New York Times,* Dec. 7, 1988, D24. Potter met Walt Disney at the Fair and, right after the event ended, joined the Disney organization where he oversaw construction of the water, sewer, and power systems for Disney World in Orlando.

21. Charles Grutzner, "Moses Sees Fair Lasting 2 Years," *New York Times,* Apr. 18, 1960, 8.

22. Kennett Love, "'64 Fair to Resort to `Skyscrapers,'" *New York Times,* Aug. 5, 1960, 1.

23. "U.S. World Fairs Start Beating Their Drum," *Business Week,* Apr. 22, 1961, 92ff.

24. "So Long at the Fair," *Time,* Mar. 9, 1962, 80–81.

25. "World's Fair '64: A Preview," *Newsweek,* Jan. 13, 1964, 43–47. Trow notes that "people from England and France were the reverse of important to Mr. Moses," especially because these countries opted to abide by the BIE's rules and declined their invitations to build pavilions at the Fair (*Within the Context,* 105).

26. Thomas Buckley, "World's Fair Forecast Is Rosy, with Profits for All–Even New York City," *New York Times,* Jan. 6, 1964, 78.

27. C. Gervin Hayden, "The Hard-Sell Fair," *Nation,* Nov. 2, 1963, 275.

28. Martin Arnold, "Fair Offers Plan for Park System," *New York Times,* Jan. 20, 1964, 5.

29. Charles G. Bennett, "Council Stalls Fair's Park Plan," *New York Times,* Mar. 11, 1964, 6. "Moses had the idea of an unbroken ribbon of green extending across Queens," observed Flushing Park historian Richard N. Post in 2003, with the fairgrounds as "the crown jewel" (John Hanc, "Flushing's Grandeur," *Newsday,* Aug. 14, 2003, B3). Trow (and others) has gone even further about Moses's agenda, claiming that he "had no particular interest in what actually happened at the Fair" (*Within the Context,* 107).

30. Joe McCarthy, "Moses (Robert) and the Promised Land," *Reader's Digest,* Sept. 1964, 117–21; Miller, "Something for Everyone," 46. This exhibition was not the first time that a man with a vision wanted to use a world's fair to create a great park out of a less-than-scenic piece of land. Brought in to design and landscape the 1893 World's Columbian Exposition in Chicago, Frederick Law Olmsted "envisioned transforming Jackson Park from a desert of sand and stagnant pools into a park unlike any other in the nation" (Larson, *Devil in the White City,* 53).

31. Caro, *Power Broker,* 1082–87.

32. "'Billion-Dollar' Affair," *New York Times,* Jan. 16, 1961, 7. This event was the second time Moses was leveraging a world's fair to improve a bridge, having used funds earmarked for the 1939 fair to construct the Whitestone Bridge (which was completed twenty-four hours before opening day of that exposition).

33. Gay Talese, "Fair Is Heralded as Biggest Event," *New York Times,* Sept. 13, 1962, 7.

34. "2 Million Advance Tickets Sold for '64 World's Fair," *New York Times,* Nov. 8, 1963, 7.

35. "3.8 Million Tickets to the World's Fair Are Sold in Advance," *New York Times,* Dec. 31, 1963, 8.

36. Joseph Lelyveld, "Sale of Tickets to World's Fair Tops $35 Million," *New York Times,* Mar. 3, 1964, 3.

37. "Triumph for the Fair," *Business Week,* Mar. 21, 1964, 111ff.

38. Philip Benjamin, "Moses Lists Work Required for Fair," *New York Times,* Aug. 12, 1959, 1.

39. "$120 Million Roads to Fair to Be Ready 90 Days in Advance," *New York Times,* Nov. 29, 1961, 2; Caro, *Power Broker,* 736–37. The Fair's impact on Queens's transportation grid and relationship to the new next-door Shea Stadium closely paralleled the infrastructural changes made for the previous fair, specifically the connecting of Grand Central Parkway to the new Moses-built Triborough Bridge and completion of what would be LaGuardia Airport (Roberts, "Sports and the Wide World of Tomorrow").

40. "Moses in the Wilderness," *Time,* Oct. 19, 1962, 70.

41. Although the NYCTA added new subway cars, Moses vetoed proposed new lines leading to the Fair because, according to Caro, they would allow low-income people, especially African Americans and Puerto Ricans, to easily get to his future park (*Power Broker,* 1086–87). Here Moses was breaking with world's fair tradition; Chicago's elevated L train was extended so that citizens of that city could more easily get to the exposition (Larson, *Devil in the White City,* 100).

42. "64 Fair Plans Set by Transit Board," *New York Times,* Apr. 27, 1960, 1.

43. "Red IRT Cars Tested on Runs to the Fair," *New York Times,* May 1, 1962, 2.

44. Peter Kihss, "IRT Line to Fair Gets 20 New Cars," *New York Times,* Sept. 27, 1963, 1.

45. Anna Petersen, "Moses Sees Tivoli as Model for Fair," *New York Times,* Aug. 21, 1960, 3.

46. "Moses Abandons Tivoli Fair Plan," *New York Times,* Oct. 26, 1960, 1.

47. "'64 Fair Layout Ready," *New York Times,* Nov. 3, 1960, 5.

48. Edith Evans Asbury, "Designers Quit Fair in a Dispute on Plan," *New York Times,* Dec. 3, 1960, 2. E. H. Praeger claimed the design committee did not resign in protest but was simply finished with its job ("Designs for World's Fair," letter to editor, *New York Times,* Dec. 24, 1960, 5).

49. Asbury, "Designers Quit Fair in a Dispute on Plan"; "U.S. World Fairs Start Beating Their Drum."

50. "So Long at the Fair."

51. Caro, *Power Broker,* 1092.

52. "World's Fair '64: A Preview."

53. Caro, *Power Broker,* 1092.

54. "1964 Fair Slogs Ahead."

55. Ira Wolfert, "Coming: The Most Marvelous Fair Ever!" *Reader's Digest,* Jan. 1964, 91–95.

56. "80% of Space at '64 Fair Committed Report Says," *New York Times,* Apr. 22, 1963, 4; John Brooks, "Onward and Upward with the Arts: Diplomacy at Flushing Meadow [*sic*]," *New Yorker,* June 1, 1963, 41–42; "Progress Report," *Time,* Feb. 8, 1963, 36. Many of the buildings constructed at the Fair were surprisingly handicapped friendly, way before laws were passed to mandate wheelchair accessibility. Not coincidentally, the disabled and blind were frequent and enthusiastic visitors to the Fair ("Handicapped Get Help at the Fair," *New York Times,* May 2, 1965, 79).

57. "New York's Billion Dollar Dream Fair," *Life,* Jan. 17, 1964, 38–50+.

58. *1965 Official Guide: New York World's Fair,* 185.

59. "1964: Who'll Be Away at the Fair?"; Mayer, "Ho Hum, Come to the Fair"; "World's Fair '64: A Preview."

60. "U.S. World Fairs Start Beating Their Drum."

61. Hayden, "The Hard-Sell Fair."

62. "Fair Outlook," *Newsweek,* Apr. 20, 1964, 68.

63. "New York City" folder, F128 T792.382, New-York Historical Society (hereafter cited as NYHS); Sheldon J. Reaven, "New Frontiers: Science and Technology at the Fair," 78; Sheppard, "Icons and Images," 180.

64. Philip Benjamin, "'Taken in' by Moses, Hunt Says," *New York Times*, Oct. 25, 1963, 3.

65. John Keating, "Wide Show Range for the Fair," *New York Times*, Jan. 14, 1962, sec. 2, p. 6.

66. Robert Fontaine, "No Fair," *Atlantic Monthly*, May 1960, 90–91; Hayden, "The Hard-Sell Fair"; "So Long at the Fair."

67. "World's Fair '64: A Preview"; Dickstein, "From the Thirties to the Sixties," 28.

68. A wax museum was a big hit at the 1958 Brussels fair, hence WFC officials' eagerness to have one in New York.

69. Wolfert, "Coming: The Most Marvelous Fair Ever!" Thousands of fairgoers in fact made worship part of their Fair experience on a daily basis, especially on Sundays (Bernard Weinraub, "Thousands Combine Worship with a Visit to the World's Fair," *New York Times*, Apr. 27, 1964, 20).

70. "Mormons Accept Fair Site," *New York Times*, Oct. 20, 1962, 6; Gereon Zimmerman, "N.Y. World's Fair Preview," *Look*, Feb. 11, 1964, 17–32.

71. "Bible—Open or Shut?" *Newsweek*, Sept. 17, 1962, 69.

72. Philip Benjamin, "Dispute Flares on Film for Fair," *New York Times*, Nov. 7, 1963, 1; Harry Gilroy, "Pavilion to Show Disputed Film," *New York Times*, Apr. 4, 1964, 5; "Fair Bids Protestants Cancel Film Showing Jesus as a Clown," *New York Times*, Apr. 9, 1964, 2.

73. Hayden, "The Hard-Sell Fair." Although more than a half-million kids were admitted free to the 1939–40 New York fair when they came with their teachers, group discounts for schoolchildren were not a standard policy for world's fairs. In fact, the recent Seattle fair did not discount by age at all, charging $1 admission to both adults and kids.

74. Leonard Buder, "Moses Rejects Plea to Cut Rate at Fair for City Students," *New York Times*, Sept. 28, 1963, 4.

75. Richard P. Hunt, "Aldrich Plans $762,500 Drive to Subsidize City Pupils at Fair," *New York Times*, Oct. 2, 1963, 5; Clayton Knowles, "Mayor Asks Fair to Cut Pupil Fees," *New York Times*, Oct. 3, 1963, 2.

76. Leonard Buder, "Cut Rate at Fair Backed by Gross," *New York Times*, Oct. 5, 1963, 2; "Moses Yields a Bit on Fair Admissions," *New York Times*, Oct. 8, 1963, 5.

77. Charles G. Bennett, "Moses Rejects Council Parley on 25c Fee for Pupils at Fair," *New York Times*, Oct. 10, 1963, 2. Moses was following the Scrooge-like path of the directors of the 1893 Chicago fair who rejected Mayor Carter Harrison's request that the city's poor children be admitted for free for one day. Coming to the rescue, Larson wrote, was Buffalo Bill, who declared a free "Waif's Day" at his "Wild West Show," throwing in a gratis train ticket and all the candy and ice cream one could eat for some fifteen thousand "waifs" (*Devil in the White City*, 251).

78. "Moses Says Fair May Cut '65 Rate," *New York Times*, Oct. 24, 1963, 8; "10% Pay Cut Urged for Fair Officers to Allow Lower Pupil Rates," *New York Times*, Oct. 27, 1963, 2.

79. Clayton Knowles, "Beame Urges City Subsidy on Fair Tickets for Pupils," *New York Times*, Nov. 4, 1963, 3; Knowles, "Mayor Rejects Fair-Fee Subsidy," *New York Times*, Nov. 5, 1963, 7; Charles G. Bennett, "Fair Will Admit Pupils for 25c When They Attend in Groups," *New York Times*, Dec. 4, 1963, 6.

80. David Anderson, "1684 Flushing 'Bulrushes' Deed Lets Mohawks Enter Fair Free," *New York Times*, Mar. 19, 1964, 6; Martin Arnold, "Mohawk at Fair? Rival Asks, How?" *New York Times*, Mar. 30, 1964, 5.

81. "World's Fair Urged to Employ Negroes," *New York Times*, June 15, 1961, 5.

82. "Urban League Lays Bias to '64–65 Fair," *New York Times*, Feb. 9, 1962, 4.

83. "Powell Inquiry Set on Negroes at Fair," *New York Times*, Mar. 12, 1962, 4.

84. "Negro Gets Post at Fair Here," *New York Times*, Apr. 21, 1962, 1. Rydell, Findling, and Pelle note the long history of discrimination against African Americans in the history of world's fairs in

the United States, which included a lack of representation on committees and commissions, racially degrading exhibits, the lack of an opportunity to demonstrate their past achievements, and bias in employment practices (*Fair America,* 23–24, 29–30, 39, 83–85, 88–90, 94–95, 98). See Caro, *Power Broker,* for (much) more on Moses and the matter of race.

85. "Integration 'Drive-in' Set for Fair Grounds," *New York Times,* July 11, 1963, 3.

86. "Negroes to Push Picketing in City in Drive for Jobs," *New York Times,* July 29, 1963, 4. Not only was discrimination against African Americans in employment at previous world's fairs a common occurrence, but blacks often protested the unfair practices. Black newspapers criticized the lack of African American construction workers hired by directors of the 1904 St. Louis fair, for example, and Mrs. Booker T. Washington (whose husband a month earlier had, ironically, given a speech at the fair to a packed house of National Education Association members) moved her meeting of the National Association of Colored Women off the grounds in protest of the lack of black women hired. Local black leaders also canceled the planned "Negro Day" at the fair when a black National Guard regiment was denied access to the barracks on the grounds. The racial tension at the 1904 St. Louis fair, combined with outbreaks of race-related violence across the nation, made many African Americans stay away from the event (Mary Delach Leonard, "Fair's Policy Was Diversity, but in Practice It Fell Short," *St. Louis Post-Dispatch,* Apr. 25, 2004, WF11).

87. "U.N. Is Picketed on Jobs at Fair," *New York Times,* Aug. 13, 1963, 5; Homer Bigart, "City Rights Panel Summons Unions to Racial Inquiry," *New York Times,* Aug. 14, 1963, 4.

88. Junius Griffin, "N.A.A.C.P. Plans Protests May 18 All Over State," *New York Times,* Apr. 13, 1964, 1.

89. "Out of the Bull Rushes," *Time,* Jan. 17, 1964, 52–57.

90. "Final Push for New York Fair," *Business Week,* Apr. 27, 1963, 31.

91. "Kennedy Starts Clock for Fair," *New York Times,* Apr. 23, 1963, 1.

92. "Another," *New Yorker,* Aug. 10, 1963, 15.

93. "Small World," *New Yorker,* Aug. 31, 1963, 20–21; John C. Devlin, "Dinosaurs Seen Coming into City," *New York Times,* Oct. 16, 1963, 1, 3, 6; Philip Benjamin, "General Electric Pavilion Sheds Colored Light on World's Fair," *New York Times,* Jan. 30, 1964, 5; Caro, *Power Broker,* 1094.

94. "A Billion-Dollar Fair Takes Shape," *U.S. News and World Report,* Dec. 30, 1963, 47–49; Clayton Knowles, "Beame Is Hopeful on City Revenues," *New York Times,* Sept. 11, 1963, 1.

95. Joseph C. Ingraham, "Garage Fees in City to Rise for the Fair," *New York Times,* Feb. 27, 1964, 6; John S. Wilson, "Cabaret Business Nears Low Point," *New York Times,* Mar. 12, 1964, 1.

96. "City Succumbs to 'Fair Fever,'" *Business Week,* Mar. 21, 1964, 120+; "Fair Outlook."

97. "World's Fair '64: A Preview"; "Fair Outlook."

98. Philip Benjamin, "Fair Plays Host to Taxi Drivers," *New York Times,* Dec. 10, 1963, 2.

99. Philip Benjamin, "Fair to Pose Test of Taxi Honesty," *New York Times,* Mar. 30, 1964, 8; "366," *New Yorker,* Nov. 10, 1962, 43–44.

100. Zimmerman, "N.Y. World's Fair Preview."

101. "Fair's Policemen Turn Away 30,000," *New York Times,* Mar. 30, 1964, 7.

102. Bernard Weinraub, "2 Boys Describe Fair Infiltration," *New York Times,* Apr. 13, 1964, 1.

103. McCandlish Phillips, "250,000 Expected," *New York Times,* Apr. 22, 1964, 8.

104. "World's Fair '64: A Preview."

105. "Salute to the New York World's Fair of 1964," Apr. 21, 1964, T90:0094, Museum of Television and Radio, New York. An equally wholesome special designed to promote the Fair was broadcast on ABC in 1965. *Electric Showcase,* a sixty-minute "spectacular," was filmed at the Fair and

included performances by Al Hirt, George and Sheila McCray, and the New Christy Minstrels. Also featured were the popular musical review "Les Poupees de Paris" (in which no fewer than two hundred puppets sang, danced, and acted to music by Sammy Cahn and Jimmy van Heusen) and a few other shows playing at the Fair.

106. "For Everybody from Everywhere," *Newsweek,* Apr. 27, 1964, 60–65; "The New York World's Fair," *Ebony,* June 1964, 166–68.

**2. Heigh Ho, Ho Hum**

1. "Jersey Student Is First Through Gate at Fair," *New York Times,* Apr. 23, 1964, 1.

2. Richard F. Shepard, "The Sun Meets Crowds at the Fair, and the Business of Pleasure Commences," *New York Times,* Apr. 24, 1964, 1.

3. Philip H. Dougherty, "4,000 in Opening Parade Slog Bravely Through the Rain with Music and Majorettes," *New York Times,* Apr. 23, 1964, 1.

4. James Restons, "Contrasts of 25 Years," *New York Times,* Apr. 23, 1964, 1, 2, 5–7; Dickstein, "From the Thirties to the Sixties," 34.

5. "The Fair," *New Yorker,* May 2, 1964, 39.

6. Homer Bigart, "Rain Soaks Crowd," *New York Times,* Apr. 23, 1964, 8.

7. Charles Mohr, "Johnson Paints Picture of Plenty," *New York Times,* Apr. 23, 1964, 1, 5, 6; Gelb, *City Room,* 382. It was not the first opening day of a world's fair in which African Americans picketed because of unfair employment practices. On April 30, 1939, opening day of the 1939–40 New York fair, more than four hundred protesters gathered outside the gates in Flushing Meadows to let organizers and fairgoers know they would not put up with discrimination in the workplace, an early and brave moment of the civil rights movement. Prior to that event, A. Philip Randolph of the Brotherhood of Railroad Sleeping Car Porters made a powerful case for equal rights for African Americans in his (quite lengthy) speech during the opening ceremonies of the 1926 Sesqui-Centennial International Exposition in Philadelphia (Rydell, Findling, and Pelle, *Fair America,* 74, 94).

8. Bigart, "Rain Soaks Crowd"; Gelb, *City Room,* 382; Mohr, "Johnson Paints Picture of Plenty."

9. "Pickets Marched in Rain but Fair Opened Anyway," *Business Week,* Apr. 25, 1964, 32.

10. Peter Kihss, "7 Injured in IRT Station," *New York Times,* Apr. 23, 1964, 6.

11. "CBS News: Opening Day at the 1964–65 World's Fair," Apr. 22, 1964, T84:0110, Museum of Television and Radio.

12. "Johnson Critical of Fair Chanting," *New York Times,* Apr. 24, 1964, 1.

13. Robert Alden, "CORE Tests Ban on Fair Pickets," *New York Times,* Apr. 29, 1964, 7.

14. Murray Illson, "Picketing at Fair Ruled a Trespass," *New York Times,* June 12, 1964, 2, 5.

15. Edward Ranzal, "Rights Picket Ban by Fair Is Upheld," *New York Times,* July 2, 1964, 3. On July 4, ten members of the Student Non-Violent Coordinating Committee were arrested for distributing leaflets at the Willets Point Boulevard subway station, and that same day another group, the Movement of Revolutionary Recovery, tossed anti-Castro leaflets out of the Swiss Sky Ride and were kicked out of the fairgrounds ("10 at Fair Station Seized in Protest," *New York Times,* July 5, 1964, 44).

16. Robert Alden, "Veterans of the Lincoln Brigade Demonstrate at Spanish Pavilion," *New York Times,* July 19, 1964, 1, 2.

17. Will Lissner, "12 Jewish Leaders Acquitted in Picketing at the World's Fair," *New York Times,* July 30, 1964, 5, 6; "4 Pickets at Fair Win Court Appeal," *New York Times,* Oct. 10, 1964, 3.

18. Martin Tolchin, "Fair a Showcase for Civil Rights," *New York Times,* June 9, 1964, 4. One sign of the embedded racism at the Fair was the perfectly acceptable motif of the "Old South." Chevrolet's New Orleans exhibit in the GM Pavilion, for example, featured riverboats, southern belles, and, somewhat anachronistically, "the nicest cars on either side of the Mississippi."

19. Douglas Dales, "Rockefeller Signs Bill to Give City a Tax Windfall," *New York Times,* Apr. 26, 1964, 1; Walter Carlson, "State Wins Praise for Fair Pavilion," *New York Times,* Apr. 24, 1964, 5. Seattleites were thrilled with the recent conversion of their fairgrounds (also once a blighted piece of land) into a parklike area offering dining, arts, a science museum, sports, crafts, and entertainment.

20. "Conversion of Area Long Planned by Many Citizens," *New York Times,* May 17, 1964, 5.

21. Newbold Morris, "Use of World's Fair Funds," *New York Times,* May 21, 1964, 5; Abraham D. Beame, "Beame Answers Morris," letter to editor, *New York Times,* May 28, 1964, 5.

22. "For Everybody from Everywhere" (see chap. 1, n. 106); "Smasheroo of a World's Fair," *Life,* May 1, 1964, 26–35; "The New York World's Fair" (see chap. 1, n. 106); "Into Stride," *Time,* May 8, 1964, 42.

23. Francis X. Clines, "Teen-agers Make Fair a Hangout," *New York Times,* Apr. 29, 1964, 5, 6; "Fair Hits and Misses," *Newsweek,* June 1, 1964, 79; Philip Benjamin, "Where's Dominic Been 9 Days?" *New York Times,* May 18, 1964, 1; McCandlish Phillips, "Fairgoer of 1884 Sees 1964 Model," *New York Times,* May 12, 1964, 4.

24. "Panhandlers Near the Fair Find the Grass Is Greener," *New York Times,* May 10, 1964, 3; "Fair Brings Rise in Pickpocketry," *New York Times,* June 30, 1964, 4. Entrepreneurs of all types have long gravitated to world's fairs because of the certainty that many would be carrying large sums of cash. "As wealthy visitors and foreign dignitaries began arriving in greater numbers" at the 1893 Chicago fair, Larson observes, they were "shadowed by a swarm of pickpockets, thugs, and petty swindlers" (*Devil in the White City,* 256).

25. "Snip of Scissors Is Music to Fair," *New York Times,* May 7, 1964, 1. For a humorous take on State Days, when delegations from a particular state visited the fairgrounds, see Trow, *Within the Context.* Most delegations, Trow writes, were shown around the grounds via Glide-a-Rides, the motorized people movers sponsored by Greyhound, and then taken to the Illinois Pavilion to see the animatronic Abraham Lincoln because the exhibit was often not crowded and near the front gate (100).

26. Walter Carlson, "Congressional Special Visits the Fair," *New York Times,* May 16, 1964, 1; Richard F. Shepard, "Trip to Fair Made by Mrs. Kennedy," *New York Times,* May 1, 1964, 2; "Into Stride"; "Labor Unit Hears Kennedy, Keating," *New York Times,* Oct. 18, 1964, 1.

27. Damon Stetson, "Johnson, at Fair, Presses His Drive for Rights Action," *New York Times,* May 10, 1964, 8.

28. "Javits Finds Subway Good Way to Travel," *New York Times,* Apr. 23, 1964, 4; "42% Have Used Bus or Subway to the Fair," *New York Times,* Apr. 29, 1964, 5; Robert Alden, "Subway Dolls Up for Night at Fair," *New York Times,* May 14, 1964, 4; "Crowd of 15,000 Calmed at Fair," *New York Times,* May 17, 1964, 4; Martin Tolchin, "Fair Takes Steps to Avoid Crush," *New York Times,* May 18, 1964, 3; "Authority to Make Bid for Bus Riders to Fair," *New York Times,* May 13, 1964, 7; "Transit Authority Speeds Token-Selling to Hurry Visitors to the Fair," *New York Times,* June 10, 1964, 2; "Lack of Business Cancels Circle Line Trips to Fair," *New York Times,* June 12, 1964, 4; Ward Allan Howe, "Nation's Rails Riding High on Passenger Boom," *New York Times,* Aug. 23, 1964, sec. 10, p. 2; "Ex-Professor, 68, Plans to Cycle Here from Texas," *New York Times,* May 5, 1964, 4. One hundred fifty cyclists rode en masse to the Fair on May 17, 1964, in an attempt to make the city's roads and bridges more bicycle friendly—foreshadowing the current Critical Mass rides that have the same aim (John C. Devlin, "150 Cycle to Fair in Rules Protest," *New York Times,* May 18, 1964, 32).

29. Horace Sutton, "The Fair—Heigh Ho or Ho Hum," *Saturday Review,* June 13, 1964, 41–42.

30. Ada Louise Huxtable, "World's Fair: International Scope," *New York Times,* May 10, 1964, sec. 2, p. 5.

31. "The World of Already" (see chap. 1, n. 12); Horace Sutton, "The Fair—Ole and So-So," *Saturday Review,* June 20, 1964, 24ff; "Take Me Out to the Fairgrounds," *Saturday Review,* Mar. 14, 1964, 86+; Wolf Von Eckardt, "As the Hucksters See Us," *New Republic,* May 30, 1964, 29–30; "Out of the Bull Rushes" (see chap. 1, n. 89); Vincent Scully Jr., "If This Is Architecture, God Help Us," *Life,* July 31, 1964, 9.

32. John Canaday, "The Fair as Art," *New York Times,* May 3, 1964, sec. 2, p. 1; "The World of Already."

33. "Fun in New York" (see chap. 1, n. 17); Sutton, "The Fair—Ole and So-So." With its amazing electrical illumination, the 1893 World's Columbian Exposition was also considered by many to be most beautiful at night. "If evenings at the fair were seductive, the nights were ravishing," writes Larson, adding that John Ingalls, a reporter for *Cosmopolitan,* believed, "Night is the magician of the fair" (*Devil in the White City,* 254).

34. Walter Carlson, "Workmen at Fair, Joining Opening Day Crowds, Find Their Handiwork Impressive," *New York Times,* Apr. 23, 1964, 1, 2, 5–7. A few buildings opening late was business as usual for many if not most world's fairs. The 1904 St. Louis fair, in fact, took a full year longer than expected to complete.

35. Martin Tolchin, "Belgian Village at Fair Deserted," *New York Times,* May 23, 1964, 5; *1965 Official Guide,* 145–46; Walter Carlson, "Fair's Belgium Village Is Dedicated," *New York Times,* Aug. 4, 1964, 2.

36. Tania Long, "Belgian Village Finished at Last," *New York Times,* Oct. 17, 1964, 1.

37. Martin Tolchin, "Workmen Accused of Lagging at Fair to Raise Overtime," *New York Times,* Apr. 17, 1964, 6.

38. Martin Tolchin, "Labor Problems Delay the Shows," *New York Times,* Apr. 24, 1964, 4; Tolchin, "Troubles Plague 2 Pavilion Shows," *New York Times,* Apr. 28, 1964, 5; Walter Carlson, "Optimism Served at Fair Luncheon," *New York Times,* Apr. 30, 1964, 5, 6.

39. Martin Tolchin, "A Garbage Duel at Fair Averted," *New York Times,* June 21, 1964, 3; Robert Alden, "High Costs Anger Pavilions at Fair," *New York Times,* June 22, 1964, 4. Disputes between union and nonunion workers at world's fairs were nothing new. In building Chicago's World's Columbian Exposition, Larson finds, union members vehemently protested the use of "imported" workers, on at least one occasion even beating them until police arrived (*Devil in the White City,* 119).

40. "Labor Costs at the World's Fair," *U.S. News and World Report,* July 6, 1964, 74. Caro claims that unions were not just allowed but encouraged by Moses to charge rates higher than usual New York rates so that they (and ultimately he) would benefit from what initially appeared like a very successful financial venture (*Power Broker,* 1088–89).

41. "The Unisphere Begins to Show a Bit of a Strain," *Business Week,* June 27, 1964, 100+.

42. Walter Carlson, "Cleaners at Fair Defend Services," *New York Times,* June 23, 1964, 4; Robert Alden, "Fair Exhibitors Meet on Security," *New York Times,* June 25, 1964, 5.

43. Martin Tolchin, "World's Fair Guards Increased to Curb Pilferage at Pavilions," *New York Times,* Apr. 18, 1964, 3.

44. John P. Shanley, "Pilferage Keeps Exhibits on Alert," *New York Times,* May 9, 1964, 7.

45. "Thieves Are Making Off with Strollers at Fair," *New York Times,* May 12, 1964, 5, 6; "2 Fair Employees Accused of Bootleg Ticket Sales," *New York Times,* May 16, 1964, 2; "Robbers Pose as Workmen

in $10,000 Holdup at Fair," *New York Times,* June 22, 1964, 1; "Thief at Fair Gets Seven-Foot Marlin Lent by Dennison," *New York Times,* Sept. 29, 1964, 1.

46. "Fire Closes Maryland Pavilion," *New York Times,* Apr. 23, 1964, 5; "7 Injured on Tour Find Hospital Isn't Open Yet," *New York Times,* Apr. 27, 1964, 4, 5. The Fair's medical department would end up treating more than fifty-three thousand visitors the first season alone (at no charge), with some of the major pavilions, like Ford's, also tending to ailing (mostly overheated) fairgoers with their own first-aid stations.

47. McCandlish Phillips, "3-Wheel Taxis Fall Prey to Mechanical Troubles," *New York Times,* Apr. 30, 1964, 2; "Ride at Fair Jams, Trapping 12 in Air," *New York Times,* July 3, 1964, 4.

48. "2,000 at Ford Pavilion Evacuated for a Fire," *New York Times,* May 1, 1964, 2; "Guard at Ford Pavilion Injured by Automatic Car," *New York Times,* June 13, 1964, 3; Walter Carlson, "Fire Forces 2,500 from Ford Show," *New York Times,* July 27, 1964, 1; "Ford Is Seeking Ideas on Its Pavilion at Fair," *New York Times,* Dec. 12, 1964, 5; Tania Long, "Post–Labor Day Doldrums Bring Sudden End to Fair's Long Lines," *New York Times,* Sept. 12, 1964, 2; "Notes and Comment," *New Yorker,* Oct. 10, 1964, 49. Ford was also upstaged by its rival at the Century of Progress in Chicago, when GM was the first to announce it would bring a working assembly line to the fair. Henry Ford, not wanting to play second fiddle, passed on exhibiting the first year of the fair but, seeing how popular it was, showed up for the second (1934) season (Rydell, Findling, and Pelle, *Fair America,* 85).

49. Robert Alden, "Amusement Area at Fair Finds Business Is Lagging," *New York Times,* May 11, 1964, 4; "The World of Already."

50. "Fair's Amusements Seek Aid of Cabbies," *New York Times,* May 14, 1964, 5; Gay Talese, "Tourists' Tipping Dismays Tippees," *New York Times,* Aug. 27, 1964, 4.

51. Robert Alden, "Fair Exhibitors Plan Road Show," *New York Times,* June 15, 1964, 3.

52. Walter Carlson, "A Second Show at Fair Puts Up Closing Notice," *New York Times,* June 3, 1964, 2; "What Can the Matter Be?" *Time,* Aug. 21, 1964, 48; "Debt Petition Filed by `Wonder World,'" *New York Times,* July 1, 1964, 1.

53. Robert Alden, "Holiday Crowds Disappoint Fair," *New York Times,* July 6, 1964, 3; "Fair Enough," *Newsweek,* Oct. 26, 1964, 108ff.

54. "Louisiana Exhibit in Fiscal Trouble," *New York Times,* May 26, 1964, 4.

55. Martin Tolchin, "Pact at Fair Bars Pirating of Labor," *New York Times,* June 10, 1964, 3.

56. "New Company Buys Fair's Louisiana Pavilion," *New York Times,* June 13, 1964, 5; "Louisiana Severs Ties with the Fair," *New York Times,* June 17, 1964, 3.

57. "Fair Cost Studied by West Virginia," *New York Times,* July 5, 1964, 4; Robert Alden, "Jovial Crowds Pour into Fair Despite Steady Rain," *New York Times,* July 9, 1964, 6.

58. Robert Alden, "Moses Bolsters Fair's Fun Area," *New York Times,* July 10, 1964, 3; "Montana's Pavilion at Fair Needs $153,000 to Pay Debt," *New York Times,* Dec. 18, 1964, 1.

59. "Material Relating to Texas," F128 T791.A67, New-York Historical Society (hereafter cited as NYHS).

60. "Pavilion Director Arrested at Fair," *New York Times,* July 31, 1964, 3, 4. Wynne's was not the only case in which a pavilion director was arrested. In September, Clafin Garst of the African Pavilion was busted for refusing to remove speakers that were deemed too loud ("Official at African Pavilion Arrested in Noise Dispute," *New York Times,* Sept. 16, 1964, 5).

61. "For Everybody from Everywhere"; "The World of Already."

62. Robert Alden, "Top of the Fair Deeply in Debt," *New York Times,* Aug. 29, 1964, 4.

63. McCandlish Phillips, "Food and Its Cost Stir Some Groans," *New York Times,* May 3, 1964, 6.

64. Martin Tolchin, "Some Restaurants Plan Higher Prices," *New York Times*, May 4, 1964, 2. The 1893 World's Columbian Exposition similarly suffered lower-than-expected attendance because no-shows believed they would get "fleeced unmercifully" at that fair, as Frederick Law Olmsted put it, especially on overpriced food (Larson, *Devil in the White City*, 275).

65. Martin Tolchin, "Fairgrounds Get a College Rush," *New York Times*, Apr. 19, 1964, 3, 4.

66. Francis X. Clines, "Boredom Becomes Fair Job Hazard," *New York Times*, May 7, 1964, 2.

67. "All's Fair," *Newsweek*, Sept. 14, 1964, 55–56.

68. Ibid.

69. Murray Schumach, "Season of Jokes Is on at the Fair," *New York Times*, Sept. 3, 1964, 1.

70. "Job News at Fair Is Bad—and Good," *New York Times*, May 31, 1964, 5, 6.

71. Martin Tolchin, "Employees Besiege Brass Rail for Long-Overdue Pay at Fair," *New York Times*, May 11, 1964, 2. There was a "gentlemen's agreement" fixing the wages of Fair hosts and host-esses at $2 to $2.50 per hour, as well as one that barred stealing employees.

72. Martin Tolchin, "500 Are Laid Off as Fair Employees," *New York Times*, May 19, 1964, 3, 4; Tolchin, "Fairgrounds Get a College Rush"; Walter Carlson, "Noble Frauleins Tend Bar at Fair," *New York Times*, May 21, 1964, 5.

73. Martin Tolchin, "'Parable' Movie Splits Fairgoers," *New York Times*, May 15, 1964, 1.

74. Robert Alden, "Protestants to Keep 'Parable' at Fair," *New York Times*, May 25, 1964, 4; Alden, "'Parable' Draws Crowds at Fair," *New York Times*, Aug. 7, 1964, 1; Walter Carlson, "Fair Faces a New Controversy over Film on School Bus Aid," *New York Times*, June 30, 1964, 5.

75. Philip H. Dougherty, "Moses Shrugs Off Low Crowds and Folding Shows at the Fair," *New York Times*, Aug. 1, 1964, 2. Even Walt Disney, whose favorite music was big band and barbershop quartets, added rock-and-roll shows to Disneyland in 1965 to attract a younger audience to the park at night, something Moses was not willing to do (Peter Bart, "Disneyland Tries to Rock 'N' Roll," *New York Times*, Apr. 28, 1965, 38.)

76. Walter Carlson, "Minister at Fair Accused by Rabbi," *New York Times*, June 12, 1964, 1; Caro, *Power Broker*, 411.

77. "Material Relating to Jordan," F128 T792.6.J8, NYHS.

78. "Fair Rejects Plea on Jordanian Mural," *New York Times*, Apr. 26, 1964, 1, 4; "Suit on Fair Mural Is Argued in Court," *New York Times*, June 5, 1964, 4.

79. "Fair in Black, Predicts 'Substantial Surplus,'" *New York Times*, June 5, 1965, 36.

80. Walter Carlson, "Fair, in Black, Predicts 'Substantial Surplus,'" *New York Times*, June 5, 1964, 36; Philip H. Dougherty, "25% of Fair's Debt to Be Paid Early," *New York Times*, June 30, 1964, 1.

81. Clarence Dean, "Hotels Here Act on Overbooking," *New York Times*, June 12, 1964, 37.

82. Sutton, "The Fair—Ole and So-So."

83. Robert Alden, "Lines at the Fair Offer Challenge," *New York Times*, Aug. 25, 1964, 1.

84. "Fair Enough." The equivalent to adults' trying to get into pavilions without waiting was kids' attempts to sneak into the Fair, especially for those children who lived nearby and had noth-ing better to do in the summers of 1964 and 1965. Talk to someone who grew up in Queens in the mid-1960s, and you are likely to hear a story about going over, through, or even under a fence at the fairgrounds.

85. Philip Benjamin, "Overtime Guests Jam Hotels Here," *New York Times*, June 9, 1964, 8.

86. "How the Fair Did: More Plus than Minus," *Business Week*, Sept. 26, 1964, 39.

87. "Six Stores Decide to Open Saturday," *New York Times*, June 19, 1964, 5; Marylin Bender, "Stores Offer Special Services to Fair Visitors," *New York Times*, June 27, 1964, 2.

88. *New York in Summer 1964,* F128 T791.A42, NYHS.

89. Walter Carlson, "Selling the Fair Is Year-Round Job," *New York Times,* May 24, 1964, 4.

90. Robert Alden, "Fair Moves to Counter Bad Publicity," *New York Times,* June 27, 1964, 4.

91. "Bad News Upsets Fair's Exhibitors," *New York Times,* July 4, 1964, 1.

92. Walter Carlson, "Crowds at Fair Dwindle in Heat," *New York Times,* July 2, 1964, 4.

93. Alden, "Holiday Crowds Disappoint Fair."

94. Walter Carlson, "Moses Says That `Observers' Magnify Reports on `Disorders,'" *New York Times,* July 25, 1964, 48; R. W. Apple Jr., "Tourism in City Hurt by Rioting," *New York Times,* July 23, 1964, 7.

95. "Moses Tells a Family It Is Safe to Visit City," *New York Times,* July 1, 1964, 5; "Safety for Visitors Is Cited by Shriners," *New York Times,* July 25, 1964, 48; Philip H. Dougherty, "Africans at Fair Shocked by Riots," *New York Times,* July 27, 1964, 8. Their reputation preceding them, the Shriners were regarded as the biggest partiers at the Fair. Immediately upon arrival at the grounds' gates, packs of Shriners would reportedly ask directions to the Schaefer Pavilion, even at nine in the morning (Bernard Weinraub, "Young Employees Say Farewells," *New York Times,* Oct. 19, 1964, 1, 8).

96. Philip H. Dougherty, "Onstage at Fair," *New York Times,* Aug. 5, 1964, 1.

97. Robert Alden, "Fair Attendance Climbs in August," *New York Times,* Aug. 31, 1964, 4.

98. Long, "Post–Labor Day Doldrums Bring Sudden End to Fair's Long Lines."

99. "The Word from Moses," *Time,* Sept. 25, 1964, 42.

100. "Rare Catch," *New Yorker,* July 4, 1964, 24.

101. Tania Long, "Moses Says Press Harmed the Fair," *New York Times,* Oct. 15, 1964, 3.

102. Robert Alden, "Fair Appraises Its First Season and Finds It Relatively Good," *New York Times,* Oct. 18, 1964, 3, 6.

103. Richard Phalon, "Fair's 1964 Profit below Estimate," *New York Times,* Oct. 14, 1964, 4.

104. Alden, "Fair Appraises Its First Season and Finds It Relatively Good."

105. Robert Alden, "The Fair Closes Its First Season," *New York Times,* Oct. 19, 1964, 1.

106. "Can the World's Fair Make a '65 Comeback?" *U.S. News and World Report,* Oct. 26, 1964, 15.

107. "Deegan Says 37.5 Million Will Visit Fair Next Year," *New York Times,* Nov. 14, 1964, 2; Farnsworth Fowle, "World's Fair Plans Sportsmen's Show and a Farm Exhibit," *New York Times,* Nov. 17, 1964, 5; "Third Year Urged for World's Fair," *New York Times,* Nov. 11, 1964, 1.

108. Clayton Knowles, "City Not Counting on Fair's Money," *New York Times,* Nov. 24, 1964, 3.

109. "How the Fair Did: More Plus than Minus."

110. Will Lissner, "Jersey City Girl Wins $5,000 for Essay on Fair's `Vitality,'" *New York Times,* Nov. 16, 1964, 4.

## 3. Second Time Around

1. Robert F. Wagner, "A New Yorker Goes to the Fair," *New York Times Sunday Magazine,* Apr. 18, 1965, 52–53.

2. "Deegan Company Leaves the Fair," *New York Times,* Jan. 29, 1965, 8. See Caro, *Power Broker,* regarding Moses's infamous collection of dossiers on men used as "documentation to destroy them if they ever refused to go along with his wishes" (727–29).

3. "Upbeat Fair," *Newsweek,* Apr. 26, 1965, 88–90.

4. Robert Alden, "Fair Unable to Repay City or Finance Queens Parks," *New York Times,* Jan. 27, 1965, 4.

5. "Moses vs. the Bankers," *Newsweek*, Feb. 1, 1965, 61. Caro found that the WFC's operating expenses were $33.3 million during the first season—twice the original budget (*Power Broker*, 1089). Interestingly, an audit of the 1893 fair in Chicago revealed that its head, Daniel Burnham, spent more than $22 million to build that exposition—more than twice than what was budgeted, resulting in a report labeling its financial management as "shamefully extravagant" (Larson, *Devil in the White City*, 293, 309). Similarly, the president of the 1904 St. Louis fair, David R. Francis, ran out of money before the grounds were completed, having to plead Congress for an additional $4.5 million to finish the job (Harper Barnes, "David Rowland Francis Brought the City to Life," *St. Louis Post-Dispatch*, Apr. 25, 2004, WF6).

6. Robert Alden, "Despite Controversies, Attendance Passes All Other Expositions," *New York Times*, Oct. 17, 1965, 2.

7. C. Welles, "Big Bash That Is Running Short of Cash," *Life*, May 14, 1965, 136–38. The average attendance drop-off for a world's fair's second season was 35 percent to 40 percent.

8. "Expresses to the Fair Scheduled on Subway," *New York Times*, Apr. 12, 1965, 7; Emanuel Perlmutter, "Subway Cars Here to Get Strip Maps Showing One Route," *New York Times*, Apr. 14, 1965, 1; "Summer Festival," *New Yorker*, June 19, 1965, 24.

9. Walter Carlson, "Advertising: A Fair in Search of Promotion," *New York Times*, Jan. 31, 1965, sec. 3, p. 3.

10. Bosley Crowther, "The Screen: 'To the Fair,'" *New York Times*, Feb. 13, 1965, 2.

11. Carlson, "Advertising: A Fair in Search of Promotion."

12. Robert Alden, "Fair Exhibitors Chart Promotion," *New York Times*, Mar. 2, 1965, 1.

13. C. W. Hall, "To Get the Most Out of the New York World's Fair," *Reader's Digest*, May 1965, 186–88+.

14. "Second Time Around," *Time*, Apr. 30, 1965, 76ff.

15. Murray Schumach, "7 Million Spent in Improvements," *New York Times*, Apr. 21, 1965, 36.

16. Michael T. Kaufman, "Top of the Fair Is Now Bankrupt," *New York Times*, Jan. 5, 1965, 8.

17. Schumach, "7 Million Spent in Improvements."

18. Gereon Zimmerman, "Fair: New York's Spectacular Opens Again," *Look*, Apr. 20, 1965, 27–33.

19. "Upbeat Fair."

20. Kaufman, "Top of the Fair Is Now Bankrupt."

21. "Upbeat Fair."

22. "Material Relating to Minnesota," F128 T791.A56, New-York Historical Society (hereafter cited as NYHS); "Material Relating to Vatican City," F128 T792.382, NYHS.

23. Robert Alden, "Free Water Show Planned at Fair," *New York Times*, Mar. 3, 1965, 5; McCandlish Phillips, "Florida Presents 2 Water Displays," *New York Times*, Apr. 21 1965, 37; "Material Relating to Hawaii," F128 T791.A95, NYHS.

24. "Improvements Listed for Fair Season," *New York Times*, Jan. 27, 1965, 1, 6.

25. "Material Relating to the United States," F128 T791.A2, NYHS. Challenge to Greatness was actually originally planned to be the central theme of the Federal Pavilion, only to be downgraded to an exhibit in 1964 and an even smaller one in 1965.

26. Welles, "Big Bash That Is Running Short of Cash."

27. John C. Devlin, "5 Bank Advisers to Fair Quit in Financial Dispute," *New York Times*, Jan. 19, 1965, 5.

28. Robert Alden, "Moses Criticizes Banker, Defends Finances of Fair," *New York Times*, Jan. 21, 1965, 1; "Text of Moses' Statement on World Fair's Finances," *New York Times*, Jan. 21, 1965, 5.

29. Robert Alden, "Finances of Fair Held Not Critical," *New York Times,* Jan. 22, 1965, 5.

30. "Plea for Success of Fair Made by Banker Who Quit as Adviser," *New York Times,* Jan. 24, 1965, 71.

31. Robert Alden, "World's Fair Had Deficit of $17,540,100 in 1964," *New York Times,* Feb. 6, 1965, 6.

32. Clayton Knowles, "Arculeo Bids City Operate the Fair," *New York Times,* Feb. 8, 1965, 3. In March, a group of local politicians and bankers asked Billy Rose, whom Moses had feuded with over the Jordanian mural incident, to take over the Fair, but he declined, which is putting it mildly. "I'd rather be hit by a baseball bat," the showman quipped, taking a last shot at Moses by adding, "Cancer in its last stages never attracted me very much" (Robert Alden, "Ford Fair Exhibit to Add Entrance," *New York Times,* Mar. 16, 1965, 1).

33. Richard Phalon, "Beame Bids City Subpoena Books of World's Fair," *New York Times,* Feb. 2, 1965, 3; Richard Phalon, "Beame Subpoenas Fair's Books but Faces a Battle," *New York Times,* Feb. 3, 1965, 3; Phalon, "Fair Bids City Drop Subpoena, but Beame Insists on an Audit," *New York Times,* Feb. 4, 1965, 5.

34. "It's Not the Money," *Newsweek,* Nov. 29, 1965, 80ff.

35. Robert Alden, "Fair's Priorities Revised by Moses," *New York Times,* Feb. 15, 1965, 1.

36. Murray Kempton, "Foul-up at the Fair," *New Republic* Feb. 20, 1965, 13–14.

37. Murray Illson, "Fair Aide Resigns, Assailing Moses on Fund Proposal," *New York Times,* Feb. 24, 1965, 6.

38. Robert Alden, "Fair Executives Divided on Moses," *New York Times,* Feb. 25, 1965, 1; "Vote on Moses," *New York Times,* Feb. 25, 1965, 2, 6. Although Moses had no intention of resigning, he was reportedly tempted to throw his hat in the ring to manage a new project proposed by President Johnson—the building of another big canal through Central America. Moses's friend Bernard Gimbel lobbied for him to be given the post, but LBJ passed, likely knowing that his administration wasn't big enough for the two of them.

39. "Deegan Company Leaves the Fair."

40. Thomas Buckley, "Deegan Explains Rift with Moses," *New York Times,* Jan. 30, 1965, 7.

41. "Exhibitors Give a Lift to Fair Beset by Feuds," *Business Week,* Mar. 13, 1965, 26; Robert Alden, "Moses Charges Wagner Broke Promises on Fair," *New York Times,* Mar. 6, 1965, 2, 3.

42. Robert Alden, "Fair's Exhibitors Plan a Campaign," *New York Times,* Feb. 5, 1965, 7.

43. Knowles, "Arculeo Bids City Operate the Fair"; Phalon, "Beame Subpoenas Fair's Books but Faces a Battle."

44. Robert Alden, "2 Banks Lend Fair $1 Million Needed to Open '65 Season," *New York Times,* Mar. 13, 1965, 4.

45. Robert Alden, "Fair Will Reopen in Gala Fashion," *New York Times,* Apr. 16, 1965, 4.

46. Philip Benjamin, "Humphrey Stars as Show Reopens," *New York Times,* Apr. 22, 1965, 1.

47. Alden, "Fair Will Reopen in Gala Fashion."

48. Tania Long, "587,218 See Fair in First 4 Days," *New York Times,* Apr. 25, 1965, 1.

49. "Visiting Princesses Spend Day Visiting," *New York Times,* May 8, 1965, 6; Robert Alden, "Eisenhower on Generals: Don't Become One," *New York Times,* May 10, 1965, 1.

50. Philip H. Dougherty, "A Stripper Lasts 2 Shows at Fair," *New York Times,* May 8, 1965, 3.

51. Ibid.; "Moses Calls Fair `Intellectual Picnic,' Lashes at Critics," *New York Times,* May 5, 1965, 4; "Well-Rounded," *New Yorker,* Feb. 6, 1965, 26–27.

52. "Night Rate Urged by Fair Pavilions," *New York Times,* Mar. 1, 1965, 1; Philip H. Dougherty, "Moses Bars a Cut in Fair Admission," *New York Times,* May 7, 1965, 1; Dougherty, "Foreign Exhibits

Bar Fair Closings," *New York Times,* May 29, 1965, 3; Robert Alden, "Fair Exhibitors Still in the Red," *New York Times,* June 1, 1965, 44.

53. Robert Alden, "Fair Rejects Bid to Cut $2.50 Fee," *New York Times,* July 9, 1965, 1.

54. Robert Alden, "Fair Attendance Is 22% Lower than in First 20 Days Last Year," *New York Times,* May 11, 1965, 6.

55. "Moses Seeks Aid of Weathermen," *New York Times,* May 19, 1965, 5.

56. "Gay Weatherman Sees Past Clouds," *New York Times,* June 9, 1965, 5.

57. Robert Alden, "'Pieta' Is Prepared for Fair Opening," *New York Times,* Apr. 10, 1965, 5; Alden, "CORE to Protest City Role on Fair," *New York Times,* Apr. 23, 1965, 1.

58. "100 CORE Pickets at Fair Challenged by Youths," *New York Times,* Apr. 26, 1965, 5; Robert Alden, "Fair Attendance Dips to New Low," *New York Times,* Apr. 27, 1965, 6, 7; Tania Long, "Fight Breaks Out in Dispute at Fair," *New York Times,* May 1, 1965, 3.

59. Tania Long, "Fair Arabs Spurn Kosher Luncheon," *New York Times,* May 2, 1965, 4.

60. Bernard Weinraub, "N.A.A.C.P. Assails Song at the Fair," *New York Times,* May 31, 1965, 1; "N.A.A.C.P. Wins Bid to Have 'Dem' Taken from Pavilion Song," *New York Times,* June 2, 1965, 3.

61. "Apology to Be Made for Ad for Blondes," *New York Times,* Apr. 17, 1965, 6.

62. Philip H. Dougherty, "Fairgoers Ignore a Peace Protest," *New York Times,* June 6, 1965, 1.

63. John Sibley, "A-Bomb Dropping Is Marked in City," *New York Times,* Aug. 7, 1965, 6.

64. Russell Lynes, "Goodbye to World's Fair," *Harper's,* Oct. 1965, 28ff.

65. Zimmerman, "Fair: New York's Spectacular Opens Again."

66. "Monsters Missing at Fair's Dinoland," *New York Times,* June 30, 1965, 4; Philip H. Dougherty, "Officer Menaced over Fair Party," *New York Times,* Aug. 7, 1965, 1.

67. "Advice on How to Avoid Crowd Pokes Fun at Fair," *New York Times,* July 25, 1965, 7.

68. Robert Alden, "Barnes Orders Moses' Signs Down," *New York Times,* Sept. 8, 1965, 36.

69. Robert Alden, "World's Fair Mismanaged, Beame Charges in Report," *New York Times,* Sept. 1, 1965, 2.

70. Robert Alden, "O'Connor Orders Inquiry into the Fair," *New York Times,* Sept. 2, 1965, 5; Douglas Robinson, "Aide of O'Connor Opens Fair Study," *New York Times,* Sept. 4, 1965, 1; Robert Alden, "Illinois Received Loan from Fair," *New York Times,* Sept. 3, 1965, 4.

71. Alden, "Despite Controversies, Attendance Passes All Other Expositions."

72. Murray Schumach, "Moses Gets Down to Earth in Opening World's Fair Site for Zoo," *New York Times,* Aug. 21, 1966, 40.

73. Robert Alden, "Moses Gives Plan on Fair Site Work," *New York Times,* Aug. 19, 1965, 8.

74. "Beame Report on World's Fair and Reply by Moses," *New York Times,* Sept. 1, 1965, 6. The site of the 1904 St. Louis fair, the western half of Forest Park, consisted mostly of woods, swampland, and the sewage-filled River Des Peres, another example of how a fair was the instrument to create ultimately a beautiful, lasting park for the host city out of an eyesore (Mary Delach Leonard, "Nearly 15,000 Workers Transformed Forest Park into the Ivory City," *St. Louis Post-Dispatch,* Apr. 25, 2004, WF6).

75. "Councilman Urges Third Fair Season," *New York Times,* Aug. 29, 1965, 5; Alden, "O'Connor Orders Inquiry into the Fair."

76. Clayton Knowles, "Wagner Seeking 27 New Schools in Works Budget," *New York Times,* Feb. 1, 1965, 6.

77. Robert Alden, "Pavilions Listed for Future Uses," *New York Times,* Mar. 5, 1965, 2; Alden, "City Asked to Raze State, U.S. Pavilions," *New York Times,* July 24, 1965, 6. Attempts to save the Singer Bowl

had precedent with the preservation of Municipal Stadium in Philadelphia and the Cotton Bowl in Dallas, each an architectural remnant of a world's fair.

78. Philip H. Dougherty, "Buyers Bid Early for Pieces of Fair," *New York Times*, July 19, 1965, 1.

79. "R.C.A. Will Install TV for Archdiocese," *New York Times*, Oct. 26, 1965, 3.

80. "The Great Souvenir Sale," *Time*, Oct. 8, 1965, 96. Wisconsin brought a 22,000-pound cheese to the 1893 World's Columbian Exposition that, to fairgoers' amazement, never molded for some inexplicable reason (Larson, *Devil in the White City*, 236).

81. Robert Alden, "Anybody Can Have Fair Pavilion Free," *New York Times*, Aug. 1, 1965, 2; Philip H. Dougherty, "For Sale at Fair: Tire and Temple," *New York Times*, June 26, 1965, 1; Alden, "Building at Fair Sought in South," *New York Times*, Aug. 18, 1985, 5; "The Great Souvenir Sale."

82. Robert Alden, "Attendance at Fair Sets 2-Year Mark of 317,310," *New York Times*, Sept. 6, 1965, 2.

83. Robert Alden, "Fair So Crowded Managers Worry," *New York Times*, Oct. 13, 1965, 8.

84. "Biggest in History," *Newsweek*, Sept. 20, 1965, 76ff.

85. Robert Alden, "Restaurants at Fair Recouping 1964 Losses," *New York Times*, Oct. 14, 1965, 1; Alden, "Despite Controversies, Attendance Passes All Other Expositions."

86. Robert Alden, "End of the Fair—Result Appraised," *New York Times*, Oct. 17, 1965, sec. 4, p. 1; "Attendance Figures for the Fair Are Given," *New York Times*, Oct. 19, 1965, 5.

87. William Borders, "Extra Police Fail to Halt Thievery," *New York Times*, Oct. 18, 1965, 4–6.

88. Robert Alden, "Vandalism Mars Last Day of the Two-Year Exposition," *New York Times*, Oct. 18, 1965, 3.

89. Borders, "Extra Police Fail to Halt Thievery."

90. "To the Bitter End," *Time*, Oct. 29, 1965, 52.

91. "Woes of N.Y. Fair Echo in Montreal," *New York Times*, Oct. 24, 1965, 1. Expo 67 would turn out to be an amazing success, bringing in fifty million visitors during its six-month run with very little of the drama that the New York Fair experienced.

92. "Survey Finds the Fair Lacks Personal Touch," *New York Times*, Apr. 22, 1965, 1–3, 6.

93. "Fair 'Grossly Overbuilt,'" *New York Times*, Feb. 11, 1965, 3, 4.

94. Robert Alden, "A Legacy of Fair: Unwanted Relics," *New York Times*, Aug. 11, 1965, 1.

95. "St. Louis Shows Interest in Fair's Spanish Pavilion," *New York Times*, Oct. 28, 1965, 6; "St. Louis Plans to Reconstruct Spanish Pavilion on River Bank," *New York Times*, Nov. 7, 1965, 7; "Mayor of St. Louis Tours Spanish Pavilion at Fair," *New York Times*, Jan. 23, 1966, 1; "Biggest in History."

96. "The Great Souvenir Sale"; "Japan Giving Fair Pavilion to Manhattanville College," *New York Times*, Oct. 13, 1965, 2; Ralph Blumenthal, "Indonesia Plans to Raze Pavilion," *New York Times*, Oct. 15, 1965, 3; "Danish Pavilion Is Bought for a Market in Westport," *New York Times*, Oct. 17, 1965, 1; Lisa Hammel, "Danish Pavilion to Be a Westport Shop," *New York Times*, Nov. 23, 1965, 1; William Borders, "'Pieta' Leaves Fair in Guarded Truck," *New York Times*, Nov. 2, 1965, 3; "The 'Pieta,' After Hazards, Is in Place in St. Peter's," *New York Times*, Nov. 14, 1965, 1.

97. "City Park to Keep State's Pavilion," *New York Times*, Dec. 17, 1965, 3.

98. Byron Porterfield, "Wreckers Press Fairgrounds Job," *New York Times*, Feb. 20, 1966, R1; "U.S. Steel Donates a Fund to Maintain Unisphere at Fair," *New York Times*, Mar. 21, 1966, 8; "Clairol's Color Carousel Set for a Tour of 18 Cities," *New York Times*, Jan. 7, 1966, 4; "Now, Even the Dinosaurs Are Heading for Florida," *New York Times*, Feb. 3, 1966, 4.

99. "Park on Fair Site Due in December," *New York Times*, Apr. 4, 1966, 7.

100. Byron Porterfield, "Fairs Come and Go but Growth They Spawned Goes on in Queens," *New York Times*, May 1, 1966, 1.

101. "Foul Lot to Fair: A Saga by Moses," *New York Times,* Apr. 11, 1966, 8.

102. Schumach, "Moses Gets Down to Earth in Opening World's Fair Site for Zoo."

103. Kempton, "Foul-up at the Fair"; "Fair Bond Holders Facing a Default," *New York Times,* Oct. 18, 1965, 38.

104. Robert Alden, "Fair Audit Calls Management Lax," *New York Times,* Dec. 22, 1965, 1.

105. "Farewell to the Fair," editorial, *New York Times,* Oct. 17, 1965, E10.

## 4. The House of Good Taste

1. Walter Carlson, "Free Enterprise Is Hailed at Fair," *New York Times,* May 2, 1964, 5.

2. *1965 Official Guide,* 140.

3. Rydell, Findling, and Pelle, *Fair America,* 11, 81–85, 91.

4. Ibid., 11.

5. Fontaine, "No Fair" (see chap. 1, n. 66).

6. "The World of Already" (see chap. 1, n. 12); Hayden, "The Hard-Sell Fair" (see chap. 1, n. 27); "Triumph for the Fair" (see chap. 1, n. 8); Richard J. H. Johnston, "400 Paid to Visit Pavilion at Fair," *New York Times,* Apr. 1, 1964, 48.

7. "Plush, and Private," *Business Week,* May 2, 1964, 28–29. There was a private "Terrace Club" at the 1939–40 fair as well.

8. *1965 Official Guide,* 100.

9. John M. Lee, "Business at Fair Seeking Prestige," *New York Times,* Apr. 18, 1964, 1.

10. Max Kozloff, "Pop on the Meadow," *Nation,* July 13, 1964, 16–18; Robert Hughes, "The Golden Grin," *Nation,* Oct. 5, 1964, 189–91.

11. *1965 Official Guide,* 74, 77.

12. "1964 Fair Buildings Urged as University," *New York Times,* Oct. 23, 1959, 1; Raymond S. Rubinow, "Concept of World's Fair: Ultimate Use as International School Seen as Spur to Wide Approval," *New York Times,* Dec. 6, 1960, 6; "Fair Science Museum to Be Sought by Moses," *New York Times,* Apr. 28, 1962, 1; Charles G. Bennett, "City Museum Plan for Fair Scored," *New York Times,* Apr. 10, 1963, 6.

13. "Shea to Urge Bid by New York for 1968 Olympics at Fair Site," *New York Times,* Sept. 11, 1960, sec. 5, p. 3.

14. Michael Strauss, "New York World's Fair Is Named Host for Olympic Rowing Trials in 1964," *New York Times,* Aug. 12, 1962, sec. 5, p. 1.

15. Sutton, "The Fair—Ole and So-So" (see chap. 2, n. 31).

16. "The World of Already"; "The New York World's Fair" (see chap. 1, n. 106).

17. Phillips, "Food and Its Cost Stir Some Groans" (see chap. 2, n. 63); Hughes, "The Golden Grin."

18. "Fun in New York" (see chap. 1, n. 17); *1965 Official Guide,* 134, 142.

19. "Fun in New York."

20. Mayer, "Ho Hum, Come to the Fair" (see chap. 1, n. 3).

21. Ibid.

22. Hayden, "The Hard-Sell Fair"; "World's Fair '64: A Preview" (see chap. 1, n. 25).

23. "The New York World's Fair."

24. "What Can the Matter Be?" (see chap. 2, n. 52).

25. Lee, "Business at Fair Seeking Prestige"; "The Fair—for $2 Fee, a Billion-Dollar Spectacle," *U.S. News and World Report,* Apr. 27, 1964, 12.

26. "The World of Already"; Sutton, "The Fair—Ole and So-So."

27. Sutton, "The Fair—Ole and So-So." Just as the Eiffel Tower was hard evidence that France was the leader in iron and steel engineering in the late nineteenth century, as Larson suggests, the Unisphere served as firm proof that the United States was now the best in the world within this realm (*Devil in the White City,* 15). Also see Larson, *Devil in the White City,* for a full account of Daniel Burnham's obsessive desire to outdo Eiffel's Tower at his 1893 Chicago fair, resulting in George Ferris's phenomenally popular wheel manufactured by Bethlehem Steel.

28. William Robbins, "Doodle Grew into the Unisphere," *New York Times,* Aug. 16, 1964, sec. 8, p. 3; Miller, "Something for Everyone," 62.

29. Robbins, "Doodle Grew into the Unisphere."

30. Charles W. Morton, "News about the Fair," *Atlantic Monthly,* June 1963, 108ff.

31. Sal Nuccio, "Advertising: Making Friends at the Fair," *New York Times,* Aug. 16, 1964, sec. 3, p. 4.

32. "Material Relating to Insurance," F128 T793.I6, New-York Historical Society (hereafter cited as NYHS).

33. *1965 Official Guide,* 90, 98, 208, 108, 82. Kodak cameras were a staple of world's fairs for many years, so much so that picture takers at the 1904 St. Louis fair were often called "Kodakers."

34. Martin Tolchin, "Big Companies Pay for Plugs at Fair," *New York Times,* May 25, 1964, 1.

35. Marylin Bender, "Pavilions to Sell Unusual Wares," *New York Times,* Apr. 22, 1964, 2, 4, 7.

36. John M. Lee, "Foreign Exhibits Stress Exports," *New York Times,* Apr. 27, 1964, 2.

37. Phillips, "Food and Its Cost Stir Some Groans."

38. Hayden, "The Hard-Sell Fair"; Caro, *Power Broker,* 927; "10 File for Space at World's Fair," *New York Times,* Aug. 22, 1960, 1.

39. "Soviet to Exhibit at '64 Fair Here," *New York Times,* Sept. 28, 1960, 2; Joseph C. Ingraham, "7-Acre G.M. Show Set for 1964 Fair," *New York Times,* Nov. 2, 1960, 1.

40. "Ready to Swing Open the Gates."

41. Sheppard, "Icons and Images," 176.

42. Lee, "Business at Fair Seeking Prestige."

43. Ibid.

44. Rydell, Findling, and Pelle, *Fair America,* 102. Disney's father, Elias Disney, Larson notes, was a carpenter and furniture maker who helped construct the White City of Chicago's 1893 fair, making one seriously wonder if that experience inspired his son to want to create magical universes of his own (*Devil in the White City,* 153, 373).

45. "Fun in New York."

46. *1965 Official Guide,* 174.

47. Mayer, "Ho Hum, Come to the Fair."

48. "For Everybody from Everywhere" (see chap. 1, n. 106). Ford's Rotunda was a major hit at the 1933 fair in Chicago, so much so that the company brought it back to Dearborn for display there.

49. Sutton, "The Fair—Ole and So-So."

50. Nuccio, "Advertising: Making Friends at the Fair."

51. Ibid.

52. "Material Relating to Automobile Rentals," F128 T793.A83, NYHS. Greyhound taxiettes also were at the 1939–40 New York fair where they played "East Side, West Side" rather than a promotional tune, a small but significant indicator of how much more commercial public events like world's fairs were in 1964 versus 1939.

53. *1965 Official Guide,* 64, 68.

54. "Material Relating to the Better Living Center," F128 T790.6.B5, NYHS; "The World of Already."

55. Douglas Lapham, vice president of the Better Living Center and director of exhibitions, interview by author, Oct. 6, 2004, New York City.

56. "Big Companies to Join the Fair with Space in Better Living Center," *New York World-Telegram and Sun,* Oct. 16, 1963, 55.

57. "Material Relating to the Better Living Center." Many visitors still have indelible images of their first encounter with a Ford Mustang at the Fair. "I stood there with my mouth open and told my husband I had to have one," Wanda Whitsell of Springfield, Virginia, recently recalled. "I begged him until late 1965, when he finally surrendered and gave it to me for Christmas," she explained, still the proud owner of her 1966 Nightmist Blue coupe (Jim Motavalli, "For Mustang Owners, the First Love Is the Sweetest," *New York Times,* Mar. 22, 2004, D12). The Mustang had appeared on the cover of both *Time* and *Newsweek* in 1964, Margolis has noted, a clear sign of the impact the car (which was in fact essentially a restyled Ford Falcon) had on the nation's psyche (*Last Innocent Year,* 193).

58. Eugenia Sheppard, "By Roller Coaster," *New York Herald Tribune,* Nov. 29, 1963, 17.

59. Lapham interview.

60. Morton, "News about the Fair."

61. Zimmerman, "N.Y. World's Fair Preview" (see chap. 1, n. 70).

62. Eugenia Sheppard, "Fashion at the Fair," *New York Herald Telegram,* Sept. 13, 1963, 19. Elsie was one of 275 live animals at the Fair, each one of which was reportedly inspected daily by the American Society for the Prevention of Cruelty to Animals (ASPCA). Another nonhuman celebrity was Gargantua the Gorilla in the Lake Amusement Area's Continental Circus, who occasionally engaged in tugs-of-war with volunteers—ten at a time (Philip H. Dougherty, "A.S.P.C.A. Inspects 275 Animals at the Fair Daily," *New York Times,* July 8, 1964, 36).

63. "Material Relating to Home Furnishings," F128 T793 H75, NYHS.

64. McCandlish Phillips, "Sleep at the Fair Is Just a Dream," *New York Times,* Apr. 29, 1964, 30.

65. Rydell, Findling, and Pelle, *Fair America,* 23.

66. Angela Taylor, "Pavilion Offers New Hair Colors," *New York Times,* Apr. 23, 1964, 1, 5.

67. *1965 Official Guide,* 72.

68. Taylor, "Pavilion Offers New Hair Colors." Clairol was the beauty queen not only of Fair visitors but for employees as well. Before the second season, Clairol offered makeup and hair-styling sessions for the (female) staffs of a handful of pavilions, with one hundred women taking the beauty experts up on their kind offer (Angela Taylor, "Guides Learn How to Be Fair Ladies," *New York Times,* Apr. 17, 1965, 15). Clairol also sponsored the exhibit Mother and Child in Modern Art, a mid-season-one replacement for the canceled Pavilion of Fine Arts exhibit (Helen A. Harrison, "Art for the Millions, or Art for the Market," 154).

69. "The World of Already."

70. "Fun in New York."

71. Lee, "Business at Fair Seeking Prestige."

72. *1965 Official Guide,* 83.

73. "ABC of World's Fair Wonders," *Vogue,* Jan. 15, 1964, 99+.

74. Rita Reif, "Kitchen of Future, with Plate-Maker, Placed on Display," *New York Times,* Apr. 25, 1964, 1, 2, 5.

75. Hayden, "The Hard-Sell Fair."

76. "Movie Man," *New Yorker,* Oct. 10, 1964, 49–52; Arthur Knight, "Films at the Fair," *Saturday Review,* Aug. 15, 1964, 26.

77. George O'Brien, "Model Homes at Fair," *New York Times,* Apr. 23, 1964, 7.

78. *1965 Official Guide,* 68.

79. J. Peter, "New Cook's Tour," *Look,* Sept. 8, 1964, M10–13.

80. "Material Relating to Homes," F128 T793.H7, NYHS.

81. "Material Relating to Home Furnishings," F128 T793.H75, NYHS.

82. "Material Relating to Homes." Just as prominent men helped get a world's fair off the ground, prominent women, that is, socialites, were always an important part of American world's fairs.

83. Ibid.

84. *1965 Official Guide,* 88.

85. O'Brien, "Model Homes at Fair"; Rosemarie Haas Bletter, "The `Laissez-Fair,' Good Taste, and Money Trees: Architecture at the Fair," 128.

86. Tolchin, "Big Companies Pay for Plugs at Fair."

87. *1965 Official Guide,* 98.

88. "The World of Already"; George O'Brien, "Contemporary Dwelling Is Built Around Courts," *New York Times,* May 20, 1964, 2; O'Brien, "History, Bit of Future Part of Fair Exhibition," *New York Times,* May 9, 1964, 4.

89. *1965 Official Guide,* 210.

90. O'Brien, "Model Homes at Fair."

91. "The Fair" (see chap. 2, n. 5); "Notes and Comment," *New Yorker,* July 18, 1964, 19.

92. Robert Alden, "Industries Wary of Future Fairs," *New York Times,* Aug. 16, 1965, 4.

93. Jay Walz, "Work Set to Begin on Montreal Fair," *New York Times,* June 6, 1965, 1.

94. Robert Alden, "Fair's Costs Here Felt in Montreal," *New York Times,* June 25, 1965, 6.

## 5. Global Holiday

1. See *Official Guide: New York World's Fair, 1964/1965.*

2. Ibid., 173.

3. Alvin Shuster, "Fulbright Blocks World's Fair Bill," *New York Times,* Sept. 22, 1961, 3. Instead of a U.S. pavilion, Senator Lausche thought federal funds should be approved for a new aquarium in Washington, D.C., or a memorial for James Madison.

4. "The U.S. at the World's Fair," *New York Times,* Mar. 14, 1962, 38.

5. Foster Hailey, "Kennedy Confers with Cambodian," *New York Times,* Sept. 26, 1961, 8.

6. "Kennedy Assailed for Role on Fair," *New York Times,* Oct. 3, 1961, 5; "Kennedy Hopeful of Aid to '64 Fair," *New York Times,* Oct. 6, 1961, 1.

7. Jacob K. Javits, "`New York, Thy Name's Delirium': Calling Our Town Names Has Been a Sport of Out-of-Towners for Years," *New York Times,* Dec. 24, 1961, sec. 6, p. 9.

8. "President Urges U.S. Role at Fair," *New York Times,* Mar. 14, 1962, 7. JFK was an enthusiastic supporter of world's fairs in general, wanting Boston to host one in 1976 to celebrate the nation's bicentennial. "As a native of the city of Boston," he wrote in his petition to the BIE for such on January 17, 1963, "I respectfully request that this city's bid for a world's fair designation be given your most serious consideration." LBJ too wanted the United States to host a world's fair to celebrate the bicentennial but was open to the site (Henry Kamm, "U.S. Proposes a Fair to Mark 200th Year," *New York Times,* June 23, 1964, 1).

9. "17 Million for Fair," *New York Times,* Apr. 11, 1962, 1.

10. Warren Weaver, "U.S. Fair Pavilion Helped by Gifts," *New York Times,* Mar. 1, 1964, 5.

11. Philip H. Dougherty, "250 Sponsors of Federal Pavilion Attend Buffet and Tour Exhibit," *New York Times,* May 1, 1964, 6. Rydell, Findling, and Pelle note the nationalizing efforts of previous world's fairs, most important how the Pledge of Allegiance was carried over from the dedication ceremonies of the 1893 World's Columbian Exposition in Chicago to the country's schools (*Fair America,* 9–10). As well, many believed at the time that the Philadelphia Centennial of 1876 played a major role in uniting the country after the Civil War.

12. "Memorabilia of Presidents Will Be Shown at Fair," *New York Times,* Jan. 12, 1965, 6.

13. Robert Alden, "Historic U.S. Documents to Be Displayed at Fair," *New York Times,* Apr. 11, 1965, 2; Alden, "Lynda Johnson Finds Ms. at Fair," *New York Times,* June 12, 1965, 1.

14. Reaven, "New Frontiers," 182.

15. *Official Guide, 1964/1965,* 68–70.

16. Ibid., 182–94. Native Americans were famously featured (and most would now argue exploited) at the 1893 World's Columbian Exposition in Chicago, the 1898 Trans-Mississippi and International Exposition in Omaha, and the 1904 St. Louis fair, all instances in which they were enlisted to stage mock battles between themselves and whites in "Wild West" shows (Rydell, Findling, and Pelle, *Fair America,* 46–47; Larson, *Devil in the White City,* 207). In the most extreme case of using indigenous peoples as entertainment at a world's fair, various tribes of Indians from North America as well as Ainu from Japan, Patagonians from South America, Pygmies from Africa, and Filipinos were exhibited at the 1904 St. Louis fair by the U.S. Government's Department of Ethnology, all of "the primitives" living on the fairgrounds in their "natural habitat," that is, dwellings they made themselves from native materials (Mary Delach Leonard, "Visitors Spent Days Seeing It All," *St. Louis Post-Dispatch,* Apr. 25, 2004, WF7).

17. "Material Relating to New England," F128 T791.A3, New-York Historical Society (hereafter cited as NYHS); "Material Relating to Louisiana," F128 T791.A78, NYHS; *Official Guide, 1964/1965,* 182, 184; "Material Relating to Minnesota" (see chap. 3, n. 22); *Official Guide, 1964/1965,* 190, 192, 195.

18. "Material Relating to West Virginia," F128 T791.A57, NYHS; "Material Relating to Missouri," F128 T791.A68, NYHS; *Official Guide, 1964/1965,* 188.

19. "Material Relating to New York State," F128 T791.A41, NYHS; *Official Guide, 1964/1965,* 192–93.

20. Robert Rosenblum, "Remembrance of Fairs Past," 18, 36.

21. "Material Relating to New York State," F128 T791.A41, NYHS; *Official Guide, 1964/1965,* 192–93.

22. Harrison, "Art for the Millions, or Art for the Market?" 157.

23. Rosenblum, "Remembrance of Fairs Past." In his book *Outlaw Representation: Censorship and Homosexuality in 20th-Century American Art,* Richard Meyer claims that Warhol's *Thirteen Most Wanted Men* mural was homoerotic, the men "wanted" by the artist himself. In any case, Warhol was likely distracted by his upcoming show at the Stable Gallery on East Seventy-fourth Street featuring his re-creations of Campbell's soup, Brillo pad, and Del Monte peach cartons, which would open in just a few weeks (Margolis, *Last Innocent Year,* 200, 265).

24. *Official Guide, 1964/1965,* 212, 214.

25. "Material Relating to New York City," F128 T791, NYHS.

26. "Material Relating to Railroads," F128 T791.R3, NYHS.

27. "Material Relating to Transportation," F128 T790.6.T8.

28. *Official Guide, 1964/1965,* 216–17.

29. Ira Henry Freeman, "Industry Taking Space in '64 Fair," *New York Times,* Jan. 31, 1960, 4.

30. Wayne Phillips, "First `Envoys' Leave for Europe to Promote '64 World's Fair," *New York Times,* Aug. 15, 1960, 2. One hundred three nations would ultimately be invited to the Fair. For a fascinating account of the WFC's wild ride to recruit countries to the Fair, check out Bruce Nicholson, *Hi, Ho, Come to the Fair: Tales of the New York World's Fair of 1964–1965.*

31. "Soviet to Exhibit at '64 Fair Here" (see chap. 4, n. 39).

32. "Mexico to Join Fair," *New York Times,* Oct. 13, 1960, 7; Emanuel Perlmutter, "World's Fair Bid to Peiping Barred," *New York Times,* June 3, 1962, 3.

33. "Consuls Told of Fair," *New York Times,* Mar. 1, 1960, 6.

34. Foster Hailey, "'64 Fair to Mark Century's Gains," *New York Times,* Aug. 16, 1960, 4.

35. A. M. Rosenthal, "64 Fair Opposed by World Group," *New York Times,* Nov. 19, 1960, 1.

36. "Doubt Boycott of Fair," *New York Times,* Nov. 20, 1960, 5.

37. Brooks, "Onward and Upward with the Arts" (see chap. 1, n. 56). Although fifty-nine countries exhibited in 1939, only twenty-seven of them were there in 1940 because of the outbreak of war in Europe.

38. "Austria Rejects World's Fair Bid," *New York Times,* Nov. 26, 1960, 4; "Austria Decides to Take Role in World's Fair Here," *New York Times,* July 18, 1962, 3; Ira Henry Freeman, "3 Nations Decline to Join Fair Here," *New York Times,* Feb. 18, 1961, 2; "Private Exhibitors Will Give Europe a Part in '64 Fair," *New York Times,* May 28, 1962, 8.

39. "Iran to Join World's Fair," *New York Times,* Jan. 12, 1961, 5; "Indonesia Offered Fair Role," *New York Times,* Jan. 25, 1961, 7; "Indonesia to Participate," *New York Times,* Jan. 29, 1961, 5; Dana Adams Schmidt, "African Envoys Have Their Day in Washington," *New York Times,* Jan. 18, 1961, 3; Sam Pope Brewer, "21 Participants in '64 Fair Listed," *New York Times,* Feb. 20, 1961, 7; "Scrolls Due at '64 Fair," *New York Times,* Feb. 16, 1961, 1; "Jordan Signs for World's Fair," *New York Times,* Mar. 2, 1961, 6; "Dead Sea Scrolls to Be at '64 Fair," *New York Times,* Aug. 1, 1962, 2; "Israel to Exhibit at World's Fair," *New York Times,* Aug. 13, 1962, 26; "Jordan and Israel to Show Dead Sea Scrolls at Fair," *New York Times,* Oct. 16, 1962, 5; "Israel Withdraws from '64–65 Fair," *New York Times,* Oct. 22, 1962, 1; "Private Concern to Build Israeli Pavilion at Fair," *New York Times,* July 22, 1963, 4; "Sidelights," *New York Times,* Nov. 2, 1963, 46.

40. "1964 Fair Triumphant but Vague on Morocco," *New York Times,* Mar. 15, 1961, 7; "Tunisia Signs for Fair," *New York Times,* Mar. 16, 1961, 7; "3 African Nations Agree to Join Fair," *New York Times,* Apr. 1, 1961, 7; Charles Grutzner, "No-Strike Pledge Given to '64 Fair," *New York Times,* May 5, 1961, 1; "Pakistan, Thailand Sign Up for '64 Fair," *New York Times,* May 16, 1961, 5; "Rainier Picks Place in Fair's Woodland for Monaco Exhibit," *New York Times,* May 27, 1961, 1; "Ethiopia Joins World's Fair," *New York Times,* June 1, 1961, 5; "1964 Fair to Get `Tower of Light,'" *New York Times,* June 8, 1961, 3; "World's Fair List Growing," *New York Times,* June 28, 1961, 4; "3 African Nations to Exhibit at Fair," *New York Times,* July 2, 1961, 2; "Paraguay Joins in Fair," *New York Times,* July 31, 1961, 5; "Arab League Joins Fair," *New York Times,* Sept. 1, 1961, 4; "Venezuela Joins in Fair," *New York Times,* Sept. 25, 1961, 1; "Cambodia to Exhibit at Fair," *New York Times,* Sept. 30, 1961, 1.

41. "Moses in the Wilderness" (see chap. 1, n. 40); "3 More Nations Sign for Fair," *New York Times,* Sept. 30, 1962, 8.

42. "Argentina Not to Join Fair," *New York Times,* May 16, 1963, 4; "Brazil to Pass Up Fair," *New York Times,* May 22, 1963, 2; "55 Tons of Steel Anchored at Fair for U.S. Pavilion," *New York Times,* June 8, 1963, 7.

43. Charles Grutzner, "Italians May Quit '64 World's Fair," *New York Times,* July 25, 1963, 20.

44. "Decision on '64 Fair Expected in Rome," *New York Times,* July 30, 1963, 1; "1964 Fair Presses Talks with Italy," *New York Times,* Aug. 2, 1963, 3; Arnaldo Cortesi, "Italian Exhibit at Fair Assured," *New York Times,* Aug. 3, 1963, 8.

45. "Italy Hopes to Join Fair Despite Ruling," *New York Times,* Sept. 19, 1963, 1.

46. "A Censored Edition of Folies Bergere [*sic*] to Appear at Fair," *New York Times,* Dec. 7, 1962, 1; Drew Middleton, "Mothball Fleet Sought for Fair," *New York Times,* May 5, 1963, 6; "New Group to Build Pavilion for France at '64 World's Fair," *New York Times,* Aug. 10, 1963, 1; "Suit for $12,799,336 Filed Against Fair," *New York Times,* Oct. 26, 1963, 1; "Poletti in Paris," *New York Times,* Jan. 11, 1964, 5.

47. Francis X. Clines, "French Exhibition Is Ordered Closed by Fair's Officials," *New York Times,* May 10, 1964, 1, 5.

48. Philip Benjamin, "French Pavilion Loses Fair Lease," *New York Times,* May 28, 1964, 1, 2.

49. "Germany Restudies World's Fair Role," *New York Times,* June 27, 1963, 8; Alfred E. Clark, "Moses Finds Fair on Schedule for Opening Time Next April," *New York Times,* June 28, 1963, 26; "Wall Will Enclose Berlin Unit at Fair," *New York Times,* June 7, 1963, 55; Robert Alden, "One German Firm to Exhibit at Fair," *New York Times,* Jan. 4, 1964, 1.

50. Brooks, "Onward and Upward with the Arts"; "Premier Tentatively Accepts Bid for Soviet Exhibit at Fair," *New York Times,* Sept. 18, 1959, 19; "Soviet to Exhibit at '64 Fair Here."

51. "Fair Inviting Soviet," *New York Times,* Dec. 5, 1960, 3; "Fair's Formal Bid Is Given to Soviet," *New York Times,* Dec. 11, 1960, 3.

52. "Soviet Seeks '67 World's Fair," *New York Times,* Mar. 9, 1960, 4; "1967 World's Fair in Moscow," *New York Times,* Oct. 28, 1960, 6.

53. "Soviet Signs Lease for Fair Site," *New York Times,* Mar. 3, 1962, 2; Max Frankel, "U.S. Insists Soviet Reciprocate on Fair," *New York Times,* May 3, 1962, 6.

54. Gay Talese, "Soviet-U.S. `Race' at Fair Expected," *New York Times,* July 22, 1962, 3.

55. Max Frankel, "Soviet Pulls Out of World's Fair," *New York Times,* Oct. 3, 1962, 4; "World's Fair '64: A Preview" (see chap. 1, n. 25); "Moses Cites Contract," *New York Times,* Oct. 3, 1962, 15; "Moses Asks Soviet Not to Leave Fair," *New York Times,* Oct. 4, 1962, 1; "Poletti Flying to Moscow to See Russians on Fair," *New York Times,* Dec. 8, 1962, 6; "Soviet Still Shuns Fair," *New York Times,* Feb. 16, 1963, 4.

56. "66 Nations Help Set Fair Record," *New York Times,* Apr. 22, 1964, 8; Walter Carlson, "Fair Sees Some Hopeful Signs That Soviet Will Exhibit in '65," *New York Times,* June 10, 1964, 5.

57. Arnaldo Cortesi, "Vatican Hints Role in 1964 Fair Here," *New York Times,* Sept. 4, 1960, 2.

58. "Fair to Show Michelangelo Art," *New York Times,* Mar. 29, 1962, 3.

59. "Material Relating to Vatican City" (see chap. 3, n. 22).

60. "Florentine's Hoax Protests Art Loan," *New York Times,* Apr. 2, 1962, 5; Gay Talese, "Fair Sees `Pieta' as Top Feature," *New York Times,* Apr. 11, 1962, 8; "Letters to the `Times,'" *New York Times,* May 25, 1962, 6.

61. Perlmutter, "World's Fair Bid to Peiping Barred"; "Greece May Send `Hermes' to '64 Fair," *New York Times,* Sept. 13, 1963, 24.

62. "Greeks Bar Sending Praxiteles Statue Here as Too Risky," *New York Times,* Nov. 18, 1963, 1; "'64 Fair Striving to Get Greek Art," *New York Times,* Dec. 8, 1963, 5. Another reason Greece was reluctant to send *Hermes* was that it had sent three ancient statues to the 1939–40 New York fair and, because of the war, it took ten years to get them back.

63. "Pope's Signal Starts Pavilion at Fair," *New York Times,* Nov. 1, 1962, 5.

64. "Moses Goes to Rome on Showing of `Pieta,'" *New York Times,* May 12, 1963, 5.

65. "Catholics Asked to Support Vatican Pavilion at Fair," *New York Times,* May 20, 1963, 49; Robert Alden, "Spellman Lauds Progress at Fair," *New York Times,* Mar. 19, 1964, 8; "Priest Deplores Vatican Pavilion," *New York Times,* Mar. 21, 1964, 3.

66. "Material Relating to Vatican City."

67. "Chances Dimming for El Greco Trip," *New York Times,* Apr. 5, 1964, 1.

68. Howard Taubman, "The Arts—a Critic's View: 1958 Brussels Exposition Set a Mark That New York Is Far from Matching," *New York Times,* Apr. 22, 1964, 1, 3.

69. Tania Long, "Spanish Pavilion Seeks Art for '65," *New York Times,* Oct. 13, 1964, 3; "Material Relating to Vatican City"; Hughes, "The Golden Grin" (see chap. 4, n. 10); I. Sheppard, "Icons and Images," 172. A persistent rumor was that the sculpture in the Vatican Pavilion was not the real *Pietà* but a very good replica, some simply refusing to believe that the pope actually allowed the masterpiece to come to Flushing Meadows.

70. John Canaday, "Spain's Aristocratic Rival to `Pieta,'" *New York Times,* Mar. 24, 1964, 1, 2.

71. "Franco Said to Hold Key in El Greco Rift," *New York Times,* Mar. 26, 1964, 4; Henry Ginigers, "3 Picassos Bought by Spain for Fair," *New York Times,* Apr. 2, 1964, 7; "Spain Bars El Greco from Fair Because of Risks of Shipment," *New York Times,* Apr. 8, 1964, 6; "Spain to Substitute Goyas and Others for El Greco at Fair," *New York Times,* Apr. 9, 1964, 5.

72. "`Santa Maria' Model Arrives for '64 Fair," *New York Times,* Dec. 4, 1963, 1. Spain brought not only a full-size replica of the *Santa María* to the 1893 Chicago fair but replicas of its sister ships, the *Niña* and the *Pinta,* as well (Larson, *Devil in the White City,* 327).

73. John C. Devlin, "New `Santa Maria' Has Troubles, Too," *New York Times,* Jan. 27, 1964, 2; "`Santa Maria' Goes Aground at Fair," *New York Times,* Feb. 3, 1964, 3.

74. "66 Nations Help Set Fair Record."

75. "Material Relating to International Plaza," F128 T792.I6, NYHS.

76. "Material Relating to Egypt," F128 T792.5.E6, NYHS; "Material Relating to Lebanon," F128 T792.6.L5, NYHS; Walter Carlson, "Poletti Recipient of Many Gifts as Fair's International Officer," *New York Times,* June 13, 1964, 1; Brooks, "Onward and Upward with the Arts."

77. "Material Relating to India," F128 T792.6.I6, NYHS; "Material Relating to Central America," F128 T791.L4, NYHS.

78. "Material Relating to Africa," F128 T792.5, NYHS.

79. "Queen Gets Bird's View of City from Helicopter," *New York Times,* Feb. 1, 1964, 8; Henry Raymont, "Fair Pavilions Get Final Touches for Opening Day," *New York Times,* Apr. 21, 1964, 1, 2; Carlson, "State Wins Praise for Fair Pavilion" (see chap. 2, n. 19); Robert Alden, "Swedish and Spanish Pavilions Are Dedicated in Contrasting Ceremonies at Fair," *New York Times,* Apr. 28, 1964, 1, 2; "676-Year-Old Stock to Be Shown at Fair," *New York Times,* Mar. 4, 1964, 5; Alden, "Portland, Ore., Hails West Berlin Mayor at Fair," *New York Times,* May 21, 1964, 6; "Moses Welcomes De Valera on Visit," *New York Times,* May 31, 1964, 5, 6; Walter Carlson, "King of Burundi Pays Visit to Fair," *New York Times,* May 22, 1964, 1; Martin Tolchin, "Shah and Empress Hold Hands at Fair," *New York Times,* June 14, 1964, 4.

80. "Vatican Indicates Pope Won't Come to the Fair," *New York Times,* Jan. 3, 1965, 2.

81. Robert Alden, "Thousands Guard Paul on Trip," *New York Times,* Oct. 5, 1965, 1.

82. *Official Guide, 1964/1965,* 118–71.

83. "Material Relating to Korea," F128 T792.6, NYHS; "Material Relating to Japan," F128 T792.6.J2, NYHS; "Sukarno Advice to Girls at Fair: Don't `Wiggle,'" *New York Times,* Jan. 24, 1965, 5; "Indonesia Halts Plans for Pavilion at Fair," *New York Times,* Mar. 12, 1965, 7.

84. "Out of the Bull Rushes" (see chap. 1, n. 89). When the previous New York fair ended, some of the chefs of European pavilions were stranded because of the war and decided to open restaurants in the city. One of them was Soule, who almost single-handedly introduced haute cuisine to the United States (Frank Zachary, "World's Fair of 1939–40 Improved City's Menus," letter to the editor, City Weekly Desk, *New York Times,* Nov. 5, 2000, 17).

85. "Out of the Bull Rushes."

86. Robert Alden, "Lebanese Treasures Damaged," *New York Times,* Apr. 17, 1964, 1, 3; "Material Relating to Lebanon."

87. "Fair Enough" (see chap. 2, n. 53).

88. With its Bel-Gem waffles, this world's fair was following a long tradition in introducing new foods, especially treats, to the public. Cracker Jack and Shredded Wheat were first seen at the 1893 World's Columbian Exposition in Chicago, Larson reminds us (*Devil in the White City,* 5), whereas the ice cream cone and Dr. Pepper were originally offered at the 1904 St. Louis World's Fair.

89. Allen Hughes, "Ethnic Dances Abound for Visitors to Fair," *New York Times,* June 15, 1964, 1.

90. "Material Relating to Switzerland," F128 T792.37, NYHS; "Material Relating to Spain," F128 T792.34, NYHS; "Material Relating to Belgium," F128 T792.32, NYHS; "Material Relating to Morocco," F128 T792.5.M7, NYHS.

91. *Official Guide, 1964/1965,* 108.

92. "Material Relating to Switzerland"; *Official Guide, 1964/1965,* 166; "Material Relating to Japan."

93. Lee, "Foreign Exhibits Stress Exports."

94. "Material Relating to Japan."

95. M. S. Handler, "Union Rules at Fair Vex Japanese," *New York Times,* Oct. 5, 1963, 2; "World's Fair '64: A Preview." Artisans from Japan similarly came to the 1893 fair in Chicago to assemble a Hoo-den temple, Larson notes (*Devil in the White City,* 225).

96. Robert Trumbull, "Fair Personnel Lead Double Life," *New York Times,* Apr. 20, 1964, 1.

97. Martin Tolchin, "Foreign Pavilions Rue Cleaning Cost," *New York Times,* May 22, 1964, 2.

98. Alden, "High Costs Anger Pavilions at Fair" (see chap. 2, n. 39).

99. "U.S. Agents Seize 19 Koreans Here," *New York Times,* Jan. 9, 1965, 1; "Koreans Employed in Pavilion at Fair Fight Return Home," *New York Times,* Nov. 21, 1964, 1; William E. Burrows, "African Dancers Keeping Busy During Off-Season at the Fair," *New York Times,* Dec. 6, 1964, 3; Peter Kihss, "Dr. King Asks Aid for 6 Zulus Seeking Asylum," *New York Times,* Apr. 5, 1965, 3; "U.N. Gets Plea on Behalf of 6 Zulus Seeking Asylum," *New York Times,* Apr. 20, 1965, 3; "African Describes Dangers to 5 Zulus," *New York Times,* Apr. 27, 1965, 38; "State Department Queried on 5 Zulus," *New York Times,* Apr. 28, 1965, 4; "Asylum Asked for Zulu Dancers," *New York Times,* May 5, 1965, 7; "U.S. Drops Its Case to Deport 5 Zulus," *New York Times,* May 28, 1965, 5. There was precedent for foreign workers at American world's fairs to try to seek asylum in the United States. Geisha girls from Japan's pavilion at the 1904 St. Louis World's Fair, for example, hired attorneys to help them stay in the States after the fair but were deported by immigration officials (*St. Louis Post-Dispatch,* Apr. 25, 2004, WF5).

100. Henry Raymont, "Fair Guides Play Diplomatic Role," *New York Times,* Apr. 26, 1964, 1, 2, 5, 6.

101. Ilse Lebrecht, "Directions to World's Fair," *New York Times,* May 12, 1964, 6.

102. Robert Dunphy, "Password to Travel," *New York Times,* May 26, 1963, sec. 10, p. 8.

103. "Esperantists Get a Bid to the Fair," *New York Times,* Mar. 15, 1964, 3.

104. William Borders, "10 Essay Winners Get a Trip to India," *New York Times,* Jan. 10, 1965, 1.

105. Hughes, "The Golden Grin."

106. "The World of Already"; Carlson, "Crowds at Fair Dwindle in Heat" (see chap. 2, n. 92).

## 6. Sermons from Science

1. John M. Lee, "Plastics Abound in Fair Buildings," *New York Times,* Apr. 26, 1964, 5. Awarding not only cities, states, and nations but also groups of workers (as well as fraternal organizations

and even African Americans) their own special days at world's fairs went back some time. Cobblers, millers, confectioners, and stenographers got their own days, for example, at the 1893 Chicago fair (Larson, *Devil in the White City*, 241).

2. John Walsh, "Science Exhibits: At Seattle Fair, Federal Funds, Scientists Helped New Yorkers Try a Different Tack," *Science*, May 31, 1963, 960–62; Raymond Moley, "Meaning of the Fair," *Newsweek*, July 12, 1965, 92; "The World of Already" (see chap. 1, n. 12). Many less memorable technological breakthroughs also had their debut at world's fairs. Few people remember the "collapsible piano" (for yachts, of course) or the three hundred–blade jackknife, each of which was first (and likely last) shown in London's Crystal Palace.

3. Hayden, "The Hard-Sell Fair" (see chap. 1, n. 27). The Century of Progress Exposition in Chicago also had a Hall of Science that carried the technocentric motto "Science Finds; Industry Applies; Man Conforms" (Rydell, Findling, and Pelle, *Fair America*, 12).

4. Walter Sullivan, "Science Section Opening at Fair," *New York Times*, June 16, 1964, 1.

5. Layhmond Robinson, "State Atom Unit Bars a Plant Now," *New York Times*, Feb. 5, 1961, 1.

6. "Atomic Playground," *Science News Letter*, June 20, 1964, 386.

7. John A. Osmundsen, "Hall of Science Dedicated by City," *New York Times*, Sept. 10, 1964, 1, 2.

8. "Material Relating to Science and Hall of Science," F128 T790.6.S3, New-York Historical Society (hereafter cited as NYHS).

9. *Science at the Fair*, F128 T790.6.S3L3, NYHS.

10. *Post Fair Expansion of the Hall of Science*, F128 T790.6.S3H3, NYHS.

11. "Material Relating to Belgium" (see chap. 5, n. 90).

12. *1965 Official Guide*, 156.

13. Rydell, Findling, and Pelle, *Fair America*, 104–5.

14. *1965 Official Guide*, 156.

15. "Material Relating to Chemicals," F128 T793.C4, NYHS.

16. "Material Relating to Science and Hall of Science."

17. "Material Relating to Chemicals."

18. "Hydrogen Fusion on Display, along with Other Wonders of the World of Science," *New York Times*, Apr. 22, 1964, 6–8.

19. "Preliminaries," *New Yorker*, Mar. 28, 1964, 33.

20. Lee, "Plastics Abound in Fair Buildings."

21. Dudley Dalton, "New Uses Found for Fiber Glass," *New York Times*, May 31, 1964, R1, 2.

22. "Material Relating to Chemicals."

23. Lee, "Plastics Abound in Fair Buildings."

24. "Kodak Pavilion at Fair Wins Concrete Group's Award," *New York Times*, Aug. 23, 1964, R9, 2.

25. "Material Relating to Film and Cameras," F128 T793.F6, NYHS.

26. Larson, *Devil in the White City*, 254.

27. "Material Relating to Electricity," F128 T793.E6, NYHS.

28. Dickstein, "From the Thirties to the Sixties," 34.

29. *1965 Official Guide*, 86, 88.

30. Ibid.

31. Wolfert, "Coming: The Most Marvelous Fair Ever!" (see chap. 1, n. 55).

32. "Preliminaries."

33. *1965 Official Guide*, 200.

34. Rydell, Findling, and Pelle, *Fair America*, 83.

35. *1965 Official Guide,* 204.

36. Ibid., 218, 220, 230.

37. Ibid., 209.

38. Ibid., 204, 218, 209.

39. Bosley Crowther, "Moon Show at the Fair," *New York Times,* May 16, 1964, 1, 2.

40. Rydell, Findling, and Pelle, *Fair America,* 103–4.

41. Richard Haitch, "Fair's Space Park 'Tutors' Visitors," *New York Times,* June 14, 1964, 1.

42. Ibid.

43. "Cooper to Lead Off Visits of Astronauts to Fair," *New York Times,* Apr. 28, 1964, 31; Philip H. Dougherty, "Gemini Capsule Arrives at Fair," *New York Times,* Aug. 4, 1965, 1.

44. Henry Raymount, "Questions Beset Corps of Guides," *New York Times,* Apr. 27, 1964, 4, 5.

45. "Material Relating to Automobiles," F128 T793.A81–3, NYHS; "Material Relating to Typewriters and Business Machines," F128 T793.T9, NYHS; "Material Relating to Japan" (see chap. 5, n. 83).

46. "Material Relating to Typewriters and Business Machines"; Walter Carlson, "Eisenhower Gets Ovation at Fair," *New York Times,* July 9, 1964, 1.

47. *1965 Official Guide,* 88, 90.

48. "Fun in New York" (see chap. 1, n. 17).

49. Mayer, "Ho Hum, Come to the Fair" (see chap. 1, n. 3).

50. Henry B. Comstock, "Inside IBM's World's Fair 'Egg,'" *Popular Science,* July 1964, 58–59; Knight, "Films at the Fair" (see chap. 4, n. 76).

51. Robert E. Tomasson, "Analysis Devices at Fair Assailed," *New York Times,* July 25, 1964, 6.

52. Murray Schumach, "Story Hour Wins Children at Fair," *New York Times,* Aug. 23, 1964, 1.

53. "Material Relating to the United States" (see chap. 3, n. 25).

54. "Material Relating to Radio," F128 T793.R2, NYHS.

55. "Material Relating to Telephone and Telegraph," F128 T793.T5, NYHS.

56. "New Time-Saving Phone Installed for Moses," *New York Times,* Oct. 8, 1963, 3.

57. "Television Phone Used from Fair to California," *New York Times,* Apr. 21, 1964, 1, 2.

58. "Science at the Fair." The Picturephone was the most impressive telecommunications feat at a world's fair since 1893, when live music played by an orchestra in New York was transmitted to Chicago by long-distance telephone (Larson, *Devil in the White City,* 247) and, before that, when Alexander Graham Bell himself showed up at the 1876 fair in Philadelphia to give the first public demonstration of his telephone. In the public debut of the Picturephone on April 23, 1964, Lady Bird spoke from Washington for five minutes with Dr. Elizabeth A. Wood, a Bell scientist in New York (Margolis, *Last Innocent Year,* 185).

59. "Picture Phones Go into Service," *New York Times,* June 25, 1964, 24.

60. Alfred R. Zipser, "World-Wide Telecast in Color Planned for Opening of '64 Fair," *New York Times,* Jan. 6, 1961, 5.

61. "Fair Has Color TV Just for Visitors," *New York Times,* May 4, 1964, 5.

62. Howard A. Rusk, M.D., "The Fair and Medicine," *New York Times,* July 12, 1964, 4, 5; Barbara Tufty, "Fair View of Future," *Science News Letter,* Apr. 11, 1964, 234.

63. "The World of Already."

64. Reaven, "New Frontiers," 96.

65. "Material Relating to Automobiles."

66. Ibid.

67. Ibid.

68. Fred M. Hechinger, "Schoolmen Take Look at 2000 A.D.," *New York Times,* July 5, 1964, 4.

69. Ibid.

70. Robert H. Terte, "Playground Gets the Wriggle Test," *New York Times,* May 1, 1964, 3, 5.

71. Arnold J. Toynbee, "At Least the Beginnings of One World," *New York Times,* Apr. 19, 1964, SMA86; Margaret Mead, "Human Nature Will Flower, If—," *New York Times,* Apr. 19, 1964, SMA96; Isaac Asimov, "Visit to the World's Fair of 2014," *New York Times,* Aug. 16, 1964, VI, 20.

72. Asimov, "Visit to the World's Fair of 2014." William Hanna and Joseph Barbera, the producers and directors of both *The Flintstones* and *The Jetsons,* credit Futurama for inspiring the Jetsons' neighborhood, Orbit City. Similarly, animators of the show based the "skypad" apartment buildings in the show on the Space Needle (Bob Goetz, "Was the Astrodome Named after a Dog?" *New York Times,* Dec. 11, 2005, sec. 8, p. 11). The Flintstones made another excursion to the Fair in a comic book, with Dino becoming smitten with one of Sinclair's fiberglass dinosaurs. Archie and the rest of his gang—Betty, Veronica, Reggie, and Jughead—too took in the Fair in a November 1964 special issue of *Life with Archie* (I. Sheppard, "Icons and Images," 186).

73. "Material Relating to Appliances," F128 T793.A7, NYHS.

74. Tania Long, "Time Capsule II to Get '64 Jazz," *New York Times,* Nov. 29, 1964, 3; Barney Lefferts, "Open in 6939," *New York Times,* Apr. 19, 1964, SMA34.

75. *Post Fair Expansion of the Hall of Science.*

76. "Science Museum May Be Expanded," *New York Times,* Jan. 26, 1965, 31.

77. "Park on Fair Site Due in December," 33 (see chap. 3, n. 99).

78. Walter Sullivan, "City Plans a Full Science Museum at Site of Fair," *New York Times,* July 14, 1966, 25.

79. Jonathan Randal, "City Science Hall Opens Officially," *New York Times,* Sept. 22, 1966, 49; Walter Sullivan, "Hopeful Future Museum," *New York Times,* Sept. 22, 1966, 58.

80. Charles Grutzner, "Life Stirs Anew at Fairgrounds," *New York Times,* Apr. 11, 1967, 44.

81. Samuel Weiss, "Future of the Fair Site Still Debated," *New York Times,* Sept. 10, 1972, 134.

82. Clayton Knowles, "New Science Hall Planned by City," *New York Times,* June 1, 1967, 33; Charles G. Bennett, "Science Museum Called Unworkable," *New York Times,* Nov. 2, 1967, 55.

83. "Queens Science Hall to Get Atomic Reactor," *New York Times,* Aug. 8, 1971, BQ75.

84. Jim Ostroff, "A Science Museum in Limbo in Queens," *New York Times,* July 9, 1972, 89.

85. Weiss, "Future of the Fair Site Still Debated."

86. David A. Andelman, "Science Hall in Flushing Will Reopen This Month," *New York Times,* Nov. 2, 1972, 47; Ira D. Guberman, "Hall of Science Gets Ready for Summer," *New York Times,* June 3, 1973, 114.

87. David C. Berliner, "Hall of Science Feels Crunch," *New York Times,* Oct. 12, 1975, 132.

88. Ibid.

89. Wolfgang Saxon, "Last Round for U.S. World's Fair Pavilion," *New York Times,* July 29, 1976, 33.

90. Howard Blum, "Political Clash Clouds Future of Science Hall," *New York Times,* Nov. 12, 1983, 25.

91. Joseph P. Fried, "Hall of Science in Queens Asks Youths to Grade It," *New York Times,* Sept. 15, 1985, 54.

92. Joseph P. Fried, "Science Hall Is to Reopen after 5 Years," *New York Times,* July 14, 1986, B2; Malcolm W. Browne, "City Again Boasts a Science Museum," *New York Times,* Sept. 5, 1986, C21; Susan Heller Anderson, "Park in Queens to Get $80 Million Restoration," *New York Times,* Nov. 19, 1987, B3.

93. Anderson, "Park in Queens to Get $80 Million Restoration"; "In Flushing Meadows–Corona Park," *New York Times,* May 27, 1990, 46.

94. Dulcie Leimbach, "For Children: From the Ashes of Flushing Meadows and Its Two World's Fairs, a Park Has Emerged That Offers a Variety of Family Activities," *New York Times,* Aug. 2, 1991, C18; Richard F. Shepard, "Flushing: Where the World Twice Met and Newcomers Dwell," *New York Times,* Apr. 28, 1989, C1.

95. David Dunlap, "A Queens Park's Past Shapes Its Future," *New York Times,* Aug. 26, 2001, RE1.

96. Fred A. Bernstein, "New Life and New Mission for a 1964 World's Fair Relic," *New York Times,* July 17, 2004, B7; "New Spin on Qns. Sphere," *New York Post,* Aug. 7, 2005, 22.

97. Dunlap, "A Queens Park's Past Shapes Its Future"; Steve Parks, "When the World Came to Corona," *Newsday,* Nov. 26, 2004, A48–49.

98. Edward Rothstein, "From Internet Arm Wrestling to the Magic of Math," *New York Times,* Nov. 24, 2004, E1, E14.

## Conclusion

1. I. Sheppard, "Icons and Images," 168.

2. There was at least one effort to infuse the Fair with a dose of hipness. Cool-jazz extraordinaire Dave Brubeck composed a song called "World's Fair," performing it for a promotional film for Clairol, *Hair Styles and Fair Styles,* shot at the Top of the Fair restaurant before opening day.

# Bibliography

Bletter, Rosemarie Haas. "The `Laissez-Fair,' Good Taste, and Money Trees: Architecture at the Fair." In *Remembering the Future: The New York World's Fair from 1939 to 1964.* New York: Rizzoli, 1989.

Caro, Robert A. *The Power Broker: Robert Moses and the Fall of New York.* New York: Knopf, 1974.

Dickstein, Morris. "From the Thirties to the Sixties: The World's Fair in Its Own Time." In *Remembering the Future: The New York World's Fair from 1939 to 1964.* New York: Rizzoli, 1989.

Doctorow, E. L. *World's Fair.* New York: Random House, 1985.

Gelb, Arthur. *City Room.* New York: G. P. Putnam's Sons, 2003.

Gelernter, David. *1939: The Lost World of the Fair.* New York: Harper Perennial, 1996.

Haddow, Robert H. *Pavilions of Plenty: Exhibiting American Culture Abroad in the 1950s.* Washington, D.C.: Smithsonian Institution Press, 1997.

Harrison, Helen A. "Art for the Millions, or Art for the Market." In *Remembering the Future: The New York World's Fair from 1939 to 1964.* New York: Rizzoli, 1989.

Larson, Erik. *The Devil in the White City: Murder, Magic, and Madness at the Fair That Changed America.* New York: Vintage Books, 2003.

Margolis, Jon. *The Last Innocent Year: America in 1964—the Beginning of the Sixties.* New York: Perennial, 1999.

May, Henry Farnham. *The End of American Innocence: A Study of the First Years of Our Own Time, 1912–1917.* New York: Columbia Univ. Press, 1994.

Meyer, Richard. *Outlaw Representation: Censorship and Homosexuality in 20th-Century American Art.* New York: Oxford Univ. Press, 2002.

Miller, Marc H. "Something for Everyone: Robert Moses and the Fair." In *Remembering the Future: The New York World's Fair from 1939 to 1964.* New York: Rizzoli, 1989.

Nicholson, Bruce. *Hi, Ho, Come to the Fair: Tales of the New York World's Fair of 1964–1965.* Huntington Beach, Calif.: Pelagian Press, 1989.

*1965 Official Guide: New York World's Fair.* New York: Time, 1965.

*Official Guide: New York World's Fair, 1964/1965.* New York: Time, 1964.

Reaven, Sheldon J. "New Frontiers: Science and Technology at the Fair." In *Remembering the Future: The New York World's Fair from 1939 to 1964.* New York: Rizzoli, 1989.

Rosenblum, Robert. "Remembrance of Fairs Past." In *Remembering the Future: The New York World's Fair from 1939 to 1964.* New York: Rizzoli, 1989.

Rydell, Robert W., John E. Findling, and Kimberly D. Pelle. *Fair America: World's Fairs in the United States.* Washington, D.C.: Smithsonian Institution Press, 2000.

Sheppard, Ilene. "Icons and Images: The Cultural Legacy of the Fair." In *Remembering the Future: The New York World's Fair from 1939 to 1964.* New York: Rizzoli, 1989.

Strasser, Susan. *Satisfaction Guaranteed: The Making of the American Mass Market.* New York: Pantheon Books, 1989.

Trow, George W. S. *Within the Context of No Context.* New York: Atlantic Monthly Press, 1997.

Wolfe, Tom. *The Electric Kool-Aid Acid Test.* New York: Bantam, 1999.

# Index

Page number in italics denotes illustration.